TRICO
A VICTORY TO REMEMBER

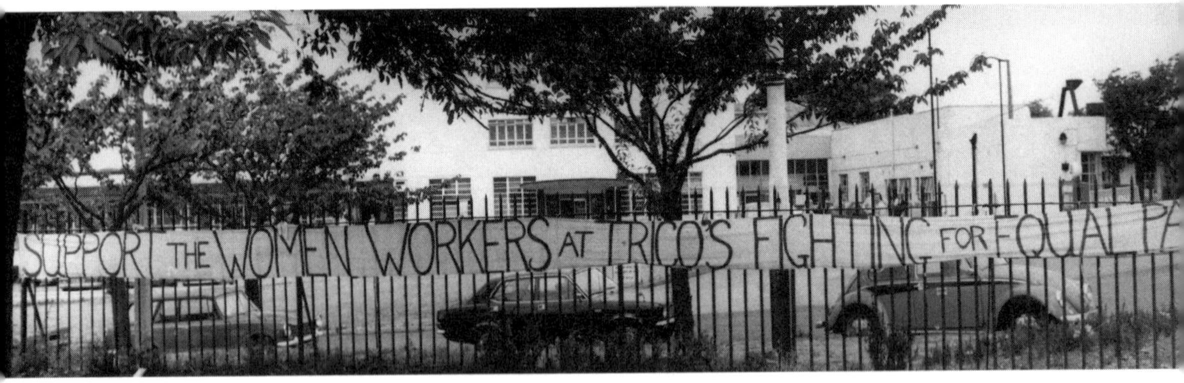
SUPPORT THE WOMEN WORKERS AT TRICO'S FIGHTING FOR EQUAL

SALLY GROVES   VERNON MERRITT

TRICO
A VICTORY TO REMEMBER

The 1976 Equal Pay Strike at Trico Folberth, Brentford

LW

LAWRENCE & WISHART
LONDON

Frontispiece: Sally Groves' banner on Trico railings.

MORNING STAR PHOTOGRAPHIC ARCHIVE, BISHOPSGATE INSTITUTE

Lawrence and Wishart Limited
Central Books Building
Freshwater Road
Chadwell Heath
RM8 1RX

This edition © Sally Groves and Vernon Merritt 2018
Published in association with Unite

The authors have asserted their rights under the Copyright, Design and Patents Act, 1998 to be identified as the authors of this work.

All rights reserved. Apart from fair dealing for the purpose of private study, research, criticism or review, no part of this publication may be reproduced, stored in a retrieval system, or transmitted, in any form or by any means, electronic, electrical, chemical, mechanical, optical, photocopying, recording or otherwise, without the prior permission of the copyright owner.

Design: Andrew Corbett

ISBN 9781912064878

British Library Cataloguing in Publication Data.
A catalogue record for this book is available from the British Library

CONTENTS

Acknowledgements: 1977 — vii
Acknowledgements: 2017 — ix
A Foreword … From the Past — xi

PART ONE: GETTING ORGANISED
Disturbing the Peace — 3
Where is Our Equal Pay? — 14
Explosion! — 22
The Early Days — 28
Hot for Equality — 39
'We're on Sex Strike Say Wives in Equal Pay Fight' — 42
Out on the Costa del Trico — 46
Into Top Gear — 50

PART TWO: THE BATTLE RAGES
Strike Breakers Incorporated — 57
More Twists and Turns — 67
They Shall Not Pass — 71
Battle at the Trico Gates — 82
'We Don't Know Anything…' — 89

PART THREE: THE RECKONING
More Determined Than Ever — 95
Tribunal Trickery — 104
Decisive Days — 114
Trico in Trouble — 125
If It's a Wiper – Black It! — 133
Stepping Up the Fight — 134
'Sardine Sidney' — 148
Victory! — 155

FORTY YEARS ON – WHAT LESSONS FOR TODAY? — 175
Trico and Grunwick — 177
Lessons for Trade Unionists — 181

Lessons for Feminism	186
Remembering Our History	188
FIGHTING FOR OUR RIGHTS	193
The Campaign for Equal Pay	198
Work of Equal Value	204
Equal Pay after 2010	208
Abbreviations	213
Appendix	217
Index	225

ACKNOWLEDGEMENTS 1977

ROLL OF HONOUR
(as completed in 1977)

The Trico Strike Committee and the Southall District Committee wishes to record its special thanks and express our everlasting gratitude to the following, who in their many different ways assisted our own efforts and made our eventual victory certain.

The husbands and wives, and families, of the strikers who patiently shared the hardship involved.

Everyone who donated money so generously and who helped organise fundraising efforts on our behalf.

Those loyal trade unionists, those from the women's movement, and others who unselfishly came to our aid at difficult times on our picket line when requested, any time of day or night.

Workers throughout industry who blacked Trico products and scab lorry firms.

The *Morning Star* and *Labour Weekly* for their honest reporting of the strike.

The members of Brent Trades Council, its Secretary Jack Dromey and Chairman Tom Durkin, for the assistance given in so many ways.

The staff and officials of the TASS section of the AUEW at

Richmond who gave invaluable help in the printing of our strike bulletins.

Harriet Harman and Jamie Ritchie of Brent Law Centre for their sound advice and help.

John Ridgely of Chippenham Posters for such professional placards.

Fred Wright for the cartoons we printed in our bulletins; the brilliance of his working class humour lifted everyone's spirits.

Bob Bunting, a retired Trico worker, for being a real inspiration on the picket line every day through five months of voluntary service.

Report Photo Agency for the magnificent photographic exhibition they donated.

A particular tribute to the AUEW Divisional and District Officials involved, John Bracher, Arthur Gibbard, Len Choulerton and, above all, Roger Butler and Bill MacLaughlin for their total dedication to our cause and the complete identity they showed with our members.

But none of this would have come about without the sheer guts and determination and solidarity of 400 women and 150 men who wrote a glorious page in the history of the working class and the fight for women's rights.

It has taken 40 years for this story finally to be completed.

In that time many of those involved have sadly died including leading figures of the strike:

Eileen Ward, Betty Aiston, Betty Humphreys …

VERNON MERRITT

ACKNOWLEDGEMENTS 2017

THIS BOOK HAS TAKEN half a lifetime in the making. It's been as big a roller coaster as the strike – if somewhat longer! I trust that the stalwarts from 1976 will consider it does justice to our epic struggle, and that it will inspire others to stand up for their rights.

Started by Vernon Merritt in 1976, and continued by me, the story is a tribute to all the gutsy women strikers and to our loyal male supporters, particularly those men that came out on strike from day one; 'the diamonds', as I called them.

I'm proud to have been part of such an amazing battle for equal rights, and proud to have fought alongside such wonderful people, a number of whom I am privileged to count amongst my dear friends.

In particular, I would like to thank the intrepid Peggy Farmer and Phyllis Green who were veritable bloodhounds in assisting me to track down old Trico strikers, and whose support and enthusiasm never flagged.

Sincere thanks are due to all those that became enthusiastically involved and contributed anecdotes and comments about the strike: Bob Banister, Loretta Braithwaite, Izzy Davies, Peggy Farmer, Ann Fitzgerald, Eric Fudge, Sandra Gray, Phyllis Green, the late and much missed Bob Mitchell, Robert (Bob) Singh, Billy Taylor, Rhoda Williams, Bella (Davis) and Brian Young. Many thanks to Margaret James for providing a vital contact.

I would also like to thank all those that read the text of the story and gave some wise comments and suggestions – that I did follow! ... Deborah Adams, Sarah Boston, Roger Butler, Peggy Farmer, Diana Holland, Robert Singh. A special thanks to George Stevenson who not only gave thoughtful comments on the text, but recognised and promoted the importance of the long forgotten Trico strike by making it his academic study. Thanks to Ann Field, Barbara Humphries (and Mick Brooks) and Dave Welsh for many helpful suggestions and promoting the cause.

A much appreciated listening ear and encouragement was provided by Martin Eady, Colin Groves, Prof. Jim Hardie and Bree Robbins. Eve Turner and Oliver New were an original spur saying, 'Get on with it!'

I very much appreciate Scott Reeves for hunting down some additional press cuttings and Ros Sitwell for featuring my article on the strike in the *Morning Star*. Many thanks to Dawn Power, who made another contribution to the story possible by so promptly passing on my contact details via the *Morning Star*.

My thanks for their assistance to the archivists and librarians at the Bishopsgate Institute, TUC Library Collection and Modern Records Centre, Warwick University.

Special thanks to Chris Davies and Andrew Wiard for giving permission to reproduce their iconic photos of the strike.

Thanks to Report Photo Agency for additional photos.

Last, but not least, gratitude to my 'computer guy', Nicholas Huzan, for his patience and expertise at critical times!

I wish to thank the following organisations and individuals for their support and generous donations to assist towards the book's publication: -

Unite the Union (Andrew Murray)

The Stevens Gradwell Memorial Fund

Margaret Manley

Ealing Trades Union Council

SALLY GROVES

A FOREWORD
... FROM THE PAST

WHAT YOU ARE about to read is an attempt to place on record a truly epic struggle, culminating in a glorious victory. It is a chapter in the history of the Labour and Trade Union movement and a landmark along the road to social justice, especially in the field of equality and human dignity. Of course it will fall short of the task, for no words set down on paper could ever adequately describe the courage, suffering, humour, depression, joy, despair, hope and finally relief and happiness, that go to make up such events.

Though it must be placed on record that a tremendous support force of countless men and women, trade unionists and others, gathered to contribute an enormous amount of time, hard work and above all money, the underlying theme of this story is that of 400 or so very remarkable women.

Having waited with commendable patience during months of frustrating and non-productive negotiation between the company and their shop stewards, and in the later stages their union officials, the women were forced to the ultimate decision to strike when the talks ended in a 'Failure to Agree' at national level.

So it was that on the afternoon of 24 May 1976 they walked out of the Trico factory at Brentford, dedicated to persuading an obdurate employer to concede their just claim for equal pay with their male colleagues doing identical work.

They had entered a new world to them and in the early stages were somewhat bemused, apprehensive and not particularly organised. However, by sheer courage and endurance they gradually formed themselves into such an impregnable unit that they succeeded in changing the course of society in this country as far as its attitude towards equality for women was concerned.

In order to understand the extent of their achievement it is necessary to examine some of the tremendous obstacles they had to overcome.

First there was the indefinable, ever present power of the establishment, entrenched in its apparently immovable bastion of authority. Allied to that was the worst inflationary situation the country had faced in decades, unemployment figures of around one and a half million and a divided squabbling nation. This, coupled with traditional male hostility, irrational tribunal decisions and a popular press campaign aimed in the main against any improvement in workers' living standards, produced an inward-looking society none too willing to accept the logic and moral justness of equality for women at work.

Not unnaturally big business interests combined to form a defence against any breakthrough in equal pay that might seriously affect their profit margins if achieved.

Last but by no means least was an unbelievably incompetent 'company policy' which seemed unable to grasp the reality of the situation, and for far too long concentrated its efforts on what had become a futile task of smashing the strike and discrediting the Amalgamated Union of Engineering Workers.

Strangely enough the company tactics, though prolonging the strike and causing terrible hardship to those involved, also had the effect of strengthening the bonds of comradeship of both the strikers and their many supporters.

These tactics included masses of propaganda sent to the homes of the strikers in an attempt to split them up, especially after a tribunal had ruled against them.

The suggestion that the strike was really just a plot hatched up by 'the Reds under the bed' totally backfired, since the only Reds involved were to be seen walking about in broad daylight and were shown to be responsible caring human beings just like the rest of us. Also there was the fact that the women themselves had made the original decision to strike and there was no indication that many of them were red or indeed pink. But it was the hiring of unsavoury back street transport gangs to form convoys to smash through the pickets that was to prove to be one of the deciding factors in the long and bitter dispute. Though the first and only real breakthrough of the picket lines by this method demoralised the strikers for a very short period, the manner in which it was achieved so outraged them that it strengthened their resolve not to give in, to a degree that was never seriously threatened again.

So it was that after twenty-one weeks of appalling hardship and courageous struggle, the strikers assembled on the morning of 15 October to hear that the company had finally agreed to give them equal pay. It was an emotional meeting with tears of joy and relief mingling with a feeling of pride in a truly great achievement. This was followed on Monday 18 October by a triumphant march back into work, with heads held high and their task completed.

In conclusion it must be said that the sheer dedication, hard work and almost total involvement of the local AUEW District Secretary Roger Butler, and the never-wavering faith and guidance of Divisional Organiser Bill MacLaughlin played a substantial part in this success. Nor would it be right not to mention that about 150 men joined the women in their struggle some three weeks after the start, when the strike was made official, and remained at their side in support to the end. These men deserve the highest praise, for they had no immediate gain to spur them, and so many of their male colleagues deserted the cause and slunk past the pickets to join the enemy inside the factory.

But as it was said earlier, the story mainly belongs to the women. It is therefore fitting that I, a mere male, having been accorded the immense privilege of writing these opening words of introduction, should express the sincere hope that if it does nothing else, this book may serve as some small tribute to the gallant band of 400 women to whom we all owe such a tremendous debt.

Fraternally yours

John Inwood
Convenor AUEW
Chairman Trico Strike Committee
1977

In memory of
EILEEN WARD
who gave outstanding leadership.
She put her heart and soul
into the Trico strike and her union,
the AUEW.

'Ordinary people do extraordinary things'

Left to Right, Angela and 'Flower' (Begonia Syed) outside Trico gates, 25 May 1976.

PETER ARKELL/REPORTDIGITAL.CO.UK

PART ONE
GETTING ORGANISED

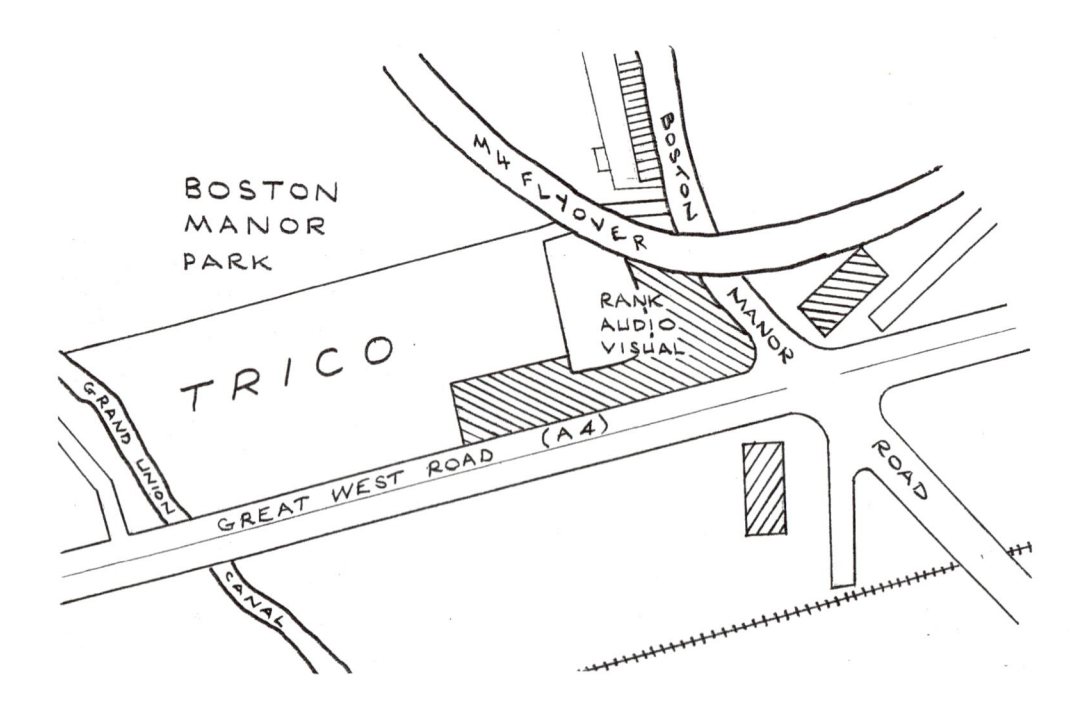

Map of Trico factory in 1976.
DRAWN BY VERNON MERRITT

DISTURBING THE PEACE

BRENTFORD, WEST LONDON, was once the home of the sprawling factory of Trico-Folberth, built in 1928. It lay in the shadow of the M4 flyover, by the side of the A4 Great West Road, one of the main routes into London, not far from the Grand Union canal. Next to it, on the corner of the busy dual carriageway and Boston Manor Road, stood Rank Audio Visual (previously the Macleans factory). On the other side was the imposing art-deco Firestone building, along with a few smaller companies. Across the road was the Fiat UK distribution centre, and further along was Booth's Distilleries and the Gillette factory. In 1962, Trico had moved there from its previous three separate workshops, to concentrate production on this prestigious site.

It is hard to imagine this today since so many of the buildings have now gone, their position usurped by the huge glass and steel edifice of GlaxoSmithKline, which rises to the sky beside the motorway. And already, by the mid-1970s, an all-too common sight for anyone driving along the Great West Road would have been the empty and decaying factories with 'To Let' or 'For Sale' signs up outside. The once proud Golden Mile was fast turning into a graveyard for manufacturing industry.[1]

Trico's Brentford factory was closed down in 1994, when the company relocated to Pontypool, South Wales, and most of the local workforce were made redundant. Yet in 1976, at the time of the strike, this American-owned multinational was still fat from the profits accumulated during its first fifty years of existence, many of which flowed from its virtual monopoly of the motor accessory market in the UK, which mainly consisted of windscreen wipers and motors.

[1] The Great West Road was officially opened by King George V on 30 May 1925, to bypass the notoriously congested Brentford High Street. Later the Brentford section became known as the Golden Mile due to the large number of factories that relocated there to take advantage of the good communications and easy availability of land. Freight was carried on the Brentford Branch railway line to Brentford Dock on the River Thames (until the dock closed in 1964, by which time the factories served by Brentford Town goods yard – which was to close in 1970 – had switched to road transport). Heathrow airport, only eight miles away, expanded its cargo transport facilities throughout the 1960s.

The recession of the mid-1970s had seen the Trico workforce decline from 2116 to 1600 over a six-year period, but it was still amongst the larger employers in West London's light industrial belt. It attracted its labour mostly from the surrounding council estates, often employing a number of relatives, or even whole families. One generation after another went to work there, and such were the family ties that people were disinclined to leave even if conditions were stagnating, while at other places they were improving.[2]

People from many lands worked on the assembly lines. A dozen and more different nationalities lent another meaning to the term multinational company. Yet all colours and creeds of workers – English, Irish, Afro-Caribbean, Indian, Spanish, Maltese, French – were treated the same by management: how could they squeeze the highest output from them and pay the lowest wages?

In 1976 Trico-Folberth had plants on several continents and was one of the world's leading manufacturers of windscreen wiper systems. It made wiper arms and blades, and wiper motors and washers, for cars, trucks and buses, as well as a range of other motor accessories. It supplied all the major British car makers: Ford, Vauxhall, Leyland and the British Motor Corporation (which comprised Austin, Morris, Jaguar, Rover and others).

For many employers at that time job segregation between men and women was a major way of holding down costs, and Trico was no exception. For this reason the company always recruited women for the daytime production assembly lines who, it was later discovered, were paid at a lower rate than their male counterparts on the night shift. The night shift was smaller, and was only introduced as a supplement during economically buoyant times. Men were employed exclusively on the night shift (though both men and women worked the back 'twilight' shift set up when the night shift closed down).

As with all engineering factories, Trico had a large tool room, and the toolmakers prided themselves on being the skilled 'craft' section of the workforce. The rest of the shop floor workers consisted of foremen, charge hands, setters (who maintained the machines), labourers, forklift truck drivers and inspectors. Apart from the inspectors, all these jobs were held entirely by men, while women did the assembly work on the day shift. It was only assembly line operators who were on piecework.

On the surface at least there seemed nothing unduly

---

[2] Some Trico workers still spoke of 'the old days', when employers on the Golden Mile would pay around £10 to an employee who introduced someone they knew, often a relative, to work in the factory.

HOW I CAME TO TRICO

PEGGY FARMER

I returned to work at Trico in 1969. I'd already worked there before that in 1960-61, before I was married, but I didn't stay very long, about eighteen months to two years, until about 1963. I worked in the Assembly Shop putting motors together. I was doing leads to put on the motors for the wiper blades. I didn't like the job. It was the foreman I didn't like – who shall remain nameless. He picked on me. I went into Inspection in 1969. Then I went to No 4 Shop and worked on the screens running the motors in the Inspection Department.

BOB BANISTER

I came to work at Trico in 1973. I'd been employed at a number of companies before that, mainly in the Wembley area. I started a job at a place called Gresham Lyon in Brentford, which made torpedo tubes in submarines. I started on the Monday and on the Friday the chief engineer called me in and said, 'I'm sorry we're going to have to let you go'. This was because of my party membership of course, although he wouldn't say so. He just hinted that it was my 'other activities' outside work. I had done nothing wrong in work. Then I got a job for another week, at a bottle washing plant in Acton, but when I went there they had a problem and said, 'Oh, just amuse yourself' – and for a whole week I was amusing myself in the drawing office, looking at drawings, looking at the sort of work I do. By the end of the week I'd decided it wasn't the sort of job I wanted – it was dead boring! So I was looking for work and then I saw this advert in the paper, 'Trico – Wanted Draughtsman.' I had worked in the motor car industry previously – I'd worked for a commercial vehicle body maker in Ruislip, so I applied and that was it.

RHODA (FRASER) WILLIAMS

I came to work at Trico in 1968. I had heard people saying they were taking workers on so I went to Personnel and they put me straight on the motor line. Joan, my niece, was already working there. Before that I had been working at Pure White laundry in Askew Road, and then at Walls in Acton. From Walls I had a job near the little market place, making enemas, but they closed it down. When I was there I was pregnant, and then afterwards I came to Trico. I decided to leave because everybody there was heading for Trico. Quite a lot of Grenadians were there. And then afterwards they put me on the motor line.

ANN FITZGERALD

When I first came over here from Ireland, in May 1964, it was the first factory where I asked for work, but there were no vacancies, so I went to Cambridge Road in Hanwell. I just went there because when I got here I had to find a job and find a bedsitter – which I did, no problem. I used to solder wires onto the back of the speedometers. But the money wasn't great there so I tried Macleans, but there were no

HOW I CAME TO TRICO

vacancies there. Something was drawing me to Trico's – so I went back to Trico's the year after, in July 1965, and got the job and never looked back.

BOB MITCHELL

I started working at Trico's in 1973 or 1974. Before that I worked as a printing apprentice for a company in Brentford which went broke and I was made redundant. I got a job in the automatic press shop at Trico's as a power press setter.

ERIC FUDGE

The board outside with a list of jobs said, 'Toolmakers and Machine Operators'. I thought, well I can't make tools so I had better go for machine operating, it can't be that difficult. And I just walked in and said I want a job doing whatever, and the people at the gate pointed me at the office and I just marched in the door there. And they said 'Oh yes sir, fill in this form'. So I filled in the form and they said 'Sit in this room and do this intelligence test'. I thought, well you don't need to be incredibly intelligent to pass this – and that was it. I got a job as a machine operator on night shift. That was several years before the strike.

ROBERT (BOB) SINGH

In January 1970 my parents left and went back home to Jamaica. I was still at school and had the intention of continuing with my schooling. Unfortunately the fact of my parents returning to Jamaica meant I needed some form of income because I had no relatives in the country at the time and I had no means of income. But in those days jobs were plentiful so I started by the Great West Road. First of all I went into Gillettes, then the next factory along was Firestone, and Trico was next door to Firestone. Firestone offered me a job as well as Trico, but for some reason – I'm not sure why – I chose Trico. My start date was January 1970, over six years before the strike.

SALLY GROVES

I was at college when my marriage broke down and I moved out. So I had to find a job as soon as possible to pay the rent of my bed-sit. I went down the job centre and asked about factory jobs as those were the best paid at the time. I was told there were two jobs available that day. One was at Walls in Acton and the other at Trico in Brentford. They were both about the same distance from my place in West Ealing, so I asked what time you had to start. I was told it was 7.30 at Walls. That was bad news as mornings are not my best time. So I asked what time at Trico and the answer was 8am. So that was it! …

remarkable about Trico that might set it aside from hundreds of similar firms. The workers were not particularly militant, nor was there any real background of industrial disputes. True, there had been a week-long stoppage in the stores and shipping departments early in 1975, but that had been quickly resolved and mostly forgotten. And you had to go back as far as 1969 to recall another strike. Trico could be said to be reasonably typical of industry in West London in its rather uneventful pattern of industrial relations.

Yet that spring something was afoot that eventually would erupt into the longest and one of the most significant and bitter strikes ever fought for equal pay. Why Trico? What happened in those months that caused the women workers of Trico to end the year as symbols of the struggle for women's rights?

One factor was the nature of the Trico Products Corporation of Buffalo, New York State. This was one of a number of American employers that were at that time becoming increasingly responsible, through their subsidiaries, for major episodes of industrial unrest in Britain, as a result of their blackmailing tactics and seemingly ham-fisted methods of handling disputes. The giant US car firms were themselves amongst its leading shareholders (the premier bloc was controlled by General Motors, the second-largest privately-owned company in the world); these were companies with records that workers everywhere held in abhorrence.

The Trico management in Britain were home grown, however, with the exception of the managing director, Rene Van Dyck, who was Australian-born. Van Dyck tended to maintain a respectable aloofness when it came to the workforce or industrial relations. But the British managers were happy to adopt Trico management techniques. The two other main members of the management team during the strike were Sidney Atkins and John Millner Slidders. Atkins was the works manager (or to give him his full title, manufacturing executive), and was the local boy made good. By this time in his fifties, he had started on the shop floor, and, with the help of a little good fortune, had risen to become chief negotiator for the company. Slidders, the other principal actor in dealings with the unions, was a newly recruited personnel executive whose arrival at Trico had been heralded by rumours of his tough approach. He had previously worked in the Irish docks and London's East End.

The three-strong board of directors was very peculiar indeed. It consisted of Van Dyck; G.B. Cooke, a senior

THE WORKFORCE AND THE COMMUNITY

PEGGY FARMER

The factory – it was brilliant. I thought it was a wonderful place to work the second time I worked there, it was more friendly. I just liked it. There were lots of people I knew there who remembered me from when I had worked there before. Even the foreman came up to me when I went on Inspection and said 'Why didn't you come back to my department, Peg?'

And I was well known because of the rest of my family living in Challis Road, including my mother. There must have been ten families down that road with people at Trico's. All round the area – the Clayponds area – you would find Trico workers. You could see them going to work in the morning. I remember there was a man, his wife and two sons from the road used to work at Trico's when I was younger, before I ever went there. I used to see the family going past – they all worked at Trico's. It was a Brentford, family-orientated, place.

Eileen Ward – I've known her since I was young, and Betty, Gladys Wells and her sister Peggy, they all worked there. Roy Sheldrick, my brothers, the Pritheroes, some of the Smiths – just talking of Challis Road. It was a good place to work.

I didn't know the management when I first went there but I got to know them well after I became Shop Steward. But I had known Sid Atkins long before. My father knew Sid Atkins, so that's going way back into the history of Trico. It was always Brentford people who worked at Trico's. I liked the atmosphere in there. It was family-orientated, everyone got on with everyone.

During the strike, so many people had family working there, and family that was out at the gate.

I think there were about 2000 working there in 1969. There were people from the Caribbean and Africa, Indian, Polish, all sorts. Everyone got on. Alright, we all stayed in our little cliques, but when we were working we all mixed in. I thought there was a great atmosphere there. I worked on the motor line as an inspector with my friend Mrs Sawney. She died two years ago, but I kept in touch with her all those years after she left to have her second child.

THE WORKFORCE AND THE COMMUNITY

LORETTA BRAITHWAITE
It was just like a family and we enjoyed each other's company from different shops. When it was a birthday or anything everybody joined in, and it became one big family. When anybody was leaving the same thing happened. Over the years you'd meet different friends of all nationalities and everybody got on quite alright.

ROBERT (BOB) SINGH
In the Press shop they were very much traditional working-class guys with their mentality: they had the real workers' mentality – very conservative in their outlook, as they felt more privileged compared to the rest of the workforce. The tool-room had the real craftsmen mentality, then you had the quality control guys, then the press setters. They were very cliquish in their outlook. The guys were predominantly white, with a few Caribbean guys.

Interestingly enough, a racist attitude was there but it didn't come out, but during the strike it did become an issue, and also after the strike. I think the main thing before the strike, though, was that I seemed to be the sort of person who read, and I was involved in the WRP at the time. Their main thing wasn't so much about colour but about my politics. They were quite derogatory – 'you're a socialist' sort of attitude.

PHYLLIS GREEN
They were all a lot of old ladies in Shipping. I was the youngest ... I'd say all the women there would have been coming up to fifty, or from fifty to seventy really. So it was just me who was younger, and then there was another couple of Irish girls there, but they'd come and go. And they used to get students as well. They used to come in for the summer holidays.

There were a lot of lovely little black girls working at Trico. There were Indian girls there as well. A lot of Irish worked at Trico's as well. I can't think of a country that there wouldn't have been someone from there, even Spain – there were Spanish people working there. It was a very mixed bunch.

RHODA (FRASER) WILLIAMS
On the motor line there was Irish, there was English, there was African, there was Grenadian, there was Barbadian, Jamaican, some Indian – a good mixture. I think we had a lot of Grenadians. I made a lot of friends.

partner in a large and long established company of City solicitors; and R.J. Oshei, the elusive American president of the Trico Corporation on the other side of the Atlantic.[3] None of the workers had ever known Oshei to visit the Brentford factory, nor could anyone tell you what he looked like. He was never seen or heard at all during the events that were about to unfold. In fact it was difficult to locate who was really responsible for day-to-day management decisions, or where the encouragement was coming from to seek to emulate the most backward of American industrial practices.

An additional factor for discontent within the factory was general wage rates, which had fallen well below the district average. This was openly admitted by the company. Far from doing anything about it, they had a range of excuses, from 'we know you're underpaid but at the moment we can't afford any more', to 'yes, we've got the money but now government restrictions won't let us pay it!'

Trade union organisation had existed at the Brentford factory for more than twenty years, but it could never have been described as really strong. A member would sometimes drop out of membership over small disagreements, or what they thought was lack of activity, and then they would join again. The fortnightly meetings of the shop stewards' committee were usually taken up with purely departmental considerations.

In 1976 about 70 per cent of the shop floor workers were unionised – mainly as members of the Amalgamated Union of Engineering Workers (AUEW), Engineering Section, now part of Unite. The AUEW was the union that had sole negotiating rights. Other manual unions – the Transport and General Workers' Union (TGWU) and the General and Municipal Workers' Union (GMWU) – had a handful of members each. A small number of staff were also members of a union, but they were split between ASTMS, APEX and TASS, which was the staff section of the AUEW.

On the other hand union organisation in the AUEW Southall District was strong and once the strike was started this became an important factor in sustaining it.

The first real signs of trouble ahead came in 1974. Sid Atkins invited the thirty shop stewards to a film show. It was a film of the plant Trico was preparing to open at Northampton on the brand new Round Spinney industrial estate. Up to 200 workers were to be taken on, and production lines transferred from Brentford. Still, the stewards were told that the business was expanding, and the new plant

---

[3] R.J. Oshei was the son of the founder of the company, John R. Oshei, a theatre manager in Buffalo, New York. The story goes that one rainy night in 1916 while driving in his automobile he struck down a man on his bicycle. It appears that the man was not seriously hurt but Oshei vowed to improve the ability of drivers to see during bad weather and therefore set up a company to manufacture and market the first windshield wiper 'Rain Rubber'. Over the years it became a multinational company that advertised itself as the 'Raining Champions'.

10 | GETTING ORGANISED

would not mean any compulsory redundancies at Brentford. Though protests were made at the lack of proper consultation, the move went ahead.

At Northampton, non-union female labour was taken on for assembly work on wages that were so low (although this did not come out until the strike began) that the Engineering Employers' Federation (EEF) had to step in to get Trico to pay the agreed national minimum rates.

But Trico was looking for ways to boost its profits still higher, and in September 1975 it dropped a bombshell! The Brentford night assembly shift was to be 'phased out' over the next six months, and would end completely in April 1976. One hundred and twenty workers were involved. The reason given was the economic recession.

Only men were employed on the night shift. They were paid an extra one-third as a shift premium, but were also paid a higher 'male' piecework rate. The obvious question for management was why employ men when they could use cheap female labour to do the same work?

In the circumstances there was little the union could do. Anxious to at least save jobs, they asked for talks. Over 100 of the men – against union advice – finally opted for a voluntary redundancy scheme. About thirty more moved onto a new specially devised 'twilight shift', from 6pm until 10pm. But five men remained, and were given the option of being transferred onto the day shift alongside the women before the end of the six months phasing-in period. They would lose their night shift premium, but would continue to be paid on the higher piecework rates that had always been given to the men on night shift. This meant they were paid about £6.50 a week more than the women.

But people talk to one another, and it wasn't long before the women working alongside these five men – who had all been put on the washer assembly line – discovered that, because of the different piecework rate, they were being paid significantly less for doing identical work.

Although nobody could have been aware of it at the time, this was to become one of the most fateful decisions in the history of the struggle for equal pay for women. Of course the Equal Pay Act itself, the result of many years of campaigning, gave the context for the dispute, but it was the management's own clumsiness that was to make their company the centre of equal pay campaigning.

THE UNION

LORETTA BRAITHWAITE

I've always been in the union. I had a choice whether I wanted to be in it or not, but it was my choice to join, because if anything happens you have to have some representation. I've always been in the union.

People had their little arguments about it, but if you didn't want to be in it you just came out. But I have always been in it. I find it all right. I never had any problem with it.

Some of the places that I worked never had a union anyway. They were only small places. I just go with the rules: if there was a union I joined it, but if there wasn't a union, there was nothing to join.

Reggie (my husband, who worked on the night shift as an Inspector) just came out with us because he was a union person, and he stayed out until we went back in.

BOB BANISTER

I worked in the drawing office at Trico for five years, until 1978. Before I went there I was already well involved with TASS, which was the technical and staff section of the AUEW. I'd been involved with the union since 1964. So I went in and made myself known to the convenor, John Inwood.

As far as staff was concerned, union organisation was a bit weak. ASTMS had a small membership there, and TASS also had a few members – at the time of the strike there were six of us in the drawing office. It wasn't a very big drawing office, probably eight or nine people.

The shop floor was organised. The convenor, John Inwood, knew his job. He seemed to be pretty competent. I'd been in non-union firms, so it was quite a relief to be in a company where the union did exist.

As a staff union we were still trying to get recognised, because staff traditionally had never been well organised. We thought staff need to be unionised, and we took it even further: we said it's not just staff we need to organise but people who call themselves managers. They need to get a union organisation around them. That was part of what I was involved in trying to push forward.

THE UNION

SANDRA (WARD) GRAY
The first thing my Mum said to me was that I had to join the union. She said that was the best thing to do, because if anything happened the union would back you up, including anything legal. And to this day I am still in the union …

BOB MITCHELL
I joined the union straight away. In my previous job I had been made redundant, I had no protection whatever, and it was something I had always believed in, that I had always wanted to do. I always felt the old corny thing of safety in numbers. I always believed that, and I still do to this day.

There was some union organisation, but it was pretty limited. Some of the guys that I worked with were quite proud to say they were union members but a handful wouldn't even talk about it. They weren't ashamed but they weren't proud either. But the ones that were in the engineering union were quite proud, and would wear badges under their overalls to identify themselves.

RHODA (FRASER) WILLIAMS
I joined the union long, long before the strike. Well obviously, for if we get into difficulty and trouble they could fight to get us out of trouble. It was very good for us to join the union. Sometimes just for our safety, just for ourselves.

WHERE IS OUR EQUAL PAY?

UNLIKE MANY more aware companies, Trico had paid little regard to the 1970 Equal Pay Act, which finally became law on 29 December 1975.

Women workers had been struggling to achieve equal pay for more than a century before the Equal Pay Act came into being. Women in the textile industry had been fighting to achieve the rate for the job long before the TUC adopted its first policy on equal pay, in 1888. More recent battles had included the strike by the Ford women sewing machinists at Dagenham in 1968, and the vigorous campaigning of the National Joint Action Campaign for Women's Equal Rights (NJACWER), which had culminated in an impressively large London demonstration in 1969. These and other events and campaigns had galvanised Barbara Castle, who was secretary of state for employment in Harold Wilson's government, to introduce the 1970 Act. (The Equal Pay Act, and the ways in which companies tried to get round its provisions, is covered in more detail in Part Four, 'Fighting for Our Rights'.)

Many people thought the Act would finally secure equal pay as a right. It was expected to be the crowning glory to what had already been achieved through women's campaigns within the trade unions and outside. But, as the case of Trico was to demonstrate only too clearly, there were still many battles ahead.

Common to industry at large, Trico had been given five years to prepare for equal pay, from the time the Act was passed until it came into force. Yet, according to the union's calculation, in all that time only £3 per week had been given to the women to close the gap, though the gap was far wider than that. For ten years and more, discriminatory rates had existed at Brentford, and the company had done little to end them. So, in the summer of 1975, negotiations were started by the union to try and ensure that, come EPA Day at the end of the year, there would at last be a common operational rate in the factory, regardless of sex.

With thorough homework, the union managed to unravel Trico's highly complex piecework formulas, which had often caused the firm's computer a nervous breakdown. They found that, based on the normal factory performance measurement, the women's piece rate of 29.2 pence per hour, when compared to the male rate of 36.7 pence per hour, once it was added to the basic wage, meant a difference at the end of a 40-hour week of about £6.50, for doing exactly the same work.[4]

Management were in no mood to concede equal pay by increasing the women's piece rate, nor to show up the deplorable state of the wage structure throughout the workforce. All they were prepared to discuss was a job evaluation exercise that they had carried out previously, which compared the women's work to the obscure job of a male capstan operator. This, they said, might entitle a small number of women to a marginal increase.

The argument they gave for not paying the male assembly operators' rate to the women doing the same job was that they were not really doing the same work. The men got more, they said, as a reward for their greater 'flexibility' – the ability to switch from one type of machine to another at the whim of management. (This was to prove one of the classic excuses for avoiding equal pay – see Part Four for more on this.)

The union quickly scotched that by producing copies of a 1969 agreement – an outcome of the strike that year – which showed that the women had also agreed to be 'flexible', in exchange for a half-penny per hour rise. As they argued, in practice both men and women were called on to exercise their talents equally.

On 8 December 1975 the stewards reported the lack of progress to a mass meeting of the women. It was decided to take the issue further and call in the local AUEW officials. More meetings were to be arranged with Atkins and Slidders. But when, on 1 January 1976, the new era dawned that should have brought equality, there had been no improvement. Some women were now making fresh gains and upsetting the status quo, but not at Trico's.

[4] At Trico piecework earnings were made up of two parts – a national supplement (i.e. the basic pay rate) and an element based on piecework. Work content in any operation was measured in minutes per 1000 pieces, known as the Unit Value or Minute Value. The rate for a particular job would be set after a work study by a Work Study Engineer who calculated the work content of the job. The operator's performance was defined as their average hourly earnings expressed in minutes: an operator returning a 120 performance measurement over the day had averaged 120 minutes per hour – or double time – for which a payment would be made at twice the basic operational rate.

AWARENESS OF THE EQUAL PAY ISSUE

"

ERIC FUDGE

They just gathered us together one day and told us that the night shift would be going to finish. Those who didn't want to move to days would be made redundant and those that did would have their pay reduced. At the end of the day they agreed that the piecework rate would remain the same and the night shift premium would go – and that was it. So I ended up with four other guys in the micro motor washer department – George Jinks, Tom Messitt, Jules de Sousa and Swabey (he was always known as Swabey!). I was surprised more didn't stay, but jobs weren't as difficult to get in those days as they are now – you could practically walk into another job.

We weren't at first aware that the piece-work rate was higher than the women's on dayshift. It was only when someone was looking at the pay slips one day, and we were all sitting there together, that someone noticed.

It was because of the shop stewards on night shift that they didn't succeed in reducing our piecework rate. As we pointed out at the time, the piecework rate was the rate for the job, but the night premium was for working nights – they were two separate things. As far as we were concerned they were not going to reduce that rate – and they agreed without too much of a fight.

They always kept the men together on days, they never put us with the ladies. We were mainly working on the micro motor line section, making armatures, the bit which is found inside an electric motor. We made the cores, which then went down the line to have the wiring wound onto them. But if they had a large stock of them we would do other things. Generally they didn't like putting us with the ladies on one of their lines, the reason being quite obvious really, with hindsight.

They probably hadn't thought through the fact that we would at some stage compare rates – and to prevent that is probably why they kept us in a little bunch separate to everyone else. They didn't want it getting out.

Unfortunately people talk to each other, we're quite sociable, and people started to see that we were in fact getting a higher rate – and they were not happy! And, of course, this caused some bad feeling, to which my response was 'Well it's not my fault; go and see the union and get something done about it'. Then there were suggestions that the company would lower our rate, to which I immediately kicked up a stink. That was not right, that was the rate for the job – they'd already taken away the night premium; we were not having that. So a further suggestion was that it would just be us that had that, and any other men starting would start on a lower rate – but no men did start!

Most of the women weren't very happy about this. We showed them our slips and they were not happy, and I agreed with them it wasn't right. What the company was trying to do was implement equal pay by reducing our pay, which I didn't reckon much of, for obvious reasons.

Every now and then there was a hiccup,

GETTING ORGANISED

AWARENESS OF THE EQUAL PAY ISSUE

and then there was a stoppage for a couple of hours or so, and then it would be 'yes, yes, we're looking into it' and all this, and then they'd all go back to work. Then someone from the union would come down and say, 'Look, you can't just stop like this, you'd better go back to work, we're negotiating', so they'd go back again. And that really wasn't working. It was quite obvious to me that as long as they pussy-footed around with endless negotiations dragging on for months on end, the company was quite happy to do that. What they needed was beating with a stick, and that was what happened in the end.

PHYLLIS GREEN

Everyone in the shipping department was saying 'Oh it doesn't affect us', as if we didn't belong to the factory. The factory was just across the footpath from where we worked, but they said, 'No, it's nothing to do with us, we don't work in the factory'. I was thinking, 'but without the factory we wouldn't be sending stuff out, we wouldn't have a job!' They were all saying we wouldn't have to go on strike, or it was nothing to do with us. For them equal pay never came into it much really. They just thought it was a local dispute.

ROBERT (BOB) SINGH

I don't think I had any recollection of an equal pay issue in the factory before the strike. I don't think any work was done with the men in the factory to make us aware that there was this issue developing. The day the strike took place, when the women went into the park, that was the first time I knew there was an issue.

BOB MITCHELL

In the area I worked, in the press shop, equal pay wasn't an issue. What was an issue was between the two shifts, day and night shift; the fact that it involved women was seen as a coincidence. The fact that the night shift had come over was seen as more important. And it wasn't until the picket line was actually up and running that I even saw some of the people that I was working with crossing the picket line.

I don't think the men were specifically invited to the mass meeting in the park. And it was considered to be a women's strike, or maybe even a nightshift strike.

PEGGY FARMER

I first remember equal pay on the agenda about eighteen months before the strike, when we walked out of that SSC meeting. That was when Sid was talking behind our backs. I said there was another meeting going on, and John Inwood and the rest of us walked out. They were talking down to us.

The five men from night shift had been transferred to the women's day shift before the end of 1975. They were still earning £6.50 a week more than the women, even after losing their shift allowance,

The management announced their solution to what they described as an 'anomaly'. It was quite simple. Government pay policy permitting (at that time there were pay policies in effect, see footnote), any future wage increases on the day shift would be awarded solely to the women: the five men working alongside them would mark time until the women caught up! In other words, the men would get a wage cut – equal pay in reverse! Their wages would be frozen for the years and years it would take for the women to catch up, during which time the high rates of inflation would be constantly forcing down the value of wages. Even the increases that were allowed under the Social Contract didn't keep up with the cost of living, and meant a big drop in living standards.[5]

It was an absurd suggestion. The company seemed to be hoping that the five men wouldn't notice that they would become £6.50 worse off in time while the rest of the factory were getting increases! If Trico were trying to be subtle, they had only managed to be inept.

In the meantime, the women on the lines were supposed not to notice that a man was working alongside them on an identical machine, and, for doing the same work, getting a higher wage. But once the men arrived on day shift, the women had visible evidence of the injustice they had been suffering. And it was enough to test anyone's patience to be given a series of phoney excuses, with no end to them apparently in sight.

The anger of the Trico women was not long in expressing itself. Spontaneous stoppages occurred in February on the washer assembly line. Stewards restored order by explaining that negotiating procedures must be used first – only after that did the women return to work.

The transfer of those five men onto day shift, alongside the women, proved to be the company's most spectacular own goal. It all added up as the final spark to a situation that had inflamed feelings beyond breaking point.

[5] The Social Contract, first developed by the Labour Party-TUC Liaison committee between 1972 and 1973, was brought in by Harold Wilson's Labour government from 1974. It was a programme of voluntary wage restraint or incomes policy, 'sold' to the trade unions as a deal in return for legal reforms, price control and a number of other measures. In 1975 the TUC consented to a more formal deal with government (Social Contract Phase I, later followed by Phase II). It had ended by the time of the Healey-Callaghan pay policy of 1978. Throughout the 1970s, high inflation constantly eroded wage settlements.

THE JOB

PHYLLIS GREEN
I worked in shipping. We used to pack things up for the post or rail delivery, or big pallets to go on the lorries. We mostly shipped the big pallets with pieces for Vauxhall or places like that. The packages contained pieces of engines, little bits of screws and other things like that.

ERIC FUDGE
It was quite good fun. Most of us working on night shift were in some way eccentric – this strange mix of people of all sorts of different races and religions but, funnily enough, everyone got along fine, mainly because we were all barking mad! A lot of them left when they shut the night shift down. I was a machine operator basically doing what the women did on the day shift. We assembled components and such like on the production line. What we'd do was make sub-assemblies for the day shift to put into other assemblies – not much else really. We were on the motor line, which made the air pressure motors for the pneumatic wipers on trucks and trains and other things. And then when we moved to the day shift we went to the washer line and micro motor line.

ANN FITZGERALD
I went back to Trico's in 1965 as an assembly worker on the blade line, and never looked back. I was on piecework – the more you did the more you got. Oh, the fingers cut! And I used to do overtime every night nearly till 7 o'clock – about two hours – and sometimes I went in Saturday morning at half eight, and it was great. I absolutely loved it, never complained about it. I was usually on the blade line but sometimes you were sent to work somewhere else. I was sent over to the arm line, and I sometimes did the squeegees, which were an awful job. You had to put the plastic bit into the machine, put your foot to open it and get the sponge in, and if you didn't get it level you had to take it out again. And then there were two screws that had to go in straight – and the times the screw wouldn't go through the plastic and it'd be a reject! And if you kept throwing them out, damaging them, you'd be told off by the charge-hand.

And then I went into the rubber room, doing the rubbers for the blades. And you had to get the rubber dead flat, and if you got bubbles on the rubber they'd come out and stop the line. You could be stopped for hours. And we did other assembly jobs

THE JOB

on the back of the wiper. You had to put the main bit in and then another one with a pair of tweezers. You had to put in tiny little green rubbers and then another metal bit on top, and then you clamped it and closed it, and you had to put them on the belt. You had so many at a time – and someone else was then sliding them on.

Oh Jesus, you couldn't stop for a minute because you'd hold up the line, and if you wanted to go out to the toilet you had to ask permission. And then if the machine broke you'd call the charge hand, and there would be a hand on your shoulder … Oh God!

I always found the money was good. You got the basic pay and then the piecework rate was added to it, but you weren't allowed to go over too much on the piecework. You had to do so many an hour, and we used to go over it, sometimes too much, and they'd cut it back. If the rate was 100 and something, 185 was the highest you could go to. But we might sometimes go to 190.

BOB MITCHELL

I worked in the automatic Press Shop as a power press setter. It was very noisy and I remember it being very greasy, but the noise protection wasn't what you'd expect now. People spoke in sign language – not recognised signs like we have now, we all made up our own signs. And you could feel the ground shake, it was that noisy.

ROBERT (BOB) SINGH

They offered me a job as a press setter in the Power Press Department. I'd never been inside a factory before, but felt like I could do it. I was sixteen when I started. One thing they told me I must do when I reported for work was to bring my mug in for tea. So, when I started I brought my mug with me to work.

The first thing that struck me was the size of the presses, the big power presses, and the noise level, extremely noisy. But it was an open environment so you could actually see the different departments and what was going on. They would be pressing out parts for the wiper blades from sheet metal, and our job was to load tools into the machine and make sure the specifications were correct when they pressed out the different bits and pieces for the wiper blades.

In our department it was all men, all press setters. The women worked mainly as operators on the machines and collected the parts as they came out. There was very much an elitist atmosphere – that the men were the ones did the real jobs. Initially there were no women in the department. Women came in and collected the parts, but later on one of the machines I worked had a woman working on it; whilst I set up the machine the woman would come and collect the bits and pieces and so on and operate the press machine. I would set up the machine and it ran automatically and it filled up the containers and they were taken off somewhere else.

RHODA (FRASER) WILLIAMS

On the motor line I worked on the BPM motor, which is 300 pieces. You did different pieces of the assembly. I would pass on to the next person and they then passed it on. We didn't do the same job every day, we used to swap around. Sometimes we had to do the welding, sometimes put in the gas stick, the cylinder, and there were panels you had to grease. The BPM motor was for the windscreen wipers on an aeroplane. I also worked on the APM, which had 200 bits – they were for cars.

The work was OK once you got hold of it. But if you forgot one piece it would just condemn the whole motor, and obviously you would have to open it up again. If it's put on the screen and it doesn't work, the inspector will pass it back and say it is not working, and we had to open it up to see what we had forgotten. If we forgot a spring or a screw, or a little bearing, it got condemned when it went for testing. You've got to remember all the pieces. You've got to know what you're doing.

On the line it was very peaceful and a lot of laughter, but you just had to settle down doing your work – you really had to study the pieces and what would be going into the motor.

Sometimes, when they didn't need the motors, or if the line broke down, they'd send us to do a little painting, touching up blades in the paint shop. And we used to break off mouldings in the press shop – you had to wear gloves for that. Sometimes I used to work on the washer line and the blade line. But my place was really the motor line.

EXPLOSION!

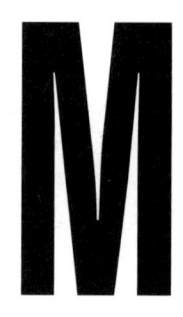

MONDAY 24 MAY was a mild, overcast day with a little hint of rain in the air. A fairly typical spring day, it was destined to be rather special in other ways.

It had just gone 12.30pm. People were walking in twos and threes, filing into Boston Manor Park for a union meeting. Soon a large crowd would gather. Everyone was in a hurry to get the meeting over with – they only had an hour for lunch. Adjoining the rear of the Trico plant, the park was ideally situated for holding mass meetings, providing the weather held. Away in the centre, near the cricket pavilion, people waited impatiently for it to start.

John Inwood, AUEW convenor at Trico, stood up to chair the meeting. There were two items on the agenda: the first one was the shop stewards' committee's recommendation for a one-day strike to support the National Day of Action on Unemployment and the Lobby of Parliament two days later, on Wednesday 26 May. The second item was a report on that morning's negotiations with the company on equal pay.

Roger Butler, Southall District secretary of the AUEW, and the union's local official responsible for the Trico factory, was to speak on both subjects. First he put across a strong case for trade unionists to support the national demonstration, which was backed by the Confederation of Shipbuilding and Engineering Unions (CSEU). Unemployment figures, at over a million and a quarter, were at record post-war levels, and local factories were closing down and throwing people on the dole. His message was that it was high time the Labour government changed its economic course, and we should be out there making our voices heard.

The recommendation was put to the vote. The meeting

was divided. Trico did not have the best reputation for supporting issues which appeared to be outside its own four walls. Some began drifting away, thinking it was all over. In the confusion there was a shout from the back for a half-day stoppage to be put. Hands went up again, and this time a majority of the members supported it.

The meeting broke up. John Inwood reminded the women to stay behind. The men – non-production manual workers, toolmakers, machine setters, labourers, fitters, maintenance, etc – returned to the factory, along with the few male assembly operators. The audience was now almost entirely female production-line workers. Roger Butler informed them that, at the second external works conference that morning, the company had made it clear that they had no intention whatsoever of implementing equal pay. They had even threatened to reduce the five male operators' rate to that of the women: the union had been forced to register a 'failure to agree'. Every effort had been made to resolve the problem through discussion, but all formal negotiating procedure had now been exhausted. The next step was up to the Trico stewards to consider, and the membership to decide.

The meeting was closed, and Roger Butler left for another engagement. It was nearly 2pm and some of the women began to drift back into work. Then word reached the factory – about 200 women had remained in the park, including the women from the washer line, and they were demanding a meeting right now. Straightaway, the other women returned and the convenor was recalled. The meeting restarted. It was in a mood for action, there and then.

There were proposals for lightning strikes, either for one or two days each week, but there was also one for all-out strike action. After some heated discussion it was quite clear what the general feeling was: nothing short of strike action would force the management's hand. The proposal for all-out strike was put first, and was carried overwhelmingly. The women from now on were on strike – and ninety-eight of them weren't even members of a union! Dazed and incredulous, they began to wonder what their decision would mean. For the great majority, for the first time in their lives they were out on strike.

All that remained was to collect their belongings and go home … and wait to see what tomorrow would bring.

24 MAY AND MASS MEETINGS

"

BOB BANISTER

The Trico drawing office was in this kind of conservatory built on the front of the building overlooking the car park, and suddenly we could see all the women streaming out the front gate and disappearing. We had a grandstand view!

It was just a moment of amazement. I sat at the drawing board looking out the window, seeing all these women streaming out of the gate, and wondering where they're going. And everybody around me was asking the same question, so I said I'd go and find out – 'I'll go and ask the convenor' – which I did. And I found John and asked 'What's up?' and he said, 'They've walked out. They left me behind. I've got to go and talk to the management now and tell them what's happened.' He told me it was about the equal pay dispute. So I asked him to keep us informed.

PHYLLIS GREEN

I came out to the park for the meeting but I wasn't sure what to do. We all left our bags and coats and everything in the factory, because everyone was telling us it was nothing to do with us! There was a lot of people, the park was full. The whole factory came out I'd say. I think the men might have come out as well just to hear what was going on – because in our department it was really about whether we would get paid for bigger jobs, and the men were afraid we would get paid for bigger jobs, and they didn't want us to get paid. I never thought about equal pay. I just thought about the bigger jobs, the jobs we were doing ... But it was great.

So we came back in, got our coats, and didn't go back for another four or five months! I think we might have clocked out. I think we queued up to clock out as well! I don't think we realised what was happening until later on, and then you got involved in things. We were kind of separated from the rest of the factory.

24 MAY AND MASS MEETINGS

ROBERT (BOB) SINGH
The day the strike took place when the women went into the park, we joined it. Besides John Inwood, the union convenor, there were the union officers and a couple of other people from the union. There couldn't have been more than ten men there. There were the five who had been on the washer line, who were directly affected.

PEGGY FARMER
When we were called into the park on 24 May, I was shocked that they were even debating to go out on strike. I voted against it. There had been a final meeting that Mac, Roger, Eileen and Betty had been at (after which there was the Failure-to-Agree), but I was shocked when Eileen said we're all over the park. Everyone thought it was great going over the park and it was just before lunchtime. But my mind was thinking of them – I voted for lightning strikes, I didn't want all out, as I was thinking of the girls who were living in rooms.

ERIC FUDGE
I vaguely remember the day we came out. Yes I think everyone was pretty much agreed that action had to be taken. I certainly didn't have any doubts. I thought we should all get out the gates. I think I wandered back in (after the meeting) and had a chat with the chaps – 'Look this isn't really good enough and we should take action'. And a couple of them said, 'Well, hang on a minute, it doesn't really affect us', to which I pointed out that it was the principle of the thing: it was not right and we should join in, we were all members of the same union, they were all our fellow workers and we should stick up for them. And so we were out. I don't think we really understood what was involved and stayed around looking at each other for a while and wondering what we were going to do next, and then people had to start saying, right, this is what we've got to do. I came back the next day and sat outside.

24 MAY AND MASS MEETINGS

BELLA (DAVIS) YOUNG
Suddenly it was a notice, you have to go to the park, and then at the meeting they said the men were on more money than the girls. The men who used to work on nights got more money than the girls. They were doing exactly the same work but they got more money. It was a mistake the company made. There was a meeting and everybody put their hand up to come out, and then we came out for the simple reason that the men were doing the same job as us but getting more money. The company made a mistake – they should have put them on another job where they did heavy work and then nobody could say anything, but they were doing exactly the same thing.

BILLY TAYLOR
I was Secretary of the AUEW Shop Stewards Committee [SSC] at Acton Works, London Underground, a factory that employed about 1500 people and had about three to four hundred AUEW members. Don Cook was the Convenor and Chairman – a very good Convenor and Chairman indeed. We got a call one morning informing us that the women at Trico had come out on strike and were seeking support. The call was from Roger Butler, the Southall District Secretary to our District Office. So Don and I went there and addressed the meeting, as we'd had the experience in 1969 – which Roger wanted to call on – of having a thirteen-week strike.

We spoke of our experience of strike and the problems the women would face and the support they would need. We pledged the support of our SSC and said we'd go to the other unions that existed in Acton Works. We were well received and the workers were well pleased that people from other factories were prepared to give such support. And we also told them they would need monetary support as well; strike pay wouldn't keep them during the strike – and told them about the money we had raised, and we gave them a booklet as to how we raised the money during our strike, running into thousands of pounds.

We then went back to report to our SSC and we pledged assistance on the picket as and when required and we reported to the

24 MAY AND MASS MEETINGS

London North District Committee. And there was a roster set up amongst our shop stewards and members, and many of them would come onto the picket line, particularly some of them would spend the evenings there. And from that the strike went on and we all assisted and right through we collected regularly. We contacted all the other departments and spread the news of the strike throughout the London Transport trade union network.

BOB MITCHELL

I remember that first meeting. It was because of our friendship together, myself and Bob Singh [later called Robert], that we both agreed straight after the mass meeting that on the following day both of us would be on strike. I left the meeting and got the bus home, and I knew on the bus journey that the following day I would be on strike.

I remember another meeting in the park, when John Inwood addressed the crowd. He asked for a show of hands, whether to support the picket line or not. A lot of guys who were still inside the factory had climbed over the fence and attended the meeting. And both myself and Bob shouted out 'They're already working. Why are you asking for their opinion?' The attitude to both of us was 'Shut up you little kids'. They called us a couple of little kids, and said we were stirring it up. 'Just because you're in a park, it's not a playground.'

THE EARLY DAYS

NEWS OF THE WOMEN'S action spread throughout the factory during the afternoon. The situation was considerably confused, but everyone knew the main issues. The frustrations of a year's fruitless negotiations had driven the women to stay outside the gate.

Discussions and arguments broke out amongst the men. Some asked why they should go on strike when the company had said they were willing to have a Tribunal resolve the issue (see below, p33). Others, whose natural inclinations were to support other workers in struggle, tried to persuade the men to come out in sympathy. After all wasn't unity strength? And they urged these men to support their trade union. One sticking point was the fact that, as yet, the strike was 'unofficial', and so a decision was put off: if the union declared it official, the rule book laid down that all members would be obliged not to cross any picket line and come out, so the situation would be more clear-cut.

But at least fifteen men did respond immediately and joined the women outside the gates. They were generally welcomed, though one or two were greeted with comments such as 'We don't need you to fight this battle, we can win it on our own', or 'Why haven't you brought the other men out here with you?' Before the strike, it had not helped understanding on either side that the men had been excluded from the meetings about equal pay. Amongst those who did support the strike were the five male assembly-line operators who were in danger of having their money taken away from them.

The final act of Monday's meeting in the park had been to make arrangements for a mass meeting of all the strikers the next morning. Once more they collected in the park. This time a slide in the play area was commandeered as a hastily converted rostrum. For the time being meetings were to be held here, or in the shelter nearby, in competition with the constant noise of the M4 flyover which towered above them.

John Inwood spoke first, and then Eileen Ward, a leading shop steward amongst the women. As a fifteen-year-old Eileen had got the sack on her very first day at Trico. But after a long interval she had returned, and had by then been working at the factory for eleven years. She told the meeting that the stewards had kept a watch on who had gone in that morning. There were no production workers – the strike was 100 per cent solid. Others were out too, including the women from the clock office, who themselves stood to gain nothing from the strike. From now on, Eileen told them, they would have to keep up a picket line and draw up a rota: 'Volunteers, please!'

It's a strange feeling being on strike. The security of the work routine – getting up to be in by eight in the morning; doing a hard job Monday to Friday; trying to reach a good piecework rate, until at last released by the factory whistle; fighting your way home at 5 o'clock in the rush-hour traffic – all this is broken almost overnight.

For many, a new routine was to replace it. They would still need to rise early: in fact it was often even earlier now. There was work to do on the picket line, and that had to be kept going from the time the very first person was likely to go in until everyone had left. A usual day was to be between 6.45am and 5.30pm, with a switch of pickets around midday.

In those first few days the picket line, like everything else, was a bit of a hit and miss affair. There were no picket armbands, no badges to show who was in charge, no official letters, just the persuasiveness of the women as they described to the lorry drivers what Trico was and why they had to strike.

Many lorries drove up to deliver supplies or collect goods, but most turned back without violating the picket line. All, that was, bar one, but the men inside refused to handle the delivery. Trico's own, easily-identified, vehicles were also put in mothballs for the duration. Soon word would get round, and fewer and fewer lorries would turn up. Trico was strike-bound.

The six-lane dual carriageway of the Great West Road, with its deafening, streaming mass of vehicles, was to become a constant companion in the weeks ahead. The factory

EARLY DAYS

ERIC FUDGE

I remember thinking all the time, 'about bloody time'. It had been dragging on for six months, and you just knew if nothing had happened it would have dragged on for another twelve months or more. The company had no inclination to do anything at all in my opinion ... I turned up at the gate the next day. There was a huge enthusiasm at the time and a huge number of people. Obviously as time goes on people don't tend to come down so much. There's always a hard core of people who are prepared to come down every day, and although a lot of other people were staying out they wouldn't necessarily come down to the picket line. But nevertheless most of them stuck to their guns and did not go back to work.

ROBERT (BOB) SINGH

I knew the women had walked out on strike, and I began to get an idea what the issues were, but at the time I didn't believe that it was going to become a major strike, a long strike. I thought it would be over in a few days. Then meetings were being called, and pickets were being set up, because it was obvious that the strike was not going to be over after a couple of days, but we still did not envisage it would be as long as it went on for. There were a few marches ... I think the women were very pleased that we were there with them on strike. I didn't get any hostility at all from the women. I just felt they were pleased that we were there, a small group of men. It was a bit of a novel thing that this small group of men were on strike with them on the picket line and it was something that they appreciated. The more the days went on, you had to organise yourselves much better, as the men were still going to work, deliveries were coming in and out, and goods being taken out, so then you had to become a lot better organised. And then you also appreciated that so many of the women on strike were sole breadwinners, so that money had to be raised.

EARLY DAYS

BOB MITCHELL
At the beginning of the strike myself and the other Bob were a bit of a novelty, because of our age. I was 19 at the time, Bob a year older than me – still is! And we both had the same name too. And we were the only two guys, the majority of people on the picket line were women. They were surprised to see us but we were accepted straight away. And from that day onwards I made a lot of friends, some of whom I kept in touch with for many years.

PHYLLIS GREEN
I went back down to Trico's the next morning at 8 o'clock. I was there for work, but not for work – for working on the picket line. And there were lorries trying to get in and lorries trying to get out – they probably wanted to get the stuff out more than get stuff in – and many of them would have driven past us. Some of the lorries going in would stop and turn round and wouldn't go in, but all the Trico lorries came out past us ... I didn't have a clue. I wouldn't have had any idea of what was going on, so I just stood my ground and stood there with my banner.

PEGGY FARMER
I was confused at the beginning of the strike. It took me at least three weeks to understand what was going on. Eileen was bewildered too. Betty Aiston was on the ball a bit. But it probably took Eileen as long as me. Roger and Sally probably knew what was going on. I think Sally knew because of her contacts. She was probably one of the ones feeding us the lines. I was as green as grass.

perimeter along the Great West Road lay back about fifteen yards from the highway. It needed to if one wasn't to choke on the dust and fumes of thousands of lorries and cars that hourly roared past.

A second picket line was necessary, to keep an eye on the back gate in Boston Manor Road: as many people used this entrance to go into Trico as used the main double gates on the A4. Shaded as it was by trees and the motorway above, this was a much more hospitable place to do picket duty.

The relationship with those who continued to cross the women's picket lines never got out of hand. Including all the office staff, there were over a thousand still working, whilst nearly 400 women were on strike, supported at this stage by fewer than twenty men.

The women were the key workers, however. Without them no production line could move. The factory therefore was brought to a progressive standstill by their action.

The ancillary workers and office staff who did walk in were quickly finding they had little of value to do – it was not much use designing and making new tools and products when the machines were not in use. In the circumstances it was not the end of the world to see the men go in, since it meant that Trico would have to bear a colossal wages bill for no output.

To Trico, however, the cost of putting up a façade of business as usual and not declaring layoffs was worth it. Whilst the men were inside they undermined the women's cause and were helping to demoralise them. In addition, there could be big dividends in the future from carrying the men and thereby dividing the workforce – and, ultimately, breaking the union. Still, it could prove a very costly policy.

The management's contempt for the strikers was barely concealed. To them they were just a rabble of women who in the past had never been able to sustain any form of united action for any length of time: this 'misunderstanding' was to be no exception. Slidders even openly boasted to the factory that the management didn't give the women more than a couple of days before they would be back inside.

But they hadn't reckoned on the strong bonds between the women, and their determination to see justice fulfilled; while, on the management's part, the lack of any experience of an important dispute situation was to prove a major factor in leading them into blunders they were to make.

On Wednesday 26 May Trico sent out a letter to all the

strikers individually, by first-class post. A copy was pinned on the firm's notice boards.

The letter contained a table which, when one read between the lines, showed that, at the average factor performance measurement of 143, the difference in wages between male and female workers on the payment by results system was £6.64 per week. The five men who were getting the higher rate would only do so for a 'limited period of time'. After that there would be 'equal pay' in the factory. Any men taken on in the future would get the present 'women's rate'. The letter concluded:

> the Company has often stated that the opinion of a Tribunal regarding their interpretation of equal pay will be welcome and they have now applied to a Tribunal for a ruling. If the Tribunal supports the Company's interpretation then it would be clear that a state of equal pay had been reached. If the Tribunal supports the Union's point of view, then the amount of increase and the effective date is already pre-determined – regardless of any industrial action that may be taken. Withdrawal of labour cannot alter the present situation! It cannot bring any more money! It can only damage the Company's commercial position and put many jobs at risk.
>
> The Company has acted as quickly as possible and has arranged a meeting with Arbitration Conciliation and Advisory Services (ACAS), the Union and Management for Wednesday 2 June. To avoid unnecessary loss of personal earnings it is recommended that you seriously consider returning to work on Thursday 1 June.
>
> TRICO-FOLBERTH LIMITED

For the first recorded time an employer, not the aggrieved workers, had taken out an application for a hearing by an Industrial Tribunal under the Equal Pay Act. This seemed a highly suspicious course of action.

The reason for this was – as is discussed in Part Four – the EPA was already being undermined by firms that exploited its many loopholes. It was becoming generally accepted that the decisions that tribunals were coming to were – to quote the Institute of Personnel Management – 'a bit odd'!

Contrary to the real intentions of the EPA, the cases that had so far been heard had exposed a strong pro-employer

LOVE LETTERS FROM SID

ERIC FUDGE
I found the company letters they sent out very useful – at night, when it got a bit chilly, we used to set fire to them to keep warm. They were a bit rough for toilet paper; the paper was low grade, like the buggers that were writing the message! They were probably responsible for half the destruction of the Amazon rain forest.

PHYLLIS GREEN
I just didn't take any notice of those letters to be quite honest. I'd been on the picket line and I'd seen what was happening so … actually I don't know if I got many, they didn't have my address anyway! I used to read other people's when I got down to the picket line. When you're living in rooms you move so often – I'm quite sure they didn't have my address. I remember people coming up to Trico with the letter and then showing it to some of the ladies who knew more about trade unions than I did, and they'd be discussing it. Luckily enough they didn't go back in.

bias. Restrictive and over-legalistic decisions were being allowed to make a mockery of the spirit of the Act. Trico was looking for a reliable get-out to avoid their responsibility, and what could be better than being able to say, in refusing to implement equal pay, that they were abiding by the law of the land! Trico from now on looked upon the Tribunal as their trump card.

The letter that was sent out was also to set another pattern – management appealing over the heads of the elected union leadership, and trying to persuade individual workers to renege on the collective decision they'd made. It was the opening shot in a propaganda war against the union, and the 'missiles' through the post were to become another major weapon in their arsenal. The strikers later came to refer to this constant stream of letters as 'love letters from Sid'!

But, alas, all their letter writing fell on deaf ears. When the

Eileen Ward addressing strikers outside Trico gates, 26 May 1976.

TRINITY MIRROR SOUTHERN (EVENING MAIL)

women received the letters most were just torn up, and some were even sent back with, written across them, the words 'Return to work when we've got EQUAL PAY' and other similar messages!

Meanwhile, the women were on the move. On Wednesday morning a mass picket gathered at the front gate, addressed by Eileen, and for the first time press photographers turned out for the occasion. A great variety of home-made placards and banners were held aloft by the cheering crowd as the photos were taken.

Then the women marched into the park for yet another meeting. Roger Butler addressed them, telling them he would be urging the weekly meeting of the District Committee the next day to give the strike its backing and declare it official. 'You've got my full support,' he said – and he proved true to his word.

A march, it was agreed, would be held the next day round the streets of Brentford. Feeling was running high. Everyone knew they had started something big, and there would be no going back until they'd won their equal pay.

That first march was very impressive, not so much for the

THE EARLY DAYS | 35

Trico strikers outside gate. On right, 'Champion', 2nd from right, Monica Harvey, 26 May 1976.

PETER ARKELL/REPORTDIGITAL.CO.UK

fact that it was sunny, which lent a carnival atmosphere to the occasion, or for the numbers involved – about 400 – but mainly as a demonstration of ordinary people who had trust and reliance in each other; and of a comradeship from already existing ties of friendship, now with a new bond made from the fight for a single united purpose. Here were women and men who had discovered the courage needed to challenge a powerful American company.

Determination and a new-found exuberance was in everyone's face on that first march. Compared to the former factory existence it was a new world. People of different ethnic backgrounds were marching along together, equal in their will to win. Gone was the backbiting that had at times existed inside the factory – it had given way to the knowledge of being part of the overall common cause. Bonds of solidarity had begun to be formed between people, some of whom had not even known one another before the strike – some of which were to endure throughout their lives.

If Trico had thought these women were going to be an easy pushover, they were going to be cruelly mistaken.

Above: Eileen Ward and Betty Aiston carrying banner on first march round Brentford, 27 May 1976.   CHRIS DAVIES/REPORT ARCHIVE/REPORTDIGITAL.CO.UK

Below: Trico strikers on first march round Brentford, 27 May 1976.   PETER ARKELL/REPORTDIGITAL.CO.UK

Trico strikers on first march. Joyce Seath foreground, left to right middle 2nd row, Peggy Farmer, Betty Humphreys, Frances Pinner, 27 May 1976.   CHRIS DAVIES/REPORT ARCHIVE/REPORTDIGITAL.CO.UK

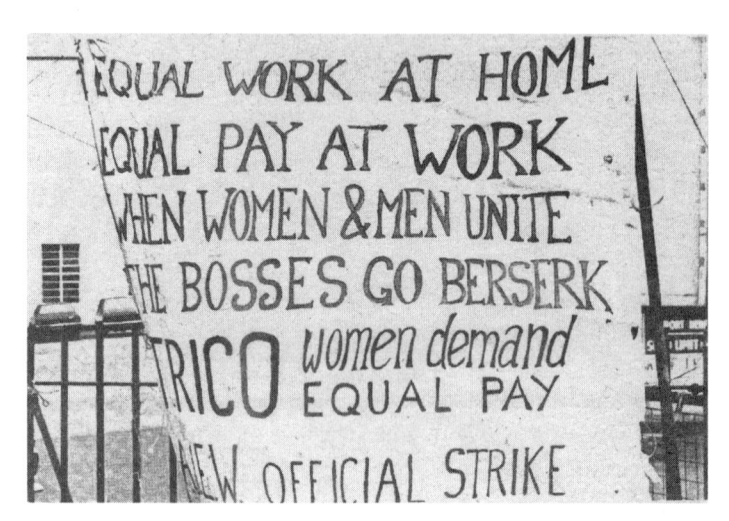

Homemade Trico banner

38 | GETTING ORGANISED

HOT FOR EQUALITY

ON THE DAY OF the march, two of the senior shop stewards, Eileen Ward and Betty Aiston, went up to the AUEW Southall District office to meet Roger Butler. Roger had contacted Bill Whyman, the AUEW Divisional Organiser covering Northampton, and asked him to approach the workers at the Northampton Trico plant, through the local District Secretary, to request support in case production was switched there.

John Inwood met with the men in the factory during this time, but a vote for all-out action in support of the women was defeated, with about 40 per cent supporting it and 60 per cent voting against. A further motion to hold a one-day stoppage on 2 June, with a possible levy of £1 a head, was passed, but the levy never became a reality. There was a feeling of some dismay amongst the women at the attitude of the men who remained working.

On the plus side, endorsement for the strike by the local AUEW District Committee was unanimous. From Thursday 27 May the women could tell everyone they were on official strike. (But, under rule, only the union's Executive Council could decide whether or not to pay dispute pay, and its deliberations could be lengthy, and issues usually took several weeks to reach the agenda.)

The 'official' tag meant other welcome things. There was now the chance of getting the remaining male AUEW members to support the strike. Financial appeal sheets were printed using the District seal, and money that would soon be very much needed started to come in from the local factories.

Roger Butler, in his report to the District Committee, stressed the importance of this strike: it was unique. It was the biggest strike by women since the Equal Pay Act had come into being, and the first in London. He urged delegates to give it priority, since all the indications were that this would be a tough nut to crack.

True to form, the ACAS meeting on 2 June did not resolve anything. The union's representatives, shop floor and official, had been summoned, not to hear that the management were prepared to put an offer of money on the table, but to listen to Trico reiterate their stand. They claimed, in so many words, that the women were being irrational and had simply misunderstood the company's position. With an attitude like this there wasn't going to be any quick solution.

On the day of the ACAS talks, a token stoppage by the men took place. But even this additional pressure was not enough to see a glimmer of light come out of the meeting. The management were digging in their heels.

By now the company had gauged the real strength of feeling amongst the men. They had held a number of what they called 'communication' meetings in the works canteen. Most had fallen for their explanation, and were visibly reluctant to support the women, even for the one-day stoppage on 2 June. Why should they lose pay over this women's 'tiff'? It was noticeable that even during the one-day stoppage the men had steered clear of showing their presence on the picket line.

Once the one-day stoppage was over, the women were isolated once again. Publicly, the union stated that the men were collecting money for the strikers out of the wages Trico were paying them to do nothing, and, if called on by the stewards to come out altogether they were confident of a response. Some in the departments had purposely stayed at work to try and persuade the others to see reason and join the women. There was still hope.

It was a different story, though, when Roger Butler and Arthur Gibbard, the AUEW Assistant Divisional Organiser, went to speak to a meeting of the men in the park: the crowd acted like a lynch mob. Roger described the meeting afterwards as very threatening: he thought they might be hung from the tree they were standing under. The meeting was totally disrupted. Right-wing elements and National Front members inside the factory had been at work, and it seemed that any traditions of trade union solidarity had never had a chance.

The press was quick to exploit the situation. The prime targets were the women who had husbands still at work in the factory. One paper, the local *Evening Mail*, even carried a half-page feature article entitled 'The tale of Mrs Striker and Mr Blackleg – or, it will never get better if you picket!' That upset everyone.

There was an understandable bitterness over the men's reaction. But the strikers had nothing to gain from any incidents on the picket line. Persuasion had failed, and those going in to work outnumbered those outside by two to one.

Adding to their problems, the company were trying out a new device to split them up. On 8 June another letter was despatched. After informing strikers that they had been advised that the Tribunal could take about eight weeks to convene, it continued:

> There are certain items of fresh information in the case which have put a new light on the situation and it is important that you should be aware of these points ... We ask you to attend a meeting at 3.00pm on Friday 11 June in the Works Canteen.

Needless to say, by now feelings amongst the women had hardened to the point where they didn't want to listen to any 'talk-in', unless it was to hear the management say they had repented and were going to give them equal pay. But a few went to the meeting. It turned out that the new information was Trico's desire to see their happy smiling faces again. The staunchly anti-union *Brentford & Chiswick Times* described the purpose of the meeting as, 'to see if a way could be found for them to return to work as quickly as possible'.[6]

The pressures were beginning to tell on the strikers. Sixteen women had returned to work, although Trico told the press that the number was thirty.

Not all, however, was against the strikers. As well as their own enthusiasm for the cause, they had other advantages.

---

[6] The nine-title Dimbleby Newspaper Group, based in west London, which included the *Brentford & Chiswick Times*, had been owned by the Dimbleby family since 1896. Between 1966 and 1986, when broadcaster David Dimbleby was managing director, the company derecognised unions and was accused by the NUJ of paying poverty wages. In 1993 David Dimbleby became sole proprietor of the group by buying out a family trust. In 2001 he sold the group to Newsquest, the UK's second largest regional newspaper publisher, for a reported £8 million. Newsquest is owned by American media group Gannett.

'WE'RE ON SEX STRIKE SAY WIVES IN EQUAL PAY FIGHT'

LIKE MOST PEOPLE who find themselves having to take strike action, the Trico women started out with no experience of dealing with the press and media in general. For them the case was simple: the company were denying them equal pay with their male colleagues who had previously been on night shift. They knew the justice of their cause.

Nothing quite prepares you for your encounters with local – let alone national – newspaper hacks, telling them your story and then finding your comments have been changed out of all recognition or horribly distorted.

It was after just such a sexist and trivialising report in the *Sun* – about women being on 'sex strike', and refusing to cook hot dinners, or even to do 'their normal wifely duties' – that the reporter, a somewhat podgy guy, got more than he bargained for when he was chased off the picket line by the furious women. The sight of him running for his life in his too snugly-fitting suit was a thing to behold!

As the weeks passed by, press coverage and media interest became quite considerable. From the start the local papers saw the dispute as a major source of interest, and local reporters were often sympathetic to the cause. The Strike Fund even received donations from their local NUJ chapels. In contrast, the editors – especially of the *Brentford & Chiswick Times* – were so sympathetic to the Trico management that one or two of their editorials were used by Trico in the letters they sent out to the strikers in their propaganda war.

Many newspapers were faced by a dilemma: they did not feel they could put the women's equal pay fight in quite the

Sally Groves with *Evening Mail* reporter at the Griffin pub strike HQ. Sandra (Ward) Gray in background.

SOURCE UNKNOWN, IN S. GROVES PRIVATE COLLECTION

same category as 'greedy trade unionists', but at the same time they looked askance at such an aggressive push for equal pay, considering that there was a perfectly good tribunal that could settle the whole matter! Certainly, once the tribunal ruled against the women (see p106), some papers took the somewhat sanctimonious view that the women should have complied with the legal remedy on offer. But some of the national press printed good features on the strike, whilst a plethora of weekly left-wing newspapers gave enthusiastic coverage of the strike's progress. These included *Militant, Newsline, Socialist Worker, Women's Voice* and *Big Flame*, while the *Morning Star*, the only daily socialist newspaper, provided supportive reporting throughout the strike.

The feminist press such as *Spare Rib* and the *Women's Charter*, the paper of the Working Women's Charter, produced in-depth features and articles on Trico, equal pay and the failures of the new Equal Pay Act, as did some national papers. In August Alan Pike wrote a well-informed article in the *Financial Times* entitled 'A long haul to equal treatment for women'. But Joan Bakewell's excellent feature in the *Daily Mirror* was relegated to the Private Opinion page. Other supportive articles came from Geoffrey Sheridan in the *Guardian*; John Fryer, Labour correspondent for *The Sunday Times*; and Caroline Moorehead in *The Times* (this was before those two papers had become right-wing mouthpieces for Rupert Murdoch).

Caroline Moorehead recognised that, as the weeks went by and more unions supported them, the Trico women saw

THE MEDIA

ROBERT (BOB) SINGH

As it went on, greater emphasis was placed on the strike by the national media. The local media and the political left-wing groups were there from the beginning. But the longer the strike went on the more the national media took a keen interest. It was also very obvious at the time that most of them were on the side of the employer – they were spouting a particular government line. I'm not saying all of them. If you built up a relationship with a particular reporter you were able to get your views over.

PHYLLIS GREEN

I didn't have money to buy papers at all during the strike. I might have bought the *New Worker* or the *Morning Star* – but they generally gave it to you if you were picketing. And then there'd be lots of newspaper people down taking photos, and a lot of them didn't really write to support us. They thought it was a holiday we were on. A lot of the papers used to say we were on the Costa del Trico. Then there was a good few left-wing papers. Yes the papers did discredit us a lot, the local papers especially. They didn't actually support us at all – why I don't know. I mean is it not good for them if people got equal pay and then they could pay their girls in the *Brentford and Chiswick Times* equal pay as well!

---

themselves fighting 'not only their own battle, but also the test case of the Equal Pay Act'. Sally Groves commented to her: 'There has never been this sort of solidarity before … It's a small revolution for us. We have suddenly found a voice. Our unity and determination will win the day.'

During the latter stages of the strike its fame had spread beyond Britain and news reports appeared in papers such as *Le Monde* in France and *24 Heures* in Lausanne.

Sally Groves took on the role of Press and Publicity Officer, and developed links with an extensive and motley assortment of press and media over the next five months. Contact was either on the picket line, in the strike HQ upstairs at the Griffin pub, or on the communal phone at the house where she had a bedsit. There were no mobile phones, PCs or internet in 1976.

Pamela and Rose, Trico strikers, outside front gates, 7 June 1976.

NLA/REPORTDIGITAL.CO.UK

OUT ON THE COSTA DEL TRICO

IT ALWAYS HELPS to have good weather, and the Trico strikers couldn't have been more fortunate. The month of June broke all weather records. Day after day the sky was clear blue and the temperature soared. For twenty days and more it topped the old 80F (almost 27C) and very often went into the 90s (over 32C), even going as high as 98F (about 37C) in the shade. An egg cracked on the tarmac at Heathrow fried splendidly! If those outside were melting one could imagine what it was like in the factory, and there was no air conditioning. But it was felt that the scabs were being duly punished as they crept daily into work! The picket line was dubbed the Costa del Trico by the women and media alike.

Coming on top of people's many and varied domestic problems, the heat could at times add to the difficulties of getting the numbers of people needed to keep the picket line going. Particularly at the front gate, you would just roast. Soon appeal after appeal would have to be made at mass meetings for more pickets.

But other things lifted the spirits. Activity was getting underway to raise support in the trade union and labour movement. Wherever the women went the response was magnificent. They were completely new to speaking at meetings, and the ins and outs of their arguments may not have always been easy to follow. But the sincerity and down-to-earth way in which they put it across convinced everybody of the inner justice of their case. Not one of the people that found themselves on strike had had any previous experience of speaking to a trade union audience outside Trico. They

Clockwise from above:

Stella North, Trico striker, outside Trico factory.
P. FARMER PHOTO IN S. GROVES PRIVATE COLLECTION

Good backing for the strike! Stella North and Ann Fitzgerald centre of photo.
SOURCE UNKNOWN, IN S. GROVES PRIVATE COLLECTION

Loretta Braithwaite and John Connors on picket line.
P. FARMER PHOTO IN S. GROVES PRIVATE COLLECTION

would be the first to say that they knew next to nothing about the different types of organisations which would be willing to help.

Betty Aiston, who hailed from Newcastle and was another leading shop steward, was the first to address an outside organisation. The occasion was a meeting in early June of Hounslow Trades Council. Then a day was spent hurriedly visiting factories in Birmingham, and after that the delegations got into full swing.

Practical assistance was needed, especially money: in particular women who had no partner or family to support them were beginning to feel the pinch. But support for the boycotting of Trico products was also important, as the company could ship in goods from their American and Australian plants to continue to supply some of their customers. Ford, which had past experience of the problems caused by a dispute at a component manufacturer, had from the start ordered supplies from alternative sources. Airport workers throughout the country were now on the lookout for Trico products. Soon the dockers were contacted: they would keep watch as well.

A delegation went to lobby a Special TUC meeting in Central Hall, Westminster, discussing the wider issues of wage restraint and cuts in public expenditure. Shop stewards with collection tins went round the crowd outside and collected a substantial sum in recognition of what the women of Trico were doing. Even people who were themselves unemployed put in money. As one of the strikers commented afterwards, 'If we'd more experience we wouldn't have got away with making a collection like that. Someone said we could have been done, it was illegal.'

Trico was fast becoming a national symbol in the fight for equal pay.

On 15 June, the AUEW Executive Council discussed Trico, with a list of recommendations from the local officials before them. The recommendation to declare the strike official was moved by Reg Birch, the Executive Councillor covering the South East. This was agreed, and dispute pay authorised as per rule, at £9 a week. The 98 who had joined the union only after having gone on strike were also to be paid strike pay but this involved a delay while their applications were being processed. Until then things would have to be shared out. A cheque was quickly sent to ease the financial problems. By the end of the week the first pay-out would be made. It was to become a common weekly ritual to queue

MALE SUPPORTERS

> **PHYLLIS GREEN**
> A lot of men did come out and stay with us and they were a great support. They could organise things – not better than us, we could organise things better than them – but they'd give you ideas, if you weren't too used to trade union things, or you could bounce ideas off people. And if there were big lorries, they would be there, definitely. They were a great support, some of them.

for your money outside the Griffin pub.

The Executive Council's decision had other repercussions. Many of the men at Trico had said they would join the strike only once it had been made official. Department meetings were now held, and 150 men, mainly from the tool room, came out. But the rest stayed. Even amongst those who now joined the strike there was still a degree of resentment. By the end of the strike it was a different story, however: most of them had become solid supporters.

All through June the weekly mass meetings were held. The strike was now settling down into a more even rhythm. The women's awareness was growing of all the types of discrimination they suffered, not only in terms of pay. They were more determined than ever to see that they weren't treated by Trico in the old way again. They had right on their side and had the confidence that they could succeed.

Arthur Gibbard, demonstrating the importance that the union gave to the dispute, told a mass meeting: 'Tremendous support for the strike is coming in from all over the country. The struggle for equal pay is going to be raised to a new level through your strike.' And he made a pledge: 'we are going to win this strike even if it means that we have to put this factory out'.

The battle lines had been drawn.

INTO TOP GEAR

SOMEWHERE BURIED in the Trico complex there were some very worried people. Atkins, Slidders and the other company executives had sat tight when the women had walked out, expecting the strike to crumble at any moment. Now they had to start facing reality.

Of course they still had the Industrial Tribunal up their sleeve.

The company was confident of getting a favourable verdict. They'd received the advice of the Engineering Employers' Federation and other learned counsel, who were positive that they could easily find an 'escape clause' in the Act.[7] They were therefore impatient for a decision from the Tribunal, but it wasn't until the last week of June that a date for the hearing was finally announced – 14 July.

For reasons that remain unclear, Trico had cited the District Committee of the AUEW as co-respondents for the Tribunal, rather than the women involved. It therefore fell to the District Committee to decide the position to be adopted. Examining the facts, they had to agree with Trico: the Equal Pay Act had become a lawyer's paradise. It was a foregone conclusion that Trico would win. But this would mean nothing. The only real settlement to the dispute would lie in negotiating equal pay across the table, not in an exercise in which the dice were loaded against it. The union therefore decided to boycott the Tribunal. The company were deliberately setting out to abuse the good intent of the law. As Sally Groves was later to comment to *Spare Rib*: 'Local papers are running editorials saying we won't go to the tribunal because we've no faith in our case. The point is we have no faith in the tribunals.'

Atkins and Co must have spent many sleepless nights – in

---

[7] For the ways in which companies sought to get round the EPA, see Part Four.

the face of the women's solidarity and the union's backing – worrying what would happen if the full moral authority of the Tribunal turned out not to bring them to heel. What then?

Whilst Trico pondered, the union was redoubling its efforts. The District Committee had decided on the date of Tuesday 29 June for a march round Brentford, and local factories had been invited to send delegations with their banners. In a highly impressive display of support, nearly 500 joined in the march. The bright sunshine once more lent a carnival atmosphere. Representatives came from Southall District Committee, Acton Rails, AEC, Magnatex, British Airways, Glacier Metals, EMI, Ranton Plastics, AUEW-TASS West London Divisional Council, as well as Hounslow, Ealing and Brent Trades Councils. The march took an hour to complete its long course – thirsty work in the midday sun. The colourful march then returned along the Great West Road, passing the Trico factory where there was a face at every window. The women were chanting, 'What do we want? ... EQUAL PAY! ... When do we want it? ... NOW!'

The march finally disbanded in Boston Manor Park before

Centre L to R: Joan Holas and Rhoda (Fraser) Williams on second march, 29 June 1976.
PHOTO YOUNG SOCIALIST

Second march round Brentford. Left to Right, Ann Fitzgerald, Betty Aiston, Bill MacLaughlin, Len Choulerton, Arthur Gibbard, Eileen Ward, 29 June 1976.

TRINITY MIRROR SOUTHERN (EVENING MAIL)

a short meeting. The steps of the children's slide were once more used as a platform as AUEW Divisional Organiser Bill MacLaughlin addressed the gathering. Long before the end of the dispute, 'Mac', as he was known, would come to be regarded by the strikers as an old friend.

Mac thanked everyone for their magnificent display of support: 'Yours is the most important strike at present going on in the country, probably the most significant since the war. It's a strike the trade union movement can't afford to lose … We are determined to end the degrading situation of women being treated as inferior, second rate citizens … Your struggle has destroyed the myth that you can't get women to fight for themselves.'

A good day's work done, the crowd went their various ways. But there were still important things to do. The first meeting of the strike committee was about to be held. The committee had been elected at the beginning of the strike, composed of the shop stewards who had joined the strike, together with others nominated from amongst the strikers themselves. But up to now it had not met.

The Griffin pub was once more our venue. The pub lay in the shadow of Brentford Football Ground, ten minutes' walk away from the picket lines, and the nearest that could be found. Between 11am and 3pm, Monday to Friday, it housed the strike headquarters. As well as being used to pay out strike monies, it would also be a general meeting place.

The first thing to do to ensure the strike committee could function properly was to allocate jobs within its ranks. The following responsibilities were handed out:

Chairman	John Inwood
Deputy Chairman	John O'Neill
Secretary/Pickets (day)	Eileen Ward
Pickets (nights)	Andy Anders
Social Security	Betty Aiston
Finance	Monica Robinson
Publicity	Sally Groves
Factory Collections	George Jinks

Before the end of the strike a number of changes were made, and others would be brought in to share the workload.

There was much to be done. The battle was on in earnest now, and good organisation, as well as determination, would be the key to success.

PART TWO
THE BATTLE RAGES

STRIKE BREAKERS INCORPORATED

THERE WAS A ROW of old flagpoles on the Great West Road outside the Trico factory. Displayed on them were the faded flags of a dozen or so countries in which Trico had an important share of the market. Amongst them were those of Brazil, South Africa, Japan and Australia, as well as many in Western Europe.[1]

An important part (Trico claimed twenty-five per cent) of the output from Brentford was sold overseas. For the duration of the strike the company would have to bear the burden of supplying these customers from Buffalo, New York State. The costs of production in the United States were much higher and there would be little profit, but at least Trico would retain their 'goodwill', and perhaps customers wouldn't even get to hear of their little local difficulty. Of more pressing concern was what to do with the UK market. The company somehow had to protect their 90 per cent share.

Northampton was still producing, and some work was also being done on the production lines at Brentford, by people who had returned to work. In addition, a few extra workers had been recruited, and existing labourers had also been asked to do some of the women's work. Most importantly, some of the men who operated the high-speed presses were still at work.

Extra shipments from America were secretly smuggled in. To get round the trade union action to prevent imports, wipers and other products were sent through small freighting firms in unmarked boxes, or under cover of one of Trico's obscure trademarks.[2] One consignment was discovered by shop stewards at Heathrow with the crates labelled 'computer

---

[1] It was from just one of these flagpoles that, a bit later during the strike, a flag with EQUAL PAY painted on it was hoisted, much to the horror and consternation of the Trico management! The escapade was the brainchild of two of the strikers' supporters from the Pirate Jenny theatre group.

[2] The products made by Trico at that time included: vacuum and air pressure windscreen wiper motors; windscreen wiper blades and arms; windscreen washers; switches; horns; flashing light signals; cigarette lighters; solvent screen washer additives; smear remover; de-icer; squeegees. Trade names of Trico-Folberth at that time included: Trico; Rainbow; Trico Duo-Matic; Trico Vaco-Matic; Roto-Matic; Aeramic; Ciglit; SR-12; Anti-Smear; Electro-Matic; Push-Matic; Pedo-Matic; Speedblade. Source: *Buyer's Guide to the Motor Industry of Great Britain 1973-1974*.

Trico strikers on picket line, Eileen Fowler on left, Emmy on right with bike, 20 July 1976.

CHRIS DAVIES/REPORT ARCHIVE/REPORTDIGITAL.CO.UK

Left to Right, Win Clark, Mary Dempsey and Betty Humphreys on the picket line, 20 July 1976.

ANGELA PHILLIPS/REPORTDIGITAL.CO.UK

parts'! It was all part of Trico's attempt to publicly play down the effects of the strike.

When it came to the media Trico were always tight-lipped about how much the strike was costing them – although the union's estimate, based on reliable information, was that the figure was in excess of £20,000 per day. All the company would say was, 'We are working under difficulties – we have two-thirds of our workforce still with us and production is still continuing.'

But the pretence couldn't be kept up for long without fresh supplies of parts being brought into the factory, or finished products being taken out. In five weeks only a few lorries had got through. Managers and sales reps were running boxes out in private cars past the pickets, which might have annoyed the strikers, but, as Roger Butler pointed out, 'You can't run the British motor industry from the boot of a car!'

Finished work was accumulating inside the factory, and stocks of materials and sheet metal were getting dangerously low. Trico would have to break the picket lines in a big way.

During the day the picket lines were well staffed, and too effective for anyone to chance an attempt to breach them. The operation to cross the picket lines, it was decided, must be carried out under the cover of darkness.

Around 2am on Thursday 1 July, a convoy of nine forty-foot lorries and a number of private cars arrived at the factory. The four pickets on duty stopped each of them in turn. Six of the drivers decided to turn around and go back – they had not been told, so they said, that there was a dispute here. But the other three went in and out again with their loads.

It had been an expensive night for Trico: the lorry owners were on special bonus rates. But the first convoy hadn't completed the strike busting – it would have to be done again, but this time better planned.[3]

On the following evening they were back. The pickets, two on each gate, knew something was up when a white Peugeot parked opposite the main entrance. The driver used a pair of binoculars and had a radio microphone. More police cars than usual were patrolling the road. Policemen were deposited to watch the gate for the first time. Then six large unmarked lorries turned up. Nose-to-tail they did a wide sweep of the Great West Road and sped into the factory. The pickets had no chance. In fact, they had to leap out of the way to avoid being hit.

Inside, company executives worked feverishly with scab

[3] It is open to question whether or not this was in fact the first convoy. All-night picketing did not commence until late in June, and, although no evidence has been found to this effect, convoys could have already been secretly entering the factory before that time.

crews to off-load and re-load the lorries. Then they were away again. Followed onto the M1 by a transport union official, they headed north. Near Luton the official was stopped by police for driving too slowly! He was detained for fifty minutes, and the lorries were away.

The whole operation was a complete success for Trico. The haulage firms, the police and the company had all worked together to perfection. But nothing could have been more guaranteed to get people's backs up. So that was the way they treated their workers! It isn't strange for lorries to cross a picket line, of course. Indeed, most serious disputes up to that time had been marked by incidents where vehicles had attempted to enter a strike-bound factory or site, while the strikers utilised various methods of 'persuasion' to get them to refrain from their scabbing activities. But what was so unacceptable about Trico's efforts was the highly organised nature of these 'midnight convoys' – the drivers were soon labelled mercenaries – that were prepared to run over anybody in the way to get their 'blood money'.

News of the strike-busting operation received wide coverage, but Trico at first made no comment. When at last they did break their silence it was to try to make out that such means were 'normal'. According to a company spokesman: 'We don't have any set times for receiving deliveries at the factory. The normal procedure is to accept goods when we need them and when we can accept them. Night time deliveries are made if we require a special consignment.'

It may have been normal practice in dealing with the organised strikes of American car workers in the 1930s, but this was Brentford, not Detroit!

For once, sexist notions backfired on an employer. To the public this was a women's strike, and the thought of women being dealt with in this heavy-handed and undignified manner, especially when considered alongside the company's American background, meant that Trico had few honest friends left. As a public relations exercise the midnight convoys were a disaster.

It seems odd that Trico should have acted in the way they did. Why not arrange for the lorries, one at a time, to go into the factory during the day? Of course it wouldn't have been so easy: no doubt the drivers would have had to put up with a degree of abuse from the strikers (although they were under no legal obligation to stop). But much of the fuss would have been avoided.

Workers had few rights in law even then. The law on picketing at that time (see Trade Union and Labour Relations Act 1974, section 15) allowed 'one or more persons' to carry out the functions of 'peacefully persuading any person to abstain from working'. In practice they had no 'right' to carry out this action by stopping lorries in order to communicate with their occupants. According to the Lords, pickets could only signal drivers to stop: they had no right to compel them to do so.

The strike committee met to discuss how to counter the latest company tactics. Effective picketing would be crucial to the successful outcome of the strike. The problem was how to mount a mass picket whenever a convoy attempted to get in, given that the police would always be on hand to aid Trico all the way.

The strain was already beginning to show on the pickets. The burden of picketing duties was falling on just fifty to sixty people, and despite every kind of verbal persuasion others would not come forward. It was decided to begin making a payment for all-night picketing, and later on this also applied to the daytime.

Problems in getting enough people for the picket line were heightened by it being a women's strike. Many of the strikers were subject to domestic pressures at home to care for husbands and children. For some there was also disapproval, which could result in marital or family conflict over any involvement in a strike at all. Increasing financial hardship was added to these pressures, which could make it difficult to travel to the picket line at all, especially for those who lived farther afield.

Significantly – and a further example of women's poorer economic situation compared with men, and hence relative lack of independence – only two women out of almost 400 had access to cars of their own.

Support had to be organised to reinforce the picket lines. The Strike Committee decided to start a 'flying picket' list of volunteers – made up of strikers, local trade unionists and women's movement activists – who would come in the event of an emergency. From early July onwards this list grew until there were over a hundred supporters who could be reached by a telephone call. In addition, Southall District Committee called on all factories to 'adopt a night' for picketing at Trico.

Trade union solidarity is a key in all disputes, and the Trico workers learnt its value quickly. Along with support

> **SOUTHALL DISTRICT COMMITTEE AUEW**
>
> (Engineering Section)
>
> urges support for Equal Pay struggles and free Collective Bargaining.

AUEW Southall District greetings

HARDSHIP

SALLY GROVES

During June, perhaps a month after we'd come out on strike, some people were getting worried about finding the money to pay the rent or electric, let alone food bills. Let's face it, the strike was very hard for a lot of people. I was lucky as I had a bit of savings, and as the strike went on I used all of it to survive and pay my rent, and so managed to avoid going to the union hardship fund.

But in June strike pay had only just begun and donations were not as yet rolling in. We'd only just started to speak at meetings and the major delegations that were to go around the country had not really started.

The Claimants' Union was very active at the time. I'd got hold of their *Handbook for Strikers*, packed full of advice about the best way to fight your corner with the DHSS. I'd read that, although Social Security said that strikers were excluded from benefit under Section 10 of the Social Security Act 1971, the SS could make discretionary payments under Section 13 of the Act in cases of hardship.

The Claimants' Union was this group of claimants who thought you had to fight things together, as Social Security was so prejudiced towards strikers. So I thought, Ah Ha! – if I got together some of the women most badly affected – single women, widows – we could confront them at the DHSS office and get them to pay out some benefit.

So a group of us gals living in the Ealing area went down to the Ealing DHSS office at Woodgrange House near Ealing Common. We stuck to our guns, requesting a payment on hardship grounds and then insisted we see the manager. I think he was gobsmacked at being confronted by a bunch of women who'd arrived out of the blue demanding their rights. The upshot was he agreed to make payments to us all.

Spurred on by this spectacular success, on 18 June I got together another group of women who lived in Hounslow, for us to go to the office there. There were nine of us squashed like sardines into my Renault 4L car, all sitting on each other's laps. Well except for me – I was driving!

The Hounslow DHSS offices were right up on the third floor of this office block. I would hardly call their response to our arrival that afternoon welcoming! But we insisted on seeing the manager after we were refused help. He also refused to assist at all. Little did we know at the time, but instructions must have been sent round to all the local offices not, on any account, to pay Trico strikers. No doubt the manager at the Ealing office had really got it in the neck!

We weren't going to give up that easily. We refused to leave until we got some help. We DID get some 'help' in the end but not quite what we'd expected!

What we began to notice was that after a while all the other claimants had departed, and we were the only ones left in the office. The staff pulled down the shutters over the counters and we heard them being locked. It all became eerily quiet. Then we heard what at first sounded like very distant thunder – until I realised it wasn't thunder at all, but the tramp, tramp, tramp of heavily-booted feet coming up the stairs!

Some of the younger girls, beginning to panic, looked to me to tell them how we were going to get out of the situation. Well, I thought we couldn't jump out the window as it was the third floor, so I said, when the police arrive and try to get hold of us we should just show passive resistance, go all floppy, and drop to the floor.

Thirteen police arrived. When one of them got hold of me I slid to the floor but the others, instead of falling to the floor, all jumped up in terror.

The police didn't exactly hang about – they just picked me up, turned me upside down and proceeded to hurtle me down the three flights of stairs head-first, with the others following behind shrieking. If they'd dropped me I doubt I'd be here today, but they didn't. They shot me out of the front door and dropped me in the gutter.

You win some, lose some!

Later some Labour MPs, Russell Kerr and Stan Orme, did take up our case with the Supplementary Benefits Commission, but they didn't get anywhere.

BRIAN YOUNG

I remember there was a notice outside the Labour Exchange – because I was doing my little rounds of trying to get a job at that point – saying 'NO TRICO WOMEN' – meaning no to getting paid, getting the dole or anything like that.

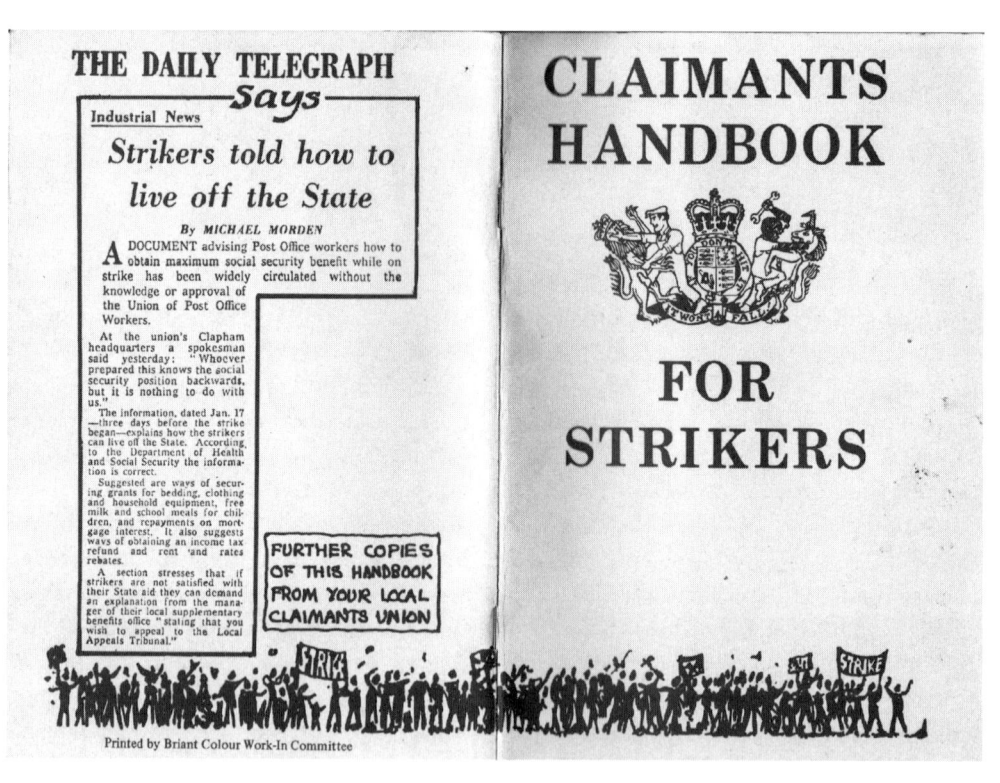

Claimants Union
Strikers Handbook
1976

from those who refused to handle Trico products, and from donations, there were endless visits to the picket line from activists in the trade union, labour and women's movements, as well as from general well-wishers, all wanting to give encouragement and offer help. The significance of the Trico strike was being recognised far beyond Trico itself – and its victory was being seen as essential for the whole of the labour movement.

Practically every day, news – or sometimes just rumours – would leak out from friends and relatives inside the factory that 'a convoy was on tonight'. The alarm bells would go and the 'telephone tree' would be activated, only to find it was all a false alarm. It soon became a delicate and dangerous art trying to distinguish the more reliable sources, and to spot other signs of activity. Sometimes strikers or their supporters would go out scouting around known convoy hiding places if one was expected.

Eric Fudge, one of the five ex-night shift operators who had been transferred onto days alongside the women, was a loyal supporter of the women's cause throughout the strike. An ex-Hell's Angel never long separated from his Suzuki

750 Kettle motorbike, he would sometimes cruise around on his bike or speed along the Great West Road searching for any hidden convoys – on occasion with Sally Groves riding pillion. On previous occasions a convoy had been known to park up in Harlequin Avenue off the Great West Road, or at the Hare and Hounds pub car park in Syon Lane.

But when the next convoy arrived it took the pickets by surprise. Although they were better organised than before, there was no time to alert anyone. Just after 1am on the morning of Sunday 11 July, seventeen lorries and fifteen private cars arrived at the gate. Leading the way was a police car, with other escorts at the rear, and the police closed off Boston Manor Road to traffic to allow the convoy to speed past the pickets into the factory. In between the arrival of each lorry, car-loads of strike-breakers were driven in – about forty men in all. They stayed until 4am. For the exit from the front gate, the police carefully positioned their cars in front of the pickets' vehicles to prevent them following. Then, just to complete their night's work, the police turned a blind eye to the lorries' number plates being covered up, and to the lorries speeding through red traffic lights as they made their way along the Great West Road.

Indignation amongst the strikers was immense. To the inexperienced, the use of police as a company force was

John Bracher addressing strikers in Boston Manor Park. Eric Fudge standing middle background with bucket.

MORNING STAR PHOTOGRAPHIC ARCHIVE, BISHOPSGATE INSTITUTE

Protest delegation to Brentford police station. Left to Right, Sally Groves, Peter Craven, Betty Humphreys, Win Clark, Ivy Chandler, Peter Tumulty, 14 July 1976.

TRINITY MIRROR SOUTHERN (EVENING MAIL)

both eye-opening and offensive. Anyone who had previously believed in their impartiality could see, when it came to workers versus employer, on whose side they really were.

In protest, on 14 July a delegation handed in a letter from the Strike Committee to Chief Inspector Charles Austen, at Brentford police station. Copies of the letter were also sent to local MPs:

> The Trico Strike Committee on behalf of its members on strike resents the interference of the police in actively assisting the Trico management's strike breaking attempts.
>
> Such blatantly partisan action can only harm future relations between trade unionists and the police in general.
>
> We request an urgent official inquiry into the role of the police in this dispute.

The strikers' request was met — for what it was worth. All summer an internal inquiry would grind on, carried out by an outside police force. No doubt it eventually produced a report that has never seen the light of day.

Publicising the role of the police and bringing it to public attention did, however, have its results: for a time the police were a bit more careful of being so clearly seen to be at the call of the Trico management.

66 | THE BATTLE RAGES

MORE TWISTS AND TURNS

AS THE EIGHTH WEEK of the strike began, prospects for a settlement looked dim. The Tribunal was due to convene during that week, immediately following on from Sunday's events. The battle appeared uphill all the way. It seemed all the company had to do was sit tight and wait for the inevitable Tribunal decision.

The events that were about to take place were therefore, at face value, inexplicable. On the Monday afternoon (12 July), Mr Roberts, a Conciliation Officer from ACAS, phoned Bill MacLaughlin at the AUEW offices to inform him Trico had had a change of heart. They had postponed going to the Tribunal and asked him to arrange a fresh meeting through the offices of ACAS.

In what appeared to be an effort to save face, a company spokesman told the press that there had been an approach from the union: 'We decided ... to defer the Tribunal so these talks can take place.' The Strike Committee was forced to make a statement to clarify that this was not what had happened. Not the best atmosphere in which to start talks!

Throughout the dispute the union had maintained the position that the issue of equal pay could only be settled by negotiations between the two sides. It had always been prepared to meet the company at any time of day or night. But until the eleventh hour had arrived, Trico had ignored this open call for talks.

On Tuesday 13 July, and again on Thursday 15 July, the two sides met under the auspices of ACAS – in separate rooms, with Roberts going from one group to the other. A series of progressively larger offers were made, in return for which the company demanded greater flexibility from the

AUEW

Amalgamated Union of Engineering Workers
(ENGINEERING SECTION)

Southall District Secretary
R Butler

to whom all communications should be addressed

AUEW House, 1 Woodlands Road
Southall, Middlesex UB1 1EG
Telephone 01-574 5361

Please confine each letter to one subject

Our ref

Your ref

District Seal ↓

To Whom It May Concern

OFFICIAL DISPUTE - TRICO-FOLBERTH LTD.
BRENTFORD

This is to inform you that this Strike has been officially endorsed by the Southall District Committee and we would appreciate your full support.

(R.C. BUTLER)
Dist. Sec.

AMALGAMATED UNION OF ENGINEERING WORKERS (Engineering Section)
General Office 110 Peckham Road, London SE15 5EL 01-703 4231

AUEW Southall District Committee Official Dispute letter of authority

women. The first day of talks was adjourned with an offer of £1.53; the second day ended with £2.33 on the table. This amount was based on a 140 piecework performance which was about the factory average.[4]

The Southall District Committee was quick to recommend outright rejection of these 'insulting offers'. A representative for the Strike Committee said of the talks: 'We thought things were moving in the right direction, but we were wrong. The outcome was an abysmal offer by management, which would not result in the implementation of our aims – equal pay for all.'

Bill MacLaughlin reported the offers to a mass meeting in the park on the following Monday, 19 July. Not a voice or hand was raised to support the company offer. Mac told the meeting that the significant thing was that: 'this employer, who has been telling the world and his wife that he had been paying equal pay, has now made two separate and different offers and both of these were supposed to represent equal pay. What is a Tribunal going to make of this?'

The Strike Bulletin also spelt out another lesson for the strikers: it is your solidarity and unity which has forced the employer to think again.

The diversion made by these offers meant a fundamental change in the dispute – Trico had conceded the principle:

Bill MacLaughlin, 'Mac', with Trico strikers after a mass meeting. Susy Arab left foreground.

MORNING STAR PHOTOGRAPHIC ARCHIVE, BISHOPSGATE INSTITUTE

[4] For an explanation of piece rates see p15 note 4.

MORE TWISTS AND TURNS | 69

Trico pickets at the back gate. Lou King foreground, Susy and Rosy Arab on wall second and third from left, 6 August 1976.

NLA/REPORTDIGITAL.CO.UK

they were not paying equal pay.

But Trico couldn't see this logic. Another application was taken out for a Tribunal hearing, to try to establish that, really, all the time, they had been obeying the Equal Pay Act. This time the company named two women members of the Strike Committee as co-respondents in addition to the AUEW: Sally Groves and Betty Aiston.

The new situation did not alter the union's attitude to the Tribunal. It was still up to the company to produce something constructive.

We were back on course again.

THEY SHALL NOT PASS

NIGHT PICKETING WAS now settling down into a steady routine. A tense atmosphere would exist every night as we waited for the next convoy. Suspicious vehicles would park opposite the gate in a lay-by. A driver would sit for half an hour writing away and then move off. Was it simply a commercial traveller innocently doing his paperwork, unaware of what was going on the other side of the road? Or was it one of Atkins' men reporting the numbers on the picket line? Each haulage lorry that approached the gates had its speed assessed. Was it going to try and get in?

The danger hours were between midnight and 2am. A pattern had been set with the first three convoys. This time was chosen for a number of reasons: firstly, there was little traffic on the roads; secondly, they wanted to use the cover of darkness; and thirdly, by 2am the twilight shift in the factory had clocked off; and finally, if the convoy left by 4am they could reach Trico's Northampton plant and off-load their freight before any of the workers had arrived. Convoys

SURVEILLANCE

PHYLLIS GREEN

It was probably in the morning I would notice the man more, when I came down the road to Northfield Avenue. He'd be at the clock in Hanwell, or the Lido, or the Plough in Northfield Avenue. And I'd think, that's strange, why do I see that man everywhere I go? And I was thinking, ah, well maybe he does shift work or something like that.

But then he started following me home as well, and I was thinking this is not just somebody who's working. I couldn't understand his interest. But he'd follow me home from the shift on the picket line. I'd never see him the whole day. He'd follow me to Trico's, and then he'd walk on straight up the Great West Road past Trico's and I'd never see him again until I'd leave the picket line. And then he'd be down near Rank Audio Visual in Boston Manor Road, sitting on the wall there, and he'd follow me home. He'd always be a good bit behind me but not enough for me not to notice him – he wouldn't be that far behind. And then as soon as I got into my house he'd go off wherever he went.

I've no idea who the man was. I thought then he might be following me because the Irish were letting off bombs in London and things like that, with me being Irish. I thought that was the problem. And then I thought he was following me just to scare me off picketing, and that he worked for Trico's, because I picketed every day.

But then one day we were in the Plough in Northfields and the same bloke came in, and he had a lot of cuts and scratches on his face, and he was drinking with the police. Another friend of ours who was there told us he was supposed to be a grass for the police. 'Somebody must have got him last night and given him a good hiding.' So that's how I found out he was working with the police. He was with about six other policemen, all big lads. That kind of scared me as well. We got out of there as quick as we could. We ran! We didn't want any truck with six-foot policemen or a man with a beat-up face!

Then when the strike was over I never saw him again. I've no idea why. But it had nothing to do with the Irish. Maybe it was down to the picketing, it was down to Trico's, no other reason. But there were no mobile phones then – so maybe that's the way they did surveillance – maybe to scare me off. But it didn't work!

That was the bit we couldn't figure out – why he would just pick on me. Every strike you have, the police are on the other side, but I'd go down a side road and then when I'd come round to the main road he'd be there again. And he wasn't scared of me seeing him – he knew I knew he was following me. He wasn't trying to hide it.

could, of course, be run at other times, but there would be more problems.

The picket line had a life of its own. It became one of the best-known clubs in London. Each evening dozens of supporters would come. Organisations had started claiming nights when they would take a turn. Tuesday and Friday nights were set aside for Brent Trades Council; on Saturdays the Working Women's Charter group would be there, along with Ealing North Constituency Labour Party. It was Ealing North's indefatigable Secretary, Jean Humphries, who ensured that no Labour Party members – including Steve Pound, later MP – ever shirked this picket duty. During the week local factories took a stint: AEC Southall led by their convenor Mick Martin on Mondays, and on Wednesdays Glacier Metal, as well as Acton Rails, British Airways, and Magnatex, amongst others. AUEW–TASS Divisional Council's day was Thursday. District Committees, other local Trades Councils and a variety of political groups also gave splendid support. And the Gay Socialists also had a slot in the rota.[5] The picket line had become a veritable Who's Who of the trade union, labour and women's movements.

And then there was the tea man. Every night at 10.30pm, and again between 1am and 2.30am, he arrived at the gates with an urn of tea, sugar and milk and served everyone with a cup. Nobody ever thought to ask who he was!

Just before 2.30 in the morning the United Biscuit trucks would park over the road and wait until it was time to return to base. To those left on the gates, seeing these trucks arrive was to know the 'all clear' had sounded for another night. The pickets could relax a bit, maybe get some sleep or just sit around telling jokes, and wait for the milk wagon to come with the sunrise.

As the days went by, the strikers became ever stronger in their determination not to see another convoy go in. There was much talk of doing anything necessary to stop the next one – the women vowed they would stand in its path: the drivers would have the choice of running them down or stopping.

When patrolling the factory perimeter at four in the morning, the limitless and devious methods one's mind dreamt up were amazing: ideas of pouring quick-drying cement over the locked gates to keep them locked for good; or smelling a gas leak and calling out some friends in the Gas Board to dig up the road; or driving stakes into the driveway

[5] The Gay Socialists came down to the Trico picket line on a regular basis to provide support with the night picketing. This shows that links were being forged between those struggling for sexual equality and the trade union movement well before the founding of Lesbians and Gays Support the Miners in 1984, famously depicted in the 2014 film *Pride*.

Trico strikers on picket line. Rosie Cook centre, 6 August 1976.

NLA/REPORTDIGITAL.CO.UK

Bob Bunting, ex-Trico worker and supporter on picket line.

SOURCE UNKNOWN, IN S. GROVES PRIVATE COLLECTION

PICKETING AND SOLIDARITY

BELLA (DAVIS) YOUNG

I can remember when we picketed in the night, some men in the lorries used to be very happy. They used to say 'Eh! – you should be washing up!' Some said, 'Stick with it mate, carry on!' Some men would be very macho-like – 'Go and cook the breakfast for your husband!'

And in the night people from the biscuit factory used to hide biscuits behind a car and they would tell us, 'The biscuits are up there', and we would go quickly and get them. This McVitie lorry came about 1 o'clock in the morning. Anyhow it was nice, we used to have a cup of tea. A man would come with a tea-urn and we would pick a biscuit and have tea and biscuits. I never knew who he was. He was a very nice bloke anyhow to do that every night. I think he was charming.

In the night it was very funny. Sarah, the French woman, would fall asleep there. I woke her up one night and said, 'Sarah you have had a very bad dream.' 'Why, what do you mean?' 'Well you've been dreaming about your boyfriend.' (This was a bloke she used to go out with.) 'The things you've been saying in your dream!' 'Ay Ay!' She was so frightened. The poor bugger, she could not sleep any more in case she had a bad dream. She used to snore!

Picketing in the middle of the night I remember dancing in the road, doing it like bull fighting!

RHODA (FRASER) WILLIAMS

We used to just sit down, and then, when we saw the cars passing by, we'd shout out and the cars would toot their horns and we'd shout out again and then afterwards we used to be a bit jolly like. I used to go down into the Great West Road and wave my arms and dance in the road. It was very nice in that way.

I was on the first march – 'We want Equal Pay. When do we want it? Now!' – and we went down past Half Acre, Brentford, past Ranton Plastics factory and then afterwards we came back. I used to shout, 'When do we want it. Right Now!' Joan, my niece, was with me.

Sometimes I stayed at the gate picketing. Yes, we used to be laughing and I used to dance in the Great West Road, shouting 'Equal Pay!'

LORETTA BRAITHWAITE

When the strike was on we picketed, you know, me and some of my friends took it in turns. It was not always happy, but we enjoyed it amongst each other, had different talks about different things. The people that came to the picket line from other places were very friendly and I got on with them alright. I found it very enjoyable. But it caused a lot of arguments with different people who didn't come out – but that is life and we just had to enjoy it.

Not that we would like to be on the picket line, but because for some reason

PICKETING AND SOLIDARITY

"

we had to, just to show our thing about it. Sometimes it was very amusing, sometimes it wasn't. It just depended who you were picketing with. Some people wanted to come to picket but just for a couple of minutes and then go, but some wanted to stay a few hours and see everything and then change over.

It was an experience. That was the first time I'd ever been out on strike anywhere I'd worked. Well you had to at that time, because if you break away then everything is lost. If you break away everything is down the drain, so it's best to stick together.

BOB MITCHELL
It was a beautiful summer, unusually so. Yes, the night picket was relatively the best time to picket because during the day it was a very uncomfortable and sun-burning time.

I got the impression that the longer it went on, the more people got involved, whether it was the trades councils – Brent Trades Council in particular – or other people I'd never met before. I knew Brent wasn't the end of the world, but it seemed like a long way. I thought if the message had got that far at least someone was listening to us – I suppose naively. Later Brent was really involved with the Grunwick strike. I was impressed by the support we were getting from outside of Brentford. The Great West Road was at the time called the Golden Mile of British industry because you had so many big firms, like Firestones, Beechams, Gillettes, lots of big companies – and we got support from all of them.

That to a certain extent changed me – the support of people that I didn't even know existed, but had just heard about the strike and had come from all over the South East. That impressed me. I thought we were doing something right if someone else agreed with it. Later in my life I've repaid the compliment, if you like, by going on other picket lines, supporting other causes. The longest one ever was outside the South African Embassy, supporting the ANC.

It sounds a bit corny, but it's a solidarity thing. I saw different groups and different individuals joining our picket line, and it was a matter of solidarity. People had come, obviously at their own expense, in their own time, to support our cause, which I had a lot of faith in. But it made me think we were getting the message through, the correct message, being delivered properly, rather than just shouting and stamping our feet. We were delivering it well, maybe very professionally, though I didn't know how to go about that sort of thing. We were very well advised, mainly, I would say, by Brent Trades Council, who must have had a lot more experience. I think the Strike Committee was very well advised. It was my first taste of anything of that sort, and we were learning every day, and learning, fortunately, from people who were very well versed in trade union action.

PICKETING AND SOLIDARITY

ANN FITZGERALD

I would come down quite early and I used to stay nearly all day, until late afternoon. I never refused to come or do anything I was asked to. But some people, as it went on, started breaking away. And sometimes I was there on my own at that little pillar at the front gate, with no-one else there. And then there was the crowd the other side, at the back gate.

Something just drew you there – the atmosphere was great, and you were always chin-wagging and chatting with someone. You weren't just sitting there and thinking, oh God, I'm on here again today. It was a social thing.

And I think that perch, that pillar, belonged to me – my name was on it! I sat in front of that pillar. I didn't have a chair. I think I was just on the ground half of the time.

We used to go down to the café sometimes and chin-wag about it. And when we went to the park everybody showed pure solidarity.

Then when it went on longer and got serious, we started going places. I think I went to Firestones shaking the tin!

PEGGY FARMER

John Inwood had said to us that we needed pickets set up so we all mucked in. I took over a lot of the picketing at the back – it was fun at the front but they could creep in the back, though once the convoys and night picket started I went to the front. When I used to do the night picket the back gates were already locked. Someone had put chewing gum in those locks so many times that they couldn't open the gates – it had gone hard! They had to lift them off. I started going round the back gates when convoys were coming in one gate, and going out the other.

We had a van we used to make tea in … Once when I was on night picket this man who worked in the City got off at Brentford station and came to the picket line. He went in the van, took off his navy pin-stripe suit, put on his jeans, and sat there all night long with us. He went back in the van in the morning, put his clothes back on and went back up to the City! He might have had some sleep as we had the deck chairs out. It was because he wanted to support the strike.

Another night this bloke was going down the Great West Road on his bike, and he saw us outside and he was looking over. Of course a few of the women whistled at him, so he came over and said 'What are you doing here'? So we said we were on strike and asked him if he wanted a cup of tea. We asked him what he was doing at that time of the morning – it was 4 in the morning. He said his wife had chucked him out, so he thought he'd take a cycle and go to work. He had no socks on but he had his sandwiches in his saddlebag, so we ate his sandwiches and then he went off to work! Never saw him again.

BOB BANISTER

I used to chat to people on the picket line and also I'd read the bulletin and find out what was happening. All through the summer I was with the girls on the picket line who were sitting in their deck chairs, often with bikinis, and blokes I knew coming into work were saying, 'I really didn't want to come into work, I'd rather be out there with them!'

PICKETING AND SOLIDARITY

"The girls used to have tea and sandwiches at some point during the evening which I think they got from a local café. Anyhow these sandwiches were apparently like doorsteps, they were very, very thick. And one of our supporters was a rather refined person, not the average working-class woman. I mean no disrespect, she was great, but she did have this, shall we say, precious way. And when she was given a sandwich she looked at this great thick sandwich and said, 'How am I supposed to eat this?' And one woman turned round and said, 'Well, whatever you do love, don't drop it on your foot for God's sake!'

PHYLLIS GREEN
It was always nice sunny weather. We were lucky. The only part that was a bit frightening was when the lorries tried to get in. They'd come right up in front of you when you were standing with the banner, and you'd feel the heat of the engine, they'd just be moving really slowly, and I used to be scared of that. But then the rest of the time people would stop and were really good to us, though you'd get the odd ones going up and down the road shouting 'Go back to work!', especially the white van men, people like that.

I was afraid of being shouted at on the picket line, I didn't like that either. Half the time I wouldn't have had any idea what was going on, so I just stood my ground and stood there with my banner.

There was a good few left-wing people that came down at night, but I also saw them in the day time – people from other factories who'd come down and do an hour or two, just chatting to us and giving us support. There were a lot of good people that helped.

Eileen and Betty were very important. They'd go off to a meeting to negotiate things and let you know what was happening – like if there were lorries going in, a convoy – when I came back on a Monday, as I didn't picket at the weekend.

Once there was a report that they were bringing the blades down the canal on a boat, I remember hearing that. They'd done that one weekend, they'd brought the boats up the canal and loaded them up. I remember thinking, God how hard up must this big multi-million-pound firm be, when they're sneaking in the back door with bloody boats for a couple of women picketing.

Everyone expected everyone to stay out because you were working right beside them on the lines, the people were your friends. It didn't really matter where you were from, you were their friend, and if you were out, you expected them to be out."

for lorries to impale their tyres on – these were some of the milder ideas!

Someway, somehow, the next convoy had to be defeated.

A fortnight had now passed since the last convoy on 11 July. Packages were piling up high outside the Shipping Department. There would have to be a move soon. Rumour had it that a few nights previously Trico had cancelled a convoy because of the size of the picket. True or not, it gave everyone new heart.

Then news came out that the next convoy had been organised for the early hours of 27 July. It looked a cast iron tip-off.

The strikers responded. The emergency flying picket list was activated.

As people arrived they were given their positions, half to the back gate, and half to the front. John O'Neill, the Irish deputy convenor, known as Big John the Gentle Giant, took charge. John had worked at Trico as a maintenance fitter for the past thirty-one years and was well liked and respected. All evening the pickets were drilled. At the back gate they stood arms linked two and three deep, but at the front gate, to prevent the police's attempt to restrict the picket, they had to keep on the move, going round and round in endless circles.

The time was dragging on and it seemed as though the convoy might have turned back. By now one hundred people had gathered and were waiting patiently. Riders were out on motorbikes trying to discover the whereabouts of the convoy. Then, just before 2am, a scout reported that the convoy was waiting a couple of miles away. Extra pickets were diverted to the rear entrance in Boston Manor Road, the gate that was likely to be used.

The Strike Bulletin later took up the story:

> Three times they had come and three times they had forced their way in. Sid Atkins, the Works Manager, and his cronies must have thought that their mercenary convoys of highly paid midnight cowboys were unbeatable. But on the fourth occasion … THEY HAD THE SHOCK OF THEIR LIVES. Seventy men and women strikers stood on the picket line to meet them.
>
> The brief encounter took place at 2am on a dry and chilly Tuesday morning. A magnificent peaceful, patient and disciplined picket line had been kept on its toes by the feeling that this was going to be the night. Then it

GROWTH OF POLITICAL AWARENESS

PHYLLIS GREEN
I suppose we went through a kind of a low patch for a while, when we were just sitting and just picketing all the time, but then as it went on you got more interested in politics – I did anyway. I didn't really know anything about politics and what the government was doing and what was happening, and then it hit you that you were out for equal pay ... that was when it hit, after maybe a month or two. It didn't really bother me at the beginning that I was out because the men were getting a couple of pounds more than me. But then when you're out there for a while, you start thinking, you know, we're entitled to it, and we're not going back until this is solved, and then it became important. It was more than Trico's then.

BOB MITCHELL
I was changing in my outlook and life in general, and politically I was growing up – for want of a better term. And looking back now I can see it did have an effect on my general outlook on life, and attitudes to women or to other races as well – I think those ideas were always there, but they grew. My feeling for that became stronger – not in a militant or active way, but just in my thoughts. It's affected me for the better I like to say – forty-something years later I still feel very strongly about it.

It did give me a completely different outlook, mainly in my relationship with Bob, because he obviously is a different race to me, and people like yourself were obviously a different sex to me. And, being nineteen, the only thing I was interested in about the women wasn't the strike! But yes I saw different races and the opposite sex with totally different eyes for a positive reason, which has stayed with me into my mid-fifties.

all started to happen. A lookout reported that the convoy had assembled in the Uxbridge Road and was on its way. Down the Boston Manor Road it steamed with lorry lights blazing. One look at the reception committee convinced them that they had met their match. They headed for the hills with their tails between their legs.

Their 'army' consisted of eight lorries and a Ford

Trico night pickets turn back convoy, 26–27 July 1976. Bob Mitchell and Robert (Bob) Singh 3rd and 4th from right.

CHRIS DAVIES/REPORT ARCHIVE/REPORTDIGITAL.CO.UK

Cortina following up the rear. Included was a removal van full of a platoon of their scab troops. Unlike last time, when their number plates and names were covered over illegally with the police turning a blind eye, this time we got their numbers and the names of three haulage firms. We will ensure that those companies do no work for any union-organised company for the duration of the strike.

As they turned into the Great West Road, followed by our scouts, the front vehicle flagged the others down and the scabs had a pow-wow. A brief conversation with Trico on a walkie-talkie and fifteen minutes later they disappeared into the night from whence they had come.

WE HAD WON! Not even eight lorries, over fifty scabs and van-loads of police lurking in the background could break our resolve. Another noble chapter in the history of the battle for equal pay and justice had been written.

The night's events had their sequel. The next day the back gate, which the strikers had chained up and the security guards had refused to unlock for the convoy, was taken off its hinges and dismantled! Trico were getting ready for the next round.

THEY SHALL NOT PASS

BATTLE AT THE TRICO GATES

THE AFFAIR OF 27 JULY had illustrated many lessons. The most important was the power of working-class unity and the need for superior organisation in overcoming an employer who holds his workers in contempt.

But the victory, although a very welcome morale boost, would mean nothing if it wasn't followed up. And the strikers now had to expect even more desperate efforts by the company.

How would the management react? Would they even make a serious attempt to reach a settlement through negotiation?

In the event the response of Atkins and Slidders to the shock they had received on Tuesday was like that of the proverbial wounded animal. Behind Trico's closed doors plans were laid to hit back. And this time there weren't going to be any half measures.

The Strike Committee couldn't afford to ignore even the slightest hint of trouble, no matter how flimsy the source. As a result, given repeated false alarms, exhaustion was affecting the strikers. But their victory on 27 July, no matter how temporary it might have been, had given them new reserves of energy.

By the afternoon of Thursday 29 July, the Trico machine was on the road. Two coachloads of police descended on the main gate shortly after 5pm. Just down the road another coachload waited. Two more were at the ready at Brentford police station just five minutes away.

Advance notice had reached the pickets, but not much could be done about it. Despite frantic phone calls, only a few of their helpers could be reached. The majority were

Eileen Ward attempts to stop convoy lorry, 29 July 1976.

CHRIS DAVIES/REPORT ARCHIVE/
REPORTDIGITAL.CO.UK

on their way home from work. Trico had chosen their time well. But there had been time to alert the press.

Only twenty-five people, mostly women, were on the picket line when the police arrived. Against them was a combined force of over one hundred.

The law wasn't there to play a passive role. They'd been given firm orders. The Superintendent commanding immediately broke up the orderly picket and gave instructions that he would only allow six people to picket.[6] The strikers protested but could do nothing. A police cordon was thrown around the entrance two deep on each side. Anyone going to talk to the six risked being manhandled back behind the police lines. To go from one side of the gate to the other meant, even for innocent passers-by, a hazardous journey across the busy carriageway and back again.

Four hundred yards from Trico, three partially loaded forty-foot lorries were parked illegally outside Firestone's. Their name boards were masked over. A police guard threatened to arrest any picket who approached them.

It all seemed a great laugh to the police – and an opportunity to push a few strikers about. Whilst they waited for the rest of the convoy to arrive, every few minutes more strikers would appear, asking what the hell was going on.

[6] As happened during the later Grunwick dispute, the police at Trico varied their interpretation of the law on picketing in the Trade Union and Labour Relations Act. See *Bravery and Betrayal*, Tom Durkin's assessment of the Grunwick strike, 1978.

BATTLE AT THE TRICO GATES | 83

Battle at the Trico gates. Sally Groves on ground attempting to stop lorry, 29 July 1976.

CHRIS DAVIES/REPORT ARCHIVE/
REPORTDIGITAL.CO.UK

The police were everywhere. 6 o'clock came and the lorries moved off. Blocking the road to turn into Trico's the lead vehicle stopped momentarily. Eileen Ward shouted at the driver's cab, 'We've been outside the factory for two months and it's the likes of you that are starving the women outside the gates.' She was dragged away by the police.

The police didn't reserve their strong arm stuff solely for the women. A BBC camera crew got it as well. They were thrown across the driveway but somehow went on filming. Shown on the 6 o'clock and 9 o'clock news that evening, this opened the eyes of millions to what was going on at Trico.

After a few more minutes three more trucks approached. The first two just sped in, but the last one had to stop as the driver had misjudged the entrance width and was jammed in front of the central gatepost. Sally Groves had managed to evade the police and thrown herself in the path of this lorry as it approached. All this was caught on photos taken by Report agency. As the lorry reversed, the police charged the pickets, pushing them apart. Eventually a path was cleared and in went the lorry.

Three people had been arrested: Paul Sheldrick, a Trico AUEW striker and Eileen Ward's nephew; a local supporter

84 | THE BATTLE RAGES

CONVOYS

ERIC FUDGE

The convoys used to hide in Harlequin Avenue and Transport Avenue and at the Hare and Hounds down Syon Lane. That was unfortunate as I used to drink in there a lot!

The convoy would turn up, and there'd be a great load of people all rushing around and lots of policemen losing their helmets – and all the usual sort of things you see at this sort of event. Nothing to write home about. At the time they seemed huge, but, looking back, it doesn't seem that way anymore. There were more police vans than there were lorries.

ROBERT (BOB) SINGH

The convoys were initially in the day time, when they would bring materials in during the day. I remember we had some big pickets to try and stop them. I remember one particular time when there was a bit of friction between us and some of the strike breakers. I remember being in a physical fight with one of them on the picket line when a convoy was going through.

BOB MITCHELL

My Dad saw the battle on TV, on a news flash. He phoned me up and said 'Your lot is on TV'. He had the car outside the house and brought me down. I remember when they were trying to break the picket line with haulage trucks, and when they were delivering the rolled steel from Sheffield – which is obviously a main ingredient of window wipers, it is one of the main materials we used to use in our Press Shop. We had rolls of steel, and obviously if you're going to move them around the country you need very large lorries. I recall seeing them going in under cover of darkness.

The police were obviously actively involved in protecting the trucks getting in, and up to the point I had thought that would be the end of it – I really believed we could turn them back. And when I saw them go through the great gate I actually cried, it had that effect on me.

CONVOYS

"

SALLY GROVES

I'll never forget 29 July and our battle we had at the gates that tea-time, when we tried to stop the convoy coming through. There were coachloads of police, and they had put this arbitrary limit of six pickets, but then even they were dragged away, including Eileen, so we couldn't speak to the lorry drivers. That was when I threw myself on the ground in the path of this lorry. I think two had already hurtled into the factory, and then this one came. In fact he came to a standstill because he'd misjudged the gate width as he swung round to speed in from the Great West Road. Lucky for me, or I might not have lived to tell the tale!

We were all gutted, quite devastated, and disgusted with the police and the way they treated us. But no one was going to knock us back for long.

The lorries left the Trico yard a few hours later, after unloading. We were pretty desperate to find out exactly where they were taking all the wipers and goods, particularly those going to the docks. I had my old Renault 4L, and it was there on the picket line outside the front gates. When we saw the lorries leaving I jumped in it and Vernon Merritt came too.

There must have been about 200 police blocking off the junction of Boston Manor Road with the Great West Road to prevent any cars following. I'll never know how I evaded the police. Maybe they weren't expecting someone to take off with a car from the picket line just outside the front gates. Maybe they weren't expecting a woman driver. Anyhow I managed to get past them all before they knew what was happening.

So we hurtled off in pursuit of the six 40-foot lorries. It was already late evening as we pursued the convoy through London going at some speed. In those days there wasn't so much traffic around by late evening. Then suddenly the convoy divided into two. Oh heck! We only had a split second to decide which three to follow. I didn't even know where I was! All we knew was that we wanted to follow the ones going to the docks. Just my luck, the three I did follow turned out to be the ones going to Northampton, not the docks.

We soon found ourselves hurtling along the M1. I was following two lorries in the middle lane, and the third was on the inside lane. Then this third lorry moved back into our lane, which meant my car was now sandwiched between the second and third lorries instead of tailing them. The guy in the lorry behind me now realised we were chasing them.

These lorries were massive, my car tiny. This guy deliberately came up – with his headlights on full beam – to within inches of the back of my car, which was juddering with the speed! As if that wasn't bad enough, the Renault had a problem with a valve in the engine which I'd never managed to sort out – sometimes when it blocked my car would completely lose

86 | THE BATTLE RAGES

power and instantly slow down. I knew if that happened now we'd be goners, as the lorry would ram the back of us.

Then the convoy, with me still sandwiched in between it, turned off onto the road to Northampton, leaving the motorway lights behind. It was really dark and must have been nearing midnight. The last lorry dropped back a bit so as we rounded a bend I took my opportunity to escape him and pulled off the road at the first chance. I couldn't see a thing as I had to switch off my lights and back away from the road. As I did so, there was an awful crunch of metal. It turned out I'd backed into some big iron gates leading to an estate.

Worse still, the last lorry had seen me as he came round the bend in the road, and he turned off too, pulling the lorry right across us so we had no means of escape. Vernon and I got out the car and ran through the gateway. As I looked over my shoulder the guy was getting down from his driver's cab.

It was pitch black. I remember in panic jumping over a low fence or garden wall into a field and running into some woodland where I threw myself face down in the dirt. I lay there for ages, too terrified to move even when I felt insects crawling over me. In the panic I'd forgotten all about poor Vernon! He had a problem with his leg so he wasn't very nimble. Later he told me he saw there was a gatehouse with a light on. He went up to the front door and banged on it. Someone came to the door, but all Vernon could blurt out in the panic was 'They're after us, they're after us!' They must have thought he was a madman, and they banged the door shut in his face!

What seemed like hours later I heard Vernon's voice calling my name in the pitch darkness. When I emerged Vernon told me that the lorry driver had come up the path behind him and accused Vernon of trying to ram his lorry! Then he saw the house with lights on, turned back to his lorry, and drove off.

Vernon and I got back into my now battered car and completed the journey to Trico's Northampton plant on the Round Spinney estate. From a vantage point we watched the lorries in the yard below being unloaded in the early hours of the morning. This story was picked up by the local *Northampton Post*, which described our escapade under the headline 'M1 Terror for Picket Girl Sally'.

and NUPE member who worked as a gardener for a local council; and Jack Dromey, Secretary of Brent Trades Council and member of the Greater London Association of Trades Councils. Dromey had simply questioned the police inspector on the interpretation of the law.

Watching these events from inside the factory were Trico workers who had been kept back to do the loading. The company wanted to avoid footing the bill of highly expensive labour imported from outside. Instead Trico would have to pay the price in terms of bad publicity.

It was the same story of police harassment when the convoy left. A squad of twenty police took up positions at the first road junction. The lorries were let through the red lights again. But this time, to prevent pickets from following, the police just stood across the road for five minutes afterwards and blocked it. Police motorcyclists were positioned farther on in lay-bys. Out of the half a dozen or so pickets' vehicles which tried to follow the convoy only one managed to slip the net and chase the convoy; this was driven by Sally Groves, accompanied by Vernon Merritt (see pp86-87).

The convoy split into two on the North Circular, three lorries heading for the docks and the other three travelling to Northampton where they off-loaded at Trico's plant, leaving before any of the workers arrived for their day shift.

The level of thuggery to which Trico had descended outraged everyone. John Inwood commented to the press the next day, 'Trico's handling of the dispute has deteriorated from rather poor judgement at the beginning to the borders of madness.'

Many of the pickets had been reduced to tears of rage and disappointment. Their hopes of getting justice had been trampled on by the police, the scabs and Trico alike. Ten weeks' hard work seemed to have gone down the drain. But spirits were soon revived and any thoughts of giving up dispelled. An impromptu meeting was held on the picket line on the evening of the strikebreaking raid. Bill McLoughlin and District Officials vowed that Trico would not get away with these tactics.

Their disappointment was overcome, and the new mood amongst the strikers was summed up by Mary Dempsey (Betty Aiston's sister), speaking to a *Labour Weekly* reporter:

> We're more determined than ever. I couldn't sleep at all last night after that business. After that we're going to stay

out till either the factory closes or we get what we want.

A mass meeting the following Monday was told that the police should hang their heads in shame. Roger Butler continued:

> Our people witnessed the police protecting property not people and so helping the company maintain cheap rates. The Trico management might be able to get lorry drivers without principles and get the police to act as company agents, but they cannot get women to work below the rate and they never will.

'WE DON'T KNOW ANYTHING ...'

ONE IMPORTANT JOB for the strikers was to hunt out the scab haulage firms in order to 'out' them and encourage all trade unionists to boycott these cowboy outfits. Over the weeks much information had been gathered, although, not surprisingly, it proved a difficult task to track companies down.

Five different firms had been identified, including one which ran an old blue Dodge with the initials SDS on it. Various firms fitted the initials but all denied involvement. It was a mystery.

Inside the factory men in a number of departments met after the incidents of 29 July. It was reported to a mass meeting that some had decided to down tools in protest – some forklift drivers, and workers from goods inward and the short order departments. Others who had stayed were refusing to co-operate with Trico's scabbing activities. ASTMS members had agreed not to supervise the moving of large rolls of steel dumped in the yard by the lorry crews. In fact many bundles had been severely damaged due to the carelessness and haste of the convoy. They were destined to remain in the yard as a reminder of Trico's stupidity.

After the 27 July and 29 July incidents there were now some fresh leads. Positive identification of three firms involved in the picket busting – all from the East End – had been made. Their transport managers were to be confronted with a strikers' delegation. Accordingly, Ivy Chandler, Mary Dempsey, Joyce Seath and Robert Singh went to the yard of one of the pirate outfits, General Express Services, along with their placards, in order to interrogate its director. They demanded to know why the company had become involved, how much were they getting for strike-breaking, and whether they would do work for Trico again. The strikers had another message – you and your activities will be boycotted by all trade unionists … until you clear yourselves.

Without exception each firm tried to deny the undeniable: 'We sold the vehicle three weeks ago, but I can't tell you who to'; 'We don't operate out Brentford way'; 'We don't know anything about it … the drivers in the photos are on holiday'. The women weren't satisfied.

Telephone calls were constantly being made to the AUEW District Office by worried company executives. The campaign was beginning to bite hard and they were 'sorry'.

In response to newspaper enquiries Roger Butler told them: 'I've had these firms ringing me up continually saying they were not responsible and that they sold their lorries to someone else before these incidents took place. Well, until they can prove it, they remain blacked.'[7]

The Managing Director of General Express Services was in real trouble. Three of his lorries had broken the picket line on 29 July, and his work centred mostly on the docks. Anxious to show he'd learnt his lesson, he wrote this letter:

To: Shop Steward,
Royal Group of Docks,
Central Road,
Labour Office, London, E.16.

Dear Sir,

With reference to your telephone conversation with our Transport Manager today, regarding an unfortunate incident at Messrs Trico works recently we would confirm without reservation:

The Company was not aware of any Industrial Dispute

---

[7] Blacking was a term widely used in the 1970s, and referred to 'secondary' industrial action taken by trade unionists in solidarity with strikers, through refusing to handle goods or services connected to the company where the strikers were based. In this text we have generally used the term 'boycott' rather than 'blacking', except, as here, when it is a direct quote. The Thatcher government restricted immunity for secondary industrial action through the 1980, 1982 and 1984 Employment Acts, and in 1990 the Trade Union Industrial Relations Act (Consolidated in 1992) made secondary action completely unlawful. Tony Blair's government did not reverse these restrictions on trade union freedoms. Although the boycotting of goods in support of the Trico strike was never fully effective, solidarity action by trade unionists in the form of picketing was indispensable to their eventual success.

Trico delegation confront transport owner, Peter Rainer of Phoenix Transport, 9 August. Left to Right, Joyce Seath, Mary Dempsey, Ivy Chandler and Robert (Bob) Singh.

CHRIS DAVIES/REPORT ARCHIVE/ REPORTDIGITAL.CO.UK

when the work was undertaken.

The management of Trico took unfair advantage of our drivers on arrival at the works, by advising the men that the dispute was a 'local' issue involving a few women employees, whilst all other of their labour force was working.

The total revenue for the work carried out will be given to charity by this Company.

The owner of a firm used on the 27 July run, Arthur A. Kent, also denied that Trico had told them the nature of the work. Trico seemed to have a habit of omitting the small detail that they were being asked to strike-break!

It looked certain that Trico were operating through a middle man in the East End: someone who could get hold of a number of one-man outfits and a few vehicles sub-contracted from others for an anti-union force.

Eventually some of the haulage firms gave us some information. 'We'll tell you who was at the centre, as long as you don't let on who told you. We might get our lorries burnt or our homes visited … these things happen out here!'

The name given was Greenwood and Gentry Ltd, of Chobham Road, Stratford. The strikers were told that Trico goods were stored in his warehouse. A somewhat risky trip to the East End was made to take a look at their yard. From a moving car photos were taken of two of the vehicles parked in the yard. One of them had been used in the 27 July convoy, and the other was the mysterious SDS vehicle that had been used on many occasions and until now had been untraceable.

Derek Coomber, editor of *Freighting World*, a weekly newspaper of international transport, might have seemed an unlikely ally for the Trico women, but he became a staunch supporter, with his featured reports and editorials exposing the haulage firms' strike-busters. He remained in close contact with Sally Groves and Roger Butler after the convoys had started smashing through the picket line, seeking to track down information on the pirate firms. Derek now contacted John Greenwood, who denied any dealings with Trico: 'It's a complete mystery to me why they think I should be involved.' That was in spite of General Express Services having admitted to him that two of their lorries that had broken the Trico picket line on 29 July had been hired out to Greenwood and Gentry late that afternoon!

The episode of the midnight convoys was nearing its end. If transport firms hadn't heard of Trico before they certainly had now. Word was being passed around … steer clear of this one. The threat of being boycotted had made them very worried, and some were members of the Road Haulage Association.

PART THREE

THE RECKONING

MORE DETERMINED THAN EVER

ON 5 AUGUST, the Labour MP for Ealing Southall, Sydney Bidwell (who, in response to a request for help from the Trico Strike Committee, had already asked employment minister Albert Booth to intervene in the dispute), promised to ask Home Secretary Roy Jenkins to investigate the picket-busting police activities. Other MPs also agreed to take up the issue. Syd Bidwell had already been in the headlines that year, when he was campaigning for Sikhs to be exempted from wearing motorcycle crash helmets.

The strikers were horrified by the blatant police collusion with the company's American gangster-style tactics. A little while back they would never have believed that Trico would be employing strike-breaking mercenary convoys of highly-paid scabs to charge through their picket lines. They would never have believed that the police would drag peaceful pickets away, preventing them from even speaking to the drivers, as they believed to be their right.

But the anger, frustration and disappointment were rapidly being translated into an increasingly steely determination. 'Disgusted', 'We're more determined than ever', 'I've changed my mind about the police' – these were just some of the reactions on the picket line given to the *Morning Star* reporter Martin Rabstein: 'We've been law-abiding and peaceful throughout the dispute. I had a great respect for the police – but not any more,' was striker Lou King's comment. Marie Lewis, another picket, told Rabstein, 'I know that I'm not going back in 'til they pay up', while someone else on the picket line told him she believed there was one law for the rich and one for the poor.

But the Trico strikers knew they were no longer alone in their struggle. As Arthur Gibbard, AUEW Assistant

DETERMINATION

❝

ANN FITZGERALD
I think then once you were out you said 'Look we've started, we'll finish'. I think that's what it came to and everybody accepted that.

BOB MITCHELL
I think our determination got stronger actually. There was a good feeling on that picket line. It just snowballed. At least once a week – because it was a time of industrial unrest throughout the country – you'd open a newspaper and see this strike had failed or that strike had failed. And I would mentally mark the days or weeks we'd been out – X amount of time longer than they had in the Midlands or wherever – and that would make me feel better. That was my memory of it. The longer it went on, day by day, the stronger our self-belief was.

ROBERT (BOB) SINGH
I wasn't surprised at how determined the women were. I felt that over the weeks of the strike a very strong sense of solidarity had developed amongst the women, and, in fact, for those women who went on strike initially not expecting it to be such a long strike, the greater the hardship they experienced, the greater their resolve became. The feeling was that they were not offering us what we want, so why should we go back to work. And so I wasn't at all surprised more women didn't go back, even though there were some real genuine cases of hardship.

Divisional Organiser, had pointed out at a mass meeting on 9 July, they were already leaving a mark on the whole trade union movement: 'If they hadn't heard of the Trico women before, they most certainly have now!' After the police used force against the pickets on 29 July to ensure the convoy

DETERMINATION

ERIC FUDGE

I think it was the bloody-mindedness of the company actually. They just were not interested at all in sorting the problem out. They were happy just to sit there and let it carry on. I think they thought that after a week or two it would all collapse and everybody would come back anyway and everything would be back to normal. And I think this attitude sort of came through to a lot of people who were out the door, and made them equally determined it wasn't going to be like that. All they were doing was generating bad feeling really, or making a bad situation worse, whatever way you like to look at it.

PHYLLIS GREEN

As time went on it made you more determined not to go back in. I definitely wouldn't have gone back if we hadn't got equal pay. I think that the majority of the women wouldn't have gone back if they hadn't got it. It just made you more determined to sit it out. I think we knew we'd get it in the end – or we didn't know, but we were determined that we'd push it to the last minute. I don't know anyone who went back. I don't know anyone who was on strike and went back.

could break through, even the BBC ran news flashes of the events.

However, good fortune was on the side of the strikers not just because of the heatwave, but also because they had a progressive and dedicated local AUEW District Committee in

Southall. Roger Butler gave unflinching leadership as District Secretary, while John Bracher, Southall District's President, was a quiet but very effective supporter of the strikers, often behind the scenes; and Bill (Mac) McLoughlin, the Divisional Organiser and another left-winger, was felt by the strikers to be ever the gentleman. Crucially for the women, negotiations with the company remained firmly under the control of these local union officials.

Then there was the invaluable assistance and support given by local Trades Councils – Hounslow and, especially, Brent, whose Secretary Jack Dromey was an organisational powerhouse, helping tremendously with the production of the Strike Bulletins and other matters. The towering figure of Tom Durkin, Chair of Brent Trades Council, became known at Trico for his unswerving support of the women's cause – as well as his irresistible urge to compose epic poems about the Trico struggle! Harriet Harman and Jamie Ritchie, at the time working at Brent Law Centre, gave the Strike Committee and AUEW District invaluable specialist advice on aspects of the new Equal Pay Act and other legal matters. All this showed what a crucial role well-represented and active Trades Councils can play helping strikers, who often struggle to organise themselves on a day-to-day basis.

In another act of solidarity, in August the Greater London Association of Trades Councils (GLATC) decided to call an emergency meeting of all its forty affiliated Trades Councils in order to co-ordinate support for the strike. This was the first time in its history that GLATC had called for a meeting on a particular dispute, and was the result of a move by Brent and Hounslow Trades Councils. The aim of the emergency meeting, scheduled to take place on 31 August, was to inform all Trades Councils about what they could do in respect of fundraising, picketing and boycotting Trico products, and to encourage them to get even more involved.

As a result of all this, the Trico women, and the male workers that had come out in support, literally picked themselves up, dusted themselves down and started all over again after the desperate events of 29 July – or, as it became known, the Battle at the Trico Gates. They were not alone, and were more determined than ever.

There was a stepping up of activity, and delegations were now being sent off all over the country, to raise money and to lobby organisations for the boycotting of Trico wipers and blades – the latter having proved to be one of the most difficult tasks.

On 2 August Roger Butler reported to a mass meeting outside the factory gates that Southall AUEW District's 16,000 members had voted overwhelmingly in favour of paying an ongoing 5p levy to support the Trico strikers. News such as this was a big morale boost.

On 10 August a delegation went to Wales. Kevin Halpin, Convenor at Acton Works, had been involved in organising this delegation, and it was led by strike committee member George Jinks, a Welshman himself, and one of the five operators who had been transferred off nights onto dayshift at Trico.

On 11 August a delegation went to Birmingham to address a meeting of the powerful British Leyland Convenors Combine Committee. Later in the day, Roger Butler and Eileen Ward, who had been the speakers at British Leyland, also spoke at a meeting of women workers at Trico's Northampton plant, along with Betty Aiston. As a result, people from the meeting, all of whom had been previously non-unionised, started joining the AUEW, and promised to support the strike. It also came to light that the women in Northampton were earning about £11 a week less than the women at Brentford. They realised that they had been duped by the Trico management.

RAISING FUNDS AND DELEGATIONS

PEGGY FARMER
Four of us went on a delegation to speak to people in Scotland. There was Peter Craven, Georgie Jinks, myself and Monica Harvey. We went by night and travelled by car. When we got there we met some delegates from the Glasgow and District TUC, and they took us to an AUEW house called Treesbank, which had just been refurbished for their meetings and for trade union people to stay there. It was a beautiful house. It was like a castle, with lovely grounds. We walked up a beautiful wide staircase with a carpet that was blue tartan all the way up. We wondered what we were coming to! It was going to be a recreational centre. We only went into the bedroom and the kitchen, but it looked like a mansion. Me and Monica slept in separate beds in one massive room, and the two boys slept in another massive room.

John Reidford drove us to Treesbank as Peter had been driving all night and had not had any sleep. We went up on Wednesday night and worked all day Thursday. On the Friday we went to about five or six factories, including Chrysler Linwood. Then on the Saturday morning we were picked up again for the *Engineering Voice* meeting in Glasgow. Then in the early afternoon we picked up our stuff and left for London. We didn't get home until the early hours of Sunday morning. It was really hectic.

John Reidford spoke mostly to the men. This is what I'm saying about Scots men – they're very man to man. We also met Arthur Millican and John Carty, the Convenor at Chrysler. He met us at the gate.

We also met a guy called Alex who was looking after the house like a caretaker. He organised most of the visits that we did through the Trades Council. We went to various factories – Massey Ferguson, Yarrow, Scots Marina, Albion Motors. The great highlight was on the Saturday morning in Glasgow, in Sauchiehall Street, when we went to the meeting with Jimmy Reid. It was absolutely marvellous – there were about 500 people there.

There were about five people already on the stage, and Peter Craven and I went on the stage as well. They wanted me to speak but I was so nervous I couldn't do it, so Peter did it. Peter was brilliant – he got up with Jimmy Reid and he spoke very well. Peter was an awfully nice person. The thing that stuck in my mind was Jimmy Reid saying, 'These lassies need our help so dig deep in your pockets, boys, and give these people money because our sisters need our help.'

I was on the stage with Jimmy Reid and I was shaking like a leaf! I think I was in awe of this man, this Jimmy Reid. When he stood up there he looked like a giant – he wasn't a giant but he looked like a giant to me because I'd heard about him. I knew what he'd done in Scotland and I was in awe of him – so you don't quite listen to what he's saying, you just hear his voice, and, my husband being a Scot as well – he sounded a bit like my Peter, the same sort of twang as Peter. It was a wonderful speech, and got a wonderful response.

Georgie Jinks and Monica were at the door with the collection and the people were very generous. I don't think anybody passed them by, and a lot of cheques came in afterwards. And the hospitality we got up there was absolutely fantastic. I thought they were wonderful.

Same with Coventry, when I went there with Eileen and Betty in the early part of the strike. We didn't go to visit anybody, we went to a union meeting, and again we had a great response. There were all types there, all belonging to the AUEW or the other unions that were up there. Betty spoke at the meeting, and a great cheer came up from them after she had told them about what we were doing.

I also went to Greenwich Trades Council with Fred Trott and Big John. Fred did the talking that day. He was a lovely speaker. He really told them the situation at Trico – a wonderful little man he was. There must have been about 100 people there. They were the only three delegations I went on.

PHYLLIS GREEN

Every Friday me and Irish Ann Fitzgerald used to go collecting money. We'd go sometimes to the gin place across the road (Booths Gin) and sometimes we'd go to Brentford Nylons, and there was another factory across the road, also something to do with cars – we didn't get much money off them. And we used to go to Firestones. They were brilliant. You'd go up with two buckets and they'd fill the buckets with money.

ROBERT (BOB) SINGH

For women who had families it was quite difficult, so the fund was set up and we went around collecting and appealing. I remember going to Sheffield and Manchester – Trafford Park estate – at the end of August.

And I remember we went to Sheffield initially – a supporter drove me and Bob up there – and we went to speak at the Trades Council, and I was just amazed at how grand the Trades Council building was. It was a solid working-class area. And it was an interesting thing because when they met us there wasn't a sense of an overwhelming feeling towards us. It was more that they went through the motions, saying yes you can come and speak and whatever to the meeting – which we did – but they'd already made a decision to give us a donation anyway. It was very much a traditional solid male-dominated working-class Trades Council meeting. But they did what they felt they had to do as trade unionists – they supported us and they gave us money.

Then we drove to Manchester and spoke

RAISING FUNDS AND DELEGATIONS

"

at a couple of meetings. We spent a night up there and then we came back down, so we went for two days. We slept in a van overnight, a Mercedes van belonging to the theatre group. The back of the van was amazing, it was very well kitted out.

ERIC FUDGE

Raising money I went first to Firestones, on the other side of the canal, and then to Duvalls up in Perivale behind the Hoover building. I think Duvalls is gone now. I used to take Ann with me, and she used to be in a very nice little number – a pair of denim hot pants and a cropped top – and she used to stand there fluttering her eyelids while the mugs put all their money in the pot trying to impress her. 'Oh, I'll chuck a fiver in, look at me.' 'Oh, thank you sir!' Well, you know, all's fair in love and war. We were certainly in the warfare situation, so use the weapons at your disposal, in this case Ann Fitzgerald! Well done that lady!

It's quite funny. At Duvalls the union rep came trotting out and was immediately quite struck like, he didn't know where to look. In fact he wasn't the union rep any more but he was scared to tell Roger. He gave more than anyone else because he was feeling guilty!

We had a list of places which had union reps in and we just used to go round them all. It was quite nice – nice sunny days, baking hot most of the time. Everybody had wonderful tans except for those that were working – they were very pale, looking like they should be haunting a castle or something.

BOB BANISTER

Once the strike had settled – it was going to be an official strike, and the pickets were going to be out there – I went to see John again and told him that, as we were part and parcel of the same union, it would normally be reasonable to expect us to come out with the others, but unfortunately there were only six of us in the office – and I hadn't even approached ASTMS at this time, who also had members in the offices. I told him that if we came out we would not have any effect on their claim. The factory had stopped anyway. I'd been down the factory and it was empty, nothing was moving. We were not going to make any difference with just six of us, and I very much doubted I could get the whole lot out. But I told him that, if he was agreeable, I'd contact the staff unions and arrange, certainly in my office, to get a weekly collection for the strike fund. And we would keep our ears open, and if we heard of any company shenanigans trying to plan something we'd let him know. And he agreed straight away, and that's what happened.

And from that time on I would go around in my office collecting money. And I also contacted ASTMS, and their rep agreed with me that that's what we'd do, we'd collect money each week. It was only a small amount of money but it was a weekly contribution. And in return we would get the bulletin, which I would then distribute. Although it has to be said that once the strike got under way, the men were picking up the bulletin themselves as they came in.

BOB MITCHELL

Sally just said we were going, and I thought, fair enough, Blackpool's a nice seaside town and the lights were on, and that was it – I didn't think anything about the Labour Party Conference. I had on this old rugby shirt and a torn motorcycle jacket. I remember Vernon saying, when we were in the B&B, you can't go in like that. I remember the landlord at the B&B asking who we were, and he said 'Oh I'll put you down as three Labours'. And he looked at me and Vernon and said 'Are you together?' And Vernon went 'No, No', and the guy said, 'Well, he's a bit young, isn't he'. But me and Vernon did share a bed in the end.

Before we went in someone gave me a shirt and tie, I can't remember who, as I had to meet Jim Callaghan. Vernon got us in, saying to the police officer 'Don't you know who Hugh Scanlon is?' Then we saw all these Right to Work marchers, and they shouted 'There's Red Robbo', and as Derek Robinson came through they all shouted to him 'Trico strikers!', and it was like the waters of the Red Sea opening for Moses. It was just 'Let them in. Let them in.' And we just walked in like royalty.

Derek Robinson was shaking people's hands and patting backs and stuff, and because I was so young he said 'It's good to have young lads like you in the movement'. I was nineteen. The next thing I remember is when the tea and scones came over, courtesy of the prime minister, Jim Callaghan. I don't think we met Scanlon. When I got back to London there was a photo of me in the *Evening Standard*.

When we drove back I fell asleep, and Sally, who was driving, fell asleep as well, and the car went off the motorway onto the embankment. Fortunately at the time there were no crash barriers, because if there had been we'd have hit one at the side of the motorway. Sally had this old Renault thing with the gear stick in the dashboard. Fortunately we did get safely back to London in the end, and Vernon woke up. We hadn't slept for about two days.

TRIBUNAL TRICKERY

OVER THE WEEKS Trico's management had lurched from one disastrous tactic to another in their attempt to demoralise and defeat the strikers and – as became increasingly evident – in an attempt to undermine and ultimately destroy the union itself. This had become a propaganda war with the union, and there was a never-ending barrage of company letters sent out to every striker. The company's tactics varied from the sublime to the ridiculous: from the massive American-style convoys of trucks organised to break through the picket line to the withholding of hard-earned holiday pay from the strikers. One surprise, given that they had told the strikers that they already had equal pay, was the inexplicable and paltry pay offers that had suddenly been made in July. These had been a further insult to the women, but the main result had been that Trico had effectively destroyed their own argument!

Following their picket-busting activities of 29 July, the company now announced that they were no longer going to 'postpone' the Tribunal, and had requested a fresh date for the hearing. True to form, the local *Brentford & Chiswick Times* newspaper chose exactly the same moment to run an editorial headed 'Judgement Day', exhorting the Trico women to stop being so stubborn and to put their case in the hands of the Tribunal! So exquisitely in tune was the editorial with the company's sentiments that Trico management sent copies of it in the post to all the strikers!

The eventual dates for the Tribunal hearing were announced as 17 and 18 August, no doubt with two days being allocated on the grounds that the women might come to their right minds and decide to attend after all. This was to be the first time that an employer presented a trade union case at a tribunal, and, given that extraordinary turn of events, it was also to be the first time that a trade union had boycotted a tribunal.

The reasons the Strike Committee and District Committee had continued with this stand were explained, yet again, in the Strike Bulletin: in the first six months' operation of the Equal Pay Act, the Industrial Tribunal had turned down seventy-nine of the equal pay applications that had been made to it and upheld only thirty-one – a failure rate of about 72 per cent. The union was concerned about the huge damage that was being done to the spirit and intent of the Act by its blatant pro-employer bias. Their view was that tribunals could be helpful to women seeking equality, but they were no substitute for strong trade union organisation. The AUEW and Strike Committee were not prepared to use a Tribunal that had allowed the new Equal Pay Act 'to become a cobweb of loopholes' for those who discriminate against women.

There is, of course, no obligation to use the tribunal route to achieve equal pay, but the world might easily have believed that it was a legal requirement, given the barrage of self-righteous moral outrage the Trico women faced from their employer and some sections of the British press and establishment. But they had chosen to take the path of direct action to achieve their goal; and this had been made possible by strong trade union organisation and the whole-hearted support of their local AUEW officials.

The company was clearly confident that the Tribunal would rule in its favour. And they had every reason to be so!

Betty Aiston and Sally Groves had been named by Trico as respondents for the Tribunal. Betty had worked at the factory for twenty years and played a leading role in the strike. Sally had been made publicity officer. She and Betty boycotted the Tribunal but they did have a clandestine supporter at the hearing. Sally Wilcox was doing research for her thesis, based on the Trico strike and women's experience of equality issues, so the strikers were well informed.

The company was represented by a lawyer named Kemp and, as was later reported in the Strike Bulletin, the two star witnesses were John Millner Slidders, Trico's Personnel Executive, and the women's old friend Sid Atkins. The Chairman of the Tribunal, Sir Jocelyn Bodily, an Oxford man, had had stints as a High Court Judge in Sudan, as Principal Crown Counsel of Hong Kong, and as Chief Justice of the Western Pacific. *Who's Who* gave his address as Vine

House, Kingston Blount, Oxon, and his club as the Royal Ocean Racing. So plenty of industrial shop-floor experience there!

The Strike Bulletin mocked the 'incredible double act of John and Jocelyn', who they regarded as committing grievous bodily harm to the cause of equality as they delved 'into the murky regions of Trico management's anti-equal pay logic'. Even Kemp, the Trico lawyer, was foxed: he commented that it was 'so complex' that 'I don't fully understand it myself'. Fun was also made of Sir Jocelyn's 'union', the Royal Ocean Racing Club, which, it was believed, had a 'few less members than the AUEW'. It was also noted that Sir Jocelyn had been fired by Sid Atkins' description of his 'commando-style' night shift.

The Tribunal decision was finally delivered on 24 August:

> it was not contended that there is currently any difference at all between the work which they (the men) are doing and that which their female counterparts are doing. So here the company must rely upon the 'escape' provision contained in sub-section (3) of section 1 of the Act.

The Tribunal had accepted without question all the evidence from the employers and had not asked any questions that might have challenged that evidence. They had also accepted the contention of the employers that the ex-night workers were more flexible than the women operators and their claim that that constituted a 'material difference'. Sub-section (3) of section 1 of the Act was the notorious 'material difference' clause, which in Trico's case turned on the fact that the men had previously worked on night shift for which they had received an enhanced rate.

As Sally Groves told the local *Evening Mail*, 'We were expecting it. The company went to the tribunal because they thought they could dodge equal pay through it.' And she added that the women were 'now more determined than ever to stay out until the company give them equal pay'. And as Roger Butler later commented to Helen Hewland of the *Morning Star*: 'If the union had attended the tribunal its decision would have stuck to us like a tar baby.'

A joint statement issued to the press by the AUEW and Trico Strike Committee immediately after the decision was published stated:

THE TRIBUNAL

ERIC FUDGE

Even if you'd had the best case in the world they'd still find against you at the tribunal. They could not be trusted to give a reasonable opinion on the situation, and, as such, I was quite happy to back the AUEW's assertion that we shouldn't bother with it, and they obviously were not to be trusted.

The company were wrong there weren't they, thinking the women would give up after the tribunal went against us. I remember thinking at the time that it was just a load of meaningless nonsense and a complete waste of everybody's time. And as far as I'm concerned nothing's changed – and that's an opinion which I told to everybody and their brother and their sister for that matter. I made sure that everybody that I spoke to knew that as far as I was concerned it was a complete waste of time, and should be completely disregarded, as it was completely biased in favour of the employers.

Hardly any women returned to work after the Tribunal decision. Good job too. They obviously realised, as I did, that the whole thing was just a load of nonsense, and frankly you had to be pretty thick not to see through it, that it was just a way of helping out the employers. It was all started up by the Government anyway, so what do you expect.

BOB MITCHELL

It was a lesson to me, that the courts were always going to be biased. That was one of the big turning points. My father said the union should have gone to the Tribunal. I wouldn't say we had arguments, we had discussions. He told me, 'That's what these organisations have been set up for – for working people'.

At the time I thought it would be like putting all our eggs in one basket, building up our hopes that we had such a strong case that we couldn't lose. That, obviously, in retrospect, wouldn't have been the way the Tribunal would have gone. But my Dad would say 'You've got a good case, go and stand up in court and you'll be given a fair hearing'. But really, in my eyes, it was more like 'Give them a fair trial and hang them'!

A lot of people expected the strike to collapse after the verdict of the Tribunal. We were all going to be on our knees, and we'd go back to work defeated. But that never happened, and it was a turning point for the strike. It was hugely important. Probably out of the six months it was probably the most important bit.

Left to right:
Frances Pinner and
Peggy Farmer

PHOTO: MORNING STAR

... the Tribunal decision further underlines the serious defects in the Equal Pay Act and illustrates that even where men and women are working alongside each other on identical work, they are unlikely to qualify for equal pay in law ... This confirms the correctness of our decision not to appear in front of the Industrial Tribunal.

The statement ended with comments about the dispute that have since held true:

This dispute is a milestone in the fight for equal pay for women and has been instrumental in highlighting the inadequacies and legal loopholes in the Equal Pay Act. Further there is now an urgent need for the TUC to press the Government to strengthen the Equal Pay Act and so to transfer the spirit and intent of the Act into the wage packet.

(It should be noted here that, even if the women had attended and won their case – almost impossible given the way the Act was worded at the time – Trico could still have found ways to avoid granting equal pay to all the women, as was to happen at Electrolux in Luton.[1])

John Inwood, the women's AUEW factory convenor, told the *Middlesex Chronicle*: 'It is unfortunate that a well-intentioned Act – and the Tribunal was set up under the Act – can be used in a manner that would negate justice: that is these women getting equal pay.'

Peggy Farmer told a *News Line* reporter: 'As far as I'm concerned the Equal Pay Act was a "puller" ... launched as part of Labour's election programme to get into office. We expected to find the Act was straightforward but now we can see the loopholes. The government knows we have been out for thirteen weeks. We would like them to step in. The way I feel there is no going back until we win. My husband is with us all the way.'

Maria (May) Wilson, a sparky Scottish striker, told the journalist: 'I don't believe the industrial tribunal set-up is for the workers. As for the Equal Pay Act, there are so many holes in it you don't know where you are. I'd never been on strike before this dispute. I've got a different outlook completely now. I never used to have much time for strikes. But this company is a stubborn mule.'

Olga Porter, a deputy shop steward, told him: 'I'll stay out indefinitely. The others feel the same. We will stay out till

---

[1] See Part Four for more details about the women workers' struggle for equal pay at Electrolux, Luton.

Left to right: Betty Humphreys, Kathy Worth and Ivy Chandler at mass picket, 23 August 1976.

PHOTO IN *INDUSTRIAL MANAGEMENT* OCT 1976

we win.' Dora (Doll) Wakefield added:

> The Company are trying to get out of paying equal money by saying there is a difference between the work the men did on night shifts and what we do on day shifts. But we are not after a night shift premium. We want the same operation rate as the men doing the same job. I'm a press operator and I've been on presses for twenty-four years. We won't give in now.

Despite the strength of feeling expressed on the picket line, the strikers did have some jitters as to whether there would be any partial collapse in support following the Tribunal decision, especially given the number of mostly older women who had simply stayed at home and were not involved in the battle and comradeship at the gates. The worry was that someone sitting at home receiving all this disinformation in the company letters, without the benefit of experiencing the huge tide of outside support and belief in our cause, was more likely to become demoralised and defeatist. Would any of them succumb to the company propaganda and walk back through the gates as a group? It was hard to judge.

TRIBUNAL TRICKERY | 109

Trico mass picket.
Left to Right, Stella North, unknown, Ann Fitzgerald, Robert (Bob) Singh, Bob Mitchell, 23 August 1976.

ANDREW WIARD (REPORT)

The truth was that the tribunal decision was another blow, and, unsurprisingly, immediately afterwards the company propaganda machine moved into top gear again.

In anticipation of the danger to striker morale once the decision became known – which happened before the formal announcement on 24 August – Roger Butler and the Strike Committee called for a mass picket and mass meeting on 23 August. The mass picket was well-attended and exuberant, as is manifestly evident in the photos taken at the time. The strikers were irrepressible, and the unwavering outside support from local Trades Councils, factories and political and women's groups was also abundantly in evidence. Those represented at the picket included British European Airways shop stewards; Fords truck plant from Langley, Bucks; Racal AUEW stewards, Wembley; Nalgo local government workers; ASTMS of Smiths Industries, Cricklewood; and the Sogat print chapel; along with Brent Working Women's Charter and many others.

Roger Butler told the mass meeting later that day in Brentford that the Tribunal had been 'an utter waste of public money' and its decision had changed nothing. He reaffirmed

Angela at Trico mass picket, 23 August 1976.

ANDREW WIARD (REPORT)

that the union would meet the company any time to negotiate a settlement based on equal pay: 'That is the only basis for a return to work. Our attitude has not changed for fourteen weeks and we'll not fall for Trico tribunal trickery!'

As if determined to alienate the women further (if that were possible), Trico management had by now started to deny the holiday pay that was due to the strikers. Bill MacLaughlin told the meeting that this was a mean and petty attempt at intimidation which would only result in angering the strikers and their supporters. As was normal at the end of each mass meeting, the decision to continue the strike action was put to all the strikers present for endorsement, and the vote was unanimous.

The AUEW protested about the withholding of holiday pay to the London Association of the Engineering Employers Federation, who then wrote to the company telling them that everyone seeking holiday pay should be paid. It became quite a joke that the company's own 'union' had had to tell

TRIBUNAL TRICKERY | 111

Fred Wright cartoon in Trico Strike Bulletin No 11, 3 September 1976

Trico to get their finger out and pay up!

As it turned out, any return to work was a mere trickle.

As part of the company's propaganda campaign after the Tribunal decision, John Slidders told the press that 'the strikers' claim could not be met on either moral or legal grounds' (reported in the *Ealing Gazette*, 27 August 1976). And the company also issued another letter to the workforce, one foolscap page in length, telling them that the tribunal ruling meant two things:

> The Company is correct in saying that the night shift is not a fair comparison to make with the day shift, and consequently there is no just comparison of rates.
>
> The five men ex the night shift now working on days are a separate arrangement, not in conflict with the Equal Pay Act, and is not an automatic cross reference for establishing a day rate. This was a humanitarian act to try and minimise problems of redundancy.

And the letter ended:

The picket lines may still be operating but there will be police on duty morning and evening, which will see that the pickets are peaceful. You are in a minority of Trico employees who are not at work. About 500 employees cross the picket line at 8 o'clock any work day. It cannot be difficult for you to join them. You have put up a tremendous struggle which was, unfortunately, proved to be on the wrong basis. However, no one wins in a situation like this. Take this chance, come back to work and start earning money again. No victimisation – no recrimination – just return to work and start earning money!

Another letter followed close on its heels, implying that layoffs or redundancy would be inevitable if there was no return to work. Eileen Ward told a mass meeting on 31 August to cheers and laughter: 'As far as those letters are concerned you can pin them on the toilet wall. The rest I leave to you.' Even the *Sun* newspaper, no friend of the women, noted the decision under the heading 'Women fight equal pay snub', and quoted Betty Aiston as saying 'The fight goes on until we have won'. Betty Humphreys, a feisty Irish woman and Trico shop steward, told a local reporter that none of the women 'would be brought to heel by threats'.

Bill MacLaughlin had told the strikers at the mass meeting on 31 August: 'Your wellbeing is invested in the trade union and its organisation. The company talks about returning to a normal way of life. The fact is that if they break the union it will be a lesser way of life.'

Sid Harroway, chair of Ford Dagenham Body Plant shop stewards committee, and Mick Case, the deputy convenor of Ford Langley, as well as George Brooks of London Transport brought messages of solidarity and promises of maximum support. As Mick Case commented: 'We get the *Daily Mirror* and the *Sun* rammed down our throats all our lives telling us nothing but a load of rubbish. But you get out and meet the people like yourselves all over this country who are working and struggling for a decent living wage.'

The Trico women and the men that genuinely supported them were learning about all this in practice. They were learning who their real friends were – the ordinary working people up and down the country, not the employers and their friends in the media or government.

DECISIVE DAYS

BEING OUT ON STRIKE was a novelty at first, even exciting and fun, especially when the sun was shining and you thought there would be some back tax or holiday pay owed. The sudden freedom from the drudgery of work had been exhilarating. But as the weeks went by with no settlement in sight, the strikers' worries and anxiety had grown in direct proportion to their mounting mortgage, rent and utility bills.

During the fourteenth week on strike Betty Aiston gave an interview to *Shrew* magazine. Talking about the hardship she said:

> Some of us now really are feeling the pinch, it's been one long struggle, they've had to do without and sacrifice holidays. The strike pay is £9 but we've been giving our members £10, we've been giving them £1 extra. On top of all that we do have a hardship fund where people come to us if they are really hard pushed; there are some young girls out on strike who pay up to £15 a week in rent, these people we try to look after as best we can and help them, because if the landlord decides to get a bit naughty when they can't pay the rent they can put them out.
>
> Social security have been a terrible headache to us. And there again, even they apply sex discrimination because a man can claim for his wife and his children – in some cases, not all – but a woman, a one-parent family, gets nothing. For the simple reason she's on strike they will not entertain her at all. In response we had a delegation went down there, of women who were wanting to claim social security – it consisted of young single girls, one-parent families, and they actually sat in there from

9 o'clock in the morning, and they had to be lifted out bodily by the police when it closed, and they still didn't get a halfpenny from them. If you consider that some of these women have worked for as long as thirty years, paid a full stamp, and when they really need money from social security, they're rejected.

Peggy Long was a widow who worked to support herself. She was always to be seen sitting on the picket line at the front gate. She told a reporter from *Women's Voice*:

I've worked here for eleven years. That means I've made a lot of money for the firm. I have no security. When this strike is over what I'll remember is the hardship … how I survived on £10 a week and hardship money.

But I've also learnt a lot, noticed a lot of things since I've been on strike. Like this morning I heard on the radio about how women get less benefits than men, even when they pay the same stamp. I never realised such things before. Normally you don't even have time to think about things, you take them for granted. I also didn't realise there were so many organisations supporting women's equality till I was on strike and I've seen all of you down here.

She went on to say:

And I think it's terrible for the women whose husbands are scabbing and going inside every morning. If I had a husband and he worked here and he didn't support me I wouldn't speak to him … Me, I believe in the union. Either you're a good trade unionist or you're a bad one. You can't be half way. How can you teach your children to stand up for what is right if you haven't got the backbone to do it yourself?

Certainly the fight did go on, and with renewed effort and improved organisation. Fundraising continued and was stepped up. There was a weekly Firestones collection, with two of the strikers, Ann Fitzgerald and Phyllis Green, causing a sensation in their hot pants! The Sikh temples around Southall raised considerable sums of money for the strike fund on a regular basis in recognition that many women from their own community were involved in the dispute. Strikers visited workplaces all over West London, but also much further afield, literally the whole length and breadth of Britain.

Betty Aiston went up to Newcastle and visited the AUEW District Committee and engineering factories, while Sally Groves visited Sheffield to meet the AUEW District Committee and spoke at factory gate meetings, including at Ambrose Shardlows and Firth Brown. Shortly after this, a couple of the most stalwart of the women's supporters, Bob (Robert) Singh and Bob Mitchell, power press operators/setters at Trico and known as 'the two Bobs', set off for Sheffield and Manchester with a supporter who worked for the feminist Pirate Jenny Theatre Company. They spoke to the Trades Council in Sheffield and then at some meetings, including a student union meeting in Manchester.

Money was pouring into the strike fund now. Women's groups as well as trade unions and factories and left-wing political groups were all raising money, and they promised to redouble their efforts in face of Trico's intransigence. By now there was not only broad recognition but admiration

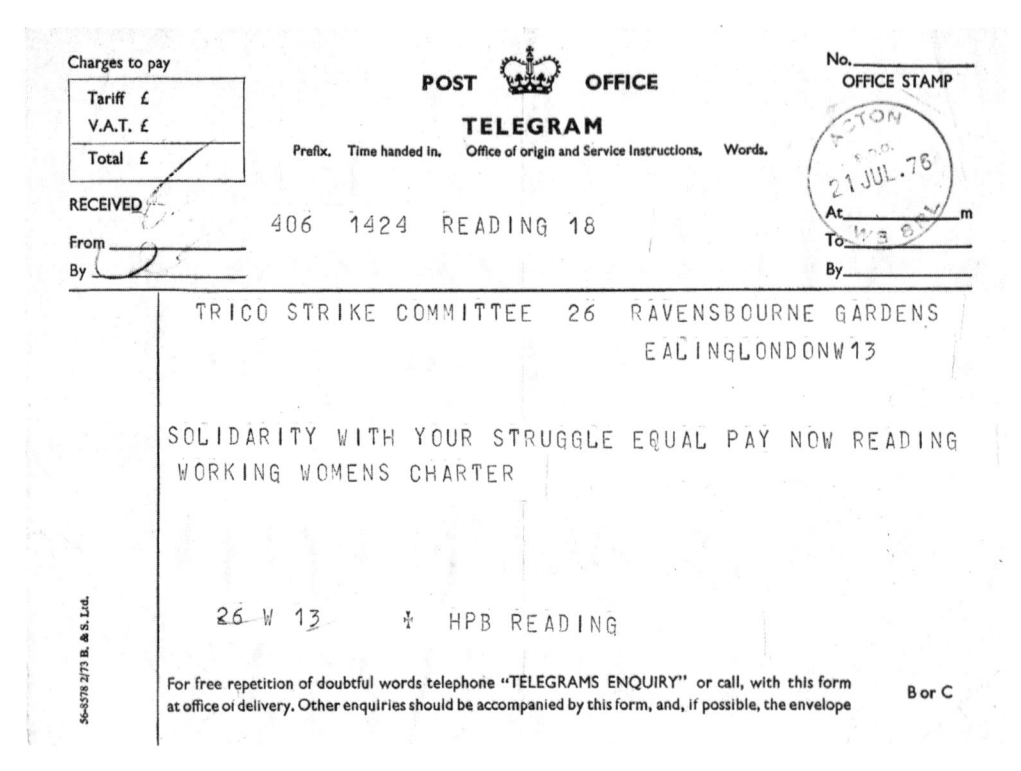

Working Women's Charter badge, and telegram of support from the Reading WWC

from people all over the country for the battle being put up by the Trico women for the principle of equal pay. There was also recognition of the hardship they were facing after fourteen weeks outside the factory gates.

Another delegation soon headed off, this time for Glasgow, led by Peggy Farmer and Peter Craven (another loyal supporter, who was a shop steward in Trico's tool room, and a delegate on Southall District Committee), along with Monica Harvey and George Jinks. A highlight of the trip was attending a 500-strong meeting of the Broad Left's *Engineering Voice*, where Jimmy Reid, of Upper Clyde Shipbuilders fame, spoke to the crowd.

A report on the visit was sent in by Arthur Milligan, a Glasgow trade unionist, and was included in the next Bulletin:

> Such was the show of solidarity by workers in the West of Scotland to the personal appeal by a visiting delegation from the Trico Strike Committee, that a further extended campaign north of the border is being planned immediately. The delegation, headed by Pete Craven, has just returned from three days of meetings with convenors and shop stewards on Clydeside and Ayrshire and they reported that 'with support like this, our determination to win is greater than ever'.
>
> Not only was immediate financial backing given but this is to be followed up by regular factory, pit and shipyard collections for the 500 strong TRICO workers, predominantly women, in their struggle for equal pay. First to weigh in with support was the 90,000 strong Glasgow and District Trades Council, whose secretary, John Reidford, said 'the TRICO strike deserves the full support of the Trade Union and Labour movement. It is ludicrous that a management is allowed to deny implementation of equal pay while, at the same time, admitting that men and women are doing the same work.' John Reidford also arranged for the delegation to stay at the new Trade Union recreational centre, TREESBANK, although it was not yet officially open, completely free of charge.
>
> A further boost for the TRICO delegation came from the instant support attitude of shop stewards at Yarrows, Scotstoun Marine, Albion Motors, Massey Ferguson, etc. It was a case of 'whatever assistance we can give, you will get' and, in fact, the suggestion that an extended

delegation visit was necessary came from the Shop Stewards themselves.

Peggy Farmer added:

> The reception that we got was out of this world. We now realise that our struggle has the active support of thousands of others. We shall never forget the warmth of our Trade Union brothers and sisters in Scotland.
>
> The climax of the visit was the opportunity to address 500 engineering shop stewards at an *Engineering Voice* meeting in Glasgow. One of the speakers was Clydeside's most well-known post-war leader, Jimmy Reid, and another was John Carty, the convenor of Chrysler Linwood. The reps from TRICO came away with an army of new allies.

This wasn't simply a matter of fine words and rhetoric: these workers were putting their money where their mouth was. Money was pouring in not only from factories and workplaces but also from miners and dockers; and from women's groups and student organisations and individuals, young and old, who had begun to hear about those Trico women taking a stand for equal pay.

In many factories and offices collections were being organised week after week by shop stewards – or by anyone who believed in the importance of working-class solidarity, never mind equal pay. These donations, large and small, were sent to the Strike Fund or Southall District, or brought along to the picket line. Money was raised at CAV Acton, London Transport's Acton Works and at Glacier Metal in Alperton and Magnatex at Harlington. John Bracher, President of Southall District Committee, and the modest but highly capable convenor of Magnatex, ensured that his factory raised hundreds of pounds for the Trico fight. Martin Bakers in Denham and the AEC joint shop stewards committee also continually raised money from factory collections. Workers at Martin Bakers also decided to donate the first week's increase under their new pay deal to the Trico strike fund, which amounted to over £460.

In Sheffield, steelmaking factories such as Ambrose Shardlows, Davey United, Firth Brown and others repeatedly sent money collected on the shop floor. Then there was Massey Ferguson in Glasgow, and the Kent miners, who started giving money very early on during the strike, sometimes £200 in a single donation, the TGWU branches at Fords and British Leyland, and dockers in the Royal Group. Meanwhile building workers constructing chalets at Prestatyn, North Wales, made contact to say that they had decided, over and above donations, to levy themselves 50p per week in support of the strike. Then there were the AUEW District Committees and Branches and Trades Councils around the country. Alongside this women's groups were also making big efforts to raise money, for example Hammersmith Working Women's Charter and Northfield Women's Liberation group in Ealing, and a host of others further afield.

Lisa Parrish, who kept the accounts for the Strike Committee, told of how touched the strikers had been by a seventy-eight-year-old man and his wife who had written a letter in support of the Trico women enclosing twenty 6½p stamps towards costs. They were both Londoners who had retired to live in Devon. Then there was the woman patient in traction at University College Hospital, London, who sent a cheque for £50, while staff at St Bernard's Hospital, Southall, also sent money. A couple living in Holland Road, London W14, also sent £100. We leave it to the imagination of the reader as to whom that couple may have been. Then there was the ex-Trico worker now living abroad who sent £25.

The Young Liberals raised about £200 at the Liberal Party conference, while the Labour Party Young Socialists raised £69.30 at a meeting they organised at the Labour Party's Blackpool conference.

One man pulled up at the picket line on the Great West Road to hand in a donation. He told the women he'd been out with his mates having a meal when they suddenly remembered the Trico women and, feeling guilty that they were able to afford a good meal, had rustled together some money.

In all the Trico strikers raised £34,644, which at 2017 value would be an astounding £262,000. This included the £6,822 that was raised from the Southall District levy. Far less money would have been raised if the strikers had not organised delegations that travelled the length and breadth of Britain appealing for help. There were no wealthy donors; it was simply ordinary men and women, ordinary trade unionists, who responded to a just cause and the principle at stake.

MORE HARDSHIP

"

BELLA (DAVIS) YOUNG

I used to picket at night because at night I got £5 from the union. With that, and the money we collected, I used to have enough money for food. Then my mother sent some money from Spain. I never asked her for it, but maybe somebody said something to her. When I got that money I said to myself, well, the strike is nearly finished, and I thought I'd got enough, so I went to buy Isabella a pair of boots (see Izzy Davis p123). I got my girl a pair of good ones.

I have very good friends and they used to give me a lot of stuff. One day, after I had done my shopping and was thinking what I was going to buy and counting my money, a Spanish woman friend of mine said, 'It's alright, Bella, I buy for you, you buy for me when you can.' I was lucky really. And also my daughter Izzy was a very good girl.

I got a little job part-time, cleaning an office with Izzy, just before the strike. You know me – I always have a little, a few pounds I'm hiding somewhere. I always manage, because I'm a very good keeper. I never buy any clothes. And I never bought anything for Izzy all that time, bless her heart, and I never gave her any pocket money, because I couldn't. I just managed with little money. It was a very hard time, but still we had to stick with each other. We didn't want to be one of the girls going in – they went in through the park to get in, as we were picketing all night.

LORETTA BRAITHWAITE

Feelings about the strike were a bit mixed. Nobody really wanted to be on strike because they were losing money, so it was a bit mixed feeling, especially if you had children – me and Reggie, both of us, were out at the same time. He was on the nights but he came out so he was off too. We had to cope, so we did. It wasn't easy, but we had to cope. Family helped.

ANN FITZGERALD

I was only in a bed-sitter, and luckily a bed-sitter at that time was only about £5 or £6 a week. But you still had to pay for it, and I had an electricity meter in my bedroom at the time, and many a time I went without having a shilling to put in it. And then you had to get your food and whatever, and bus fares – I found it very hard. And I didn't know about the extra (hardship) money at first. Then someone told me about it and I asked for it, but I felt guilty to be honest – but I couldn't tell you what I got. That was all from money coming in, and they distributed it as best they could.

RHODA (FRASER) WILLIAMS

I was married and had a little daughter. My husband was working as a conductor on the buses, so he used to pay the bills and do the shopping and everything like that, so I didn't have a lot of trouble about that. We

MORE HARDSHIP

never talked about the strike. It was up to me. Some men will quarrel. He didn't say anything. I was about 24, and my daughter was two. I could pay the bills even though the money was small. We were renting a room in his brother's house.

I didn't used to so grieve towards the strike because my ex-husband used to take care of the bills, take care of his child. In those days things were a bit cheaper – the nanny was just £3 and the rent was £4. The money was small but where you were putting your children was small as well. My ex-husband didn't say anything at all. He just stayed quiet. He never told me you have to go and get the next job, you'd better not wait for that strike to be over. He never said a word. Some people's husbands gave them a lot of trouble if they talked about the strike. The others I knew never talked about the hardship.

SANDRA (WARD) GRAY
My Mum was worried about people not being able to pay their bills, and not being able to put food on the table, and what their husbands would think when they got home. She was constantly worried about that. She worried about it all the time and she used to talk to my Dad a lot about it. My Dad was very sympathetic – he came out on strike as well for Trico's, which was good. So the whole household was on strike, and there was hardly any money coming in, and she also worried about that as well. We lived off family really. Family would help us out here, there and everywhere. They were supportive.

ERIC FUDGE
I had to try and find a way of getting some money, so I got a bit of part-time work here and there. I had a friend who had a courier company and he used to give me a bit of work.

PHYLLIS GREEN
It was only as the strike went on that you realised the seriousness of it. The first couple of weeks or months was a bit of fun, but then the money ran out, and my friends used to feed me – I'd go round for meals to their house. They were Irish people I knew from the village where I came from. I'd go round and they'd give me Sunday dinner and things like that. But it did get hard – it wasn't as funny in the end as it was at the beginning.

On Fridays we used to go down to the pub (the Griffin) because they used to pay out strike pay from the room upstairs. At first we would have had a week in hand, and maybe a couple of weeks' holiday pay, so I suppose it would have started up after that money had run out. But the union was good to the single girls – and there were a lot of foreigners, and people living in one room in people's houses. They paid my rent.

MORE HARDSHIP

"

Any time you went into the café and there were bus drivers there they'd always get you a big plate of mixed grill and so you'd be alright – so at least you'd get a meal three times a week.

But there were times when you would be thinking, Christ, I've only got 20p or 30p left, and you would be wondering what to do, and then you had to put money in the meter for the electric, as well as paying for the room. I used to borrow candles from the Catholic church and light them up instead of using electric. I remember people coming to the strike committee with gas bills and electric bills, but I only paid into the meter so I didn't have a three-month bill, so it was easier I suppose. But it would have been hard on them.

A lot of Irish girls went on holidays to Ireland and stayed there in the family home until the strike was over, and that was hard for them. I knew a few of them who did that, and you couldn't blame them really. At home they would have got their food and everything they wanted.

When I had only a few pence left I'd generally go to some of my friends or my cousins and borrow money off them. I never paid them back. I'd just ask for money and they'd give me a pound or two. But then you'd probably get two dinners for a pound at that time. And then the union paid my rent so I didn't have to worry about being thrown out. So long as I had a roof over my head, I thought, that's fine. You can starve and you can go cold, but you need somewhere to sleep. That was the most important thing.

But then I was only in once a day. You'd never have breakfast. You'd buy a packet of biscuits and they'd do you for breakfast and then you'd have the dinner. Either someone would buy it for you in the café, or you'd have your £1 from picketing for the day so you'd be able to get some rolls and a pint of milk or stuff like that – which would be fine really. Actually I don't think I was ever really worried about starving as I knew people who would help me. I knew I'd be looked after, I suppose, and that if you did go to the union they'd probably give you more money anyway. They weren't going to let you starve. I never went to the hardship fund. I didn't even know about it but I didn't need it anyway. As I said, I had the money to pay the rent. My rent was only £5 a week, and they were giving me a tenner. So I had a fiver left over, and that would have bought food.

I lived in Hanwell, not that far away, about half an hour's walk, and then I moved to Northfields, and that was also about half an hour's walk. I never really took a bus.

Loads of times we wondered if some women would return to work. I remember some of the older women would have a gas bill or electric bill to pay, and other things like that, and they'd say, 'Oh it's not worth it, we're not going to get anywhere.' And you'd be worried when you went down to the picket line, but they never did go in. There were loads of times when you thought 'Oh no, they're going to go in', but if they didn't turn up on a Monday, you were alright until the next Monday.

IZZY DAVIS

Well it wasn't an easy time at all, because my mother is Spanish and she didn't have any family members living nearby. She was on her own and she was a single parent. She was looking after me, a teenager, with hardly any money at all coming in. It was really hard. She used to feel really sad because she could never give me pocket money or buy me new shoes or any nice things to wear. And it was hard for her to carry on with the strike knowing that she was struggling so much at home, with a mortgage to pay and a child to look after.

I remember on one occasion her mother sent her a cheque. I think it was about £50. And Mum had seen me keep looking at this lovely pair of platform boots (well it was the 70s, wasn't it!). Really nice, they were, and I kept looking at them every time we were on our way to Tesco's. 'Look Mum, these boots are lovely, aren't they?'

And she just gave me all of the money that her Mum had sent her, and she said, 'Look Izzy, go and get yourself those lovely boots.' And I thought that was such a kind thing to do. As a teenager or young adult you know when it's serious, when you can't pester your parents because you know that there isn't any money – you know it wouldn't be fair because you can see that they're sad for you that they can't give you what they want to.

But, you know what, as a daughter it's awe-inspiring to watch your mother have this fighting spirit to stand up for her principles and her rights, and to see her with a smile on her face when she went off to that picket line, saying in her broken English, 'I will not be a scab. No! Flimmin' scabs! I'm not going to be a scab. Those scabs, they go in there …'

And she was fiercely fighting for her rights, fiercely. At the same time the softer maternal instincts were so obvious; she was in conflict, but she stood up for herself and for me. That's very inspiring, to see your mother standing up for what they think is right. And she wasn't just standing up for herself, she was also standing up for her workmates as well, and her thoughts were for them too.

So it was a really funny time. I hadn't really got a clue myself. I wasn't very political. I was just a fifteen-year-old teenager, and was just interested in normal things a teenager is interested in.

But I did learn a lot from that, and from the hardship too, and what it's like to have nothing. Even the groceries were very basic you know. She would buy things but she would be very careful and buy things

MORE HARDSHIP

that were on offer. And when she was out on the picket line it affected me because I had to get my own dinner. She would buy things that were easy for me to make so I could go home after school and cook my own supper.

And there were a lot of fun times as well. My mother has got such a great sense of humour, she's absolutely hilarious, and she's an optimistic person. And she was determined to get through that strike; she was determined not to be a 'flimmin' scab'! As for me walking around with old shoes and hardly anything nice to wear – actually that didn't matter too much. I think it mattered more to my mother and, of course, she had the worry of a mortgage to pay as well. And I don't know how she did it but she managed to juggle every penny so that we were kept warm and had enough money for the meter and there was food.

Really the actual strength she showed at that time was enormous. When she came home from that picket line she didn't have a family member to go to and say 'look, you know, I need help, I need a bit of extra money.' She had nobody nearby apart from her good friends ... there wasn't anybody. And when she did get that one cheque from her mother, she gave it to me to buy that gorgeous pair of black platform boots that I kept admiring!

I don't know how she did it. She is so warm and she is a very optimistic person and she always knows how to count her blessings. Sometimes she would say to me if she saw me looking remotely sad or something, 'Look Izzy, never look at people better off than you. You don't have to look far to see someone worse off.' She would say, 'I know things are hard at the moment but there are people even worse off, so we must count our blessings that we have.' And those snippets, those things that you are exposed to, you take them with you through life and learn how to survive hard times and stand up for your principles – the importance of doing that, not just for yourself but also for your workmates. If there's a will there's a way; that sheer determination, guts and courage even when you're upset and sad and on the breadline.

TRICO IN TROUBLE

ON 1 SEPTEMBER, WITHOUT prior warning, Trico management called a meeting for all the employees still working in the factory, where they were told that, as from end of work time that Friday 3 September, 445 men and 77 women shop floor workers from the Brentford and Northampton plants would be laid off. The management admitted that there had only been an insignificant return to work following the decision of the Tribunal. (A very different picture of numbers returning had been given to the press and in company letters before this!) A spokesman for the company later told reporters that neither the strikers nor the office staff were included in the layoffs, and that if the strikers returned to work, the people laid off would be taken straight back.

This was clearly an admission of failure on the part of the company to break the strike.

On Monday 31 August Eileen Ward had urged the women at the mass meeting to ignore threats of intimidation from Trico – and they had! Over the weekend the company had sent out letters urging the strikers to cross the picket line with police protection, and making threats of layoff or redundancy should they not do so. Eileen described these letters as an attempt by management to get them to 'rat' on their workmates, and continued: 'We must stand united as the company is watching us like hounds now. We've got to show them what we're made of.' Eileen Ward was always able to lift the strikers' spirits with her direct way of talking, rock-solid determination and humour. She received special tribute at that meeting for her contribution to the struggle.

Bill MacLaughlin argued that it was the company that had brought about the layoffs, and that they should bear full

LAYOFFS

BOB MITCHELL
In that period when the rest of the workforce got laid off – though they didn't actually lose their jobs – they weren't treated like they probably expected to be, like returning heroes or something!

ERIC FUDGE
I had no sympathy for them being laid off at all. If they had all come out at the start of the strike – everybody – it would never have dragged on for so long. All they did was generate a lot of bad feeling. Their self-interest is all they're interested in. Nobody matters apart from them. They were not prepared to stand up and fight for their fellow workers at the factory, so, as far as I'm concerned, their opinion doesn't count for anything and I really don't give a damn about them, and that's it really.

ROBERT (BOB) SINGH
I think the layoffs caused a bit of a tension, because people who had been working blamed us for being laid off, and it did cause quite a bit of friction between us and the non-strikers.

responsibility for the situation. The layoffs could have been avoided if the company had carried out the spirit and intent of the Equal Pay Act in the first place, instead of finding devious methods to resist it, and legal loopholes through which to crawl: 'It is wishful thinking on the part of the company to believe that there will be any collapse of the dispute':

> If there was ever a time it is now to deliver a shattering blow. We are not only going to carry on the fight, but we are going to step up the fight so that the company is compelled to meet the union. Everyone outside the gate has a common interest to see that this strike does not last any longer than is necessary. The efforts of all should be turned to putting such pressure on the employer that a speedy victory is assured.

Friday, layoff day, soon arrived. There was an element of tension and friction on the picket line as the scabs were turned out of the factory. Some of the strikers noticed a few scruffy bits of paper pinned to the trees near the front gate, with NF (National Front) scrawled on them, alongside some abusive words. They had already known that there were National Front sympathisers, and possibly members, in the factory, but these scrappy notes showed them up as a rather pathetic rag, tag and bobtail outfit. On reflection, this reaction was symptomatic of the unpleasant, sneering attitude towards the women of many of the men still working.

This attitude was picked up, unsurprisingly, by the *Brentford & Chiswick Times* and the *Hounslow Evening Mail*, which gave considerable print space to a Trico machine tool fitter who had just been laid off, and who told the paper that many of the skilled men had no sympathy left for the women. His daughter was reported as saying that the strikers should 'stop poncing about and get back to work'.

One of the Trico shop stewards from the tool room, who held a senior position on the shop stewards committee, had from the beginning refused to support the women or his union; he had crossed the picket line every day throughout the strike and had been very abusive towards the women on the picket line. This man now turned to the media to make a full-scale attack on the union leadership, claiming that the striking women had been misled by left-wing activists. He alleged, in a letter to the *Financial Times* and to a local paper, that about 317 union members still working at Trico had signed a letter to Hugh Scanlon, President of the AUEW, in

STRIKE BREAKERS

ROBERT (BOB) SINGH
Obviously there were very strong feelings against them because they were breaking the strike, they weren't prepared to make a sacrifice on a point of principle – the way I saw it. So there was a bit of strong feelings against them and I'm sure they felt the same. And that came out after the strike. Only two of us came out from our department. None of the others came out. The majority of men stayed in.

Racist attitudes. Interestingly enough it was there before the strike but it didn't come out, but during the strike it did become an issue – and after the strike.

BELLA (DAVIS) YOUNG
Harry, the foreman, said to me, 'You shouldn't be out there because you've got a daughter. Come in and work, and the people will follow you.' I said, 'I will live on bread and water before I come in through the gate.' Harry used to say, 'You are very stubborn Isobel. Two or three girls are going in to work.' I would say, 'Well, let them in to work.' Or he would say, 'Isobel, you've got your daughter. If you come to work, you will get your wages.' 'No, I'd rather live on bread and water. I can't because I would know it was wrong.'

We used to follow the scabs through the park, 'Eh, you a scab!' They went over the railings. I remember stopping a lot of lorries and all. Some guys were nasty but some just turned back.

But we had a lot of men against us. It was very hard. The men were very nasty. Well some of them were alright but some were very macho. They think we are doing it for the fun of doing it. They used to say 'Ay, come back to work'; 'Come and do the washing up'; 'Come down, do the cleaning in the house'; 'Get home, do some work.' But some used to say 'You stick up, girl.' One showed his arse in the window of a van! Some were nasty but some cheered us up.

BRIAN YOUNG
Because they got called scab every five minutes, half of them left, didn't they! They went to other factories and people said, 'That was a scab from Trico!'

BOB MITCHELL
I would say 50 per cent of my workshop came out on strike. Brian Robinson, who was a Steward, he crossed the line on the very first day. After that he stayed out, but no one heard from him for a very long time. He just saw it as an excuse to stay away from work and he went doing private work. They lost touch rather than make a big thing about being seen to cross the picket line. I know there were some that were going through the park and climbing

STRIKE BREAKERS

over the fence to get in and not be seen.

Then in the Press Shop it became a safety issue that they couldn't operate the presses on their own, unsupervised, or without another member of staff in the event of something going wrong. And so the management actually stopped the presses running. 'We can't have you running this machine if there's no one here, if you cut yourself, or you pass out or whatever.' Then they had to stay out. They had no option because management have got a legal liability to their employees. They're responsible for their safety. So the management actually shut the machines down.

ANN FITZGERALD

I was with Tony at the time, and although I could go to his family and stay there at weekends and they would feed me, he couldn't come near me when I was on the picket line. He was working in the factory.

I never remember him coming to the front entrance. There was a back way in – and some went over the fence. I think I was going home to my own bed-sit and I don't think we saw each other socially that much, because you couldn't really pass any information or talk about it. I couldn't really say how much of him I saw while that five months was going on.

PHYLLIS GREEN

I didn't really care about the men who stayed in. It never came into my head. I used to chat to the ones that were going in past me and people used to say 'Why are you talking to them?' And I used to think, well I'm going to be there working with them in a couple of months. There were a few of the men in my department who didn't talk to us for about three months after we went back, but then they got fed up as they'd nobody else to talk to, so they started talking again.

ERIC FUDGE

Obviously you all work in the same place and you have to get on with the job, and at some stage you've got to speak to them, but as far as I'm concerned I hadn't much time for them. I'd talk to them about work or whatever or something that needed doing, but there was never that friendly sort of banter again, not for me anyway. They did try to behave as though nothing had happened but I wasn't really interested in them any more.

TRICO IN TROUBLE

which they expressed their lack of confidence in the union executive that was responsible for the strike, and were heavily critical of the local shop stewards and convenor. The steward said that he accepted the company's case that the equal pay claim was based on false premises, and that all the strike had achieved was to split the membership, and this would lead to the loss of jobs if the strike continued.

He told the *Brentford & Chiswick Times* that he had been summoned to appear before the AUEW Southall District Committee at their next meeting, on 9 September, to give an explanation of his actions, but had not yet decided whether to attend. But regardless of what eventually happened, he vowed to spend the last two years of his working life 'trying to blow this communist-dominated District Office'.

The strikers did not appear unduly flustered by these 'reds under the beds' scare stories that were suddenly appearing in the media. This was in large part due to the level of trust that had built up between the striking women and their shop stewards and union leadership over sixteen weeks of strike, and their lack of respect for the men – especially stewards – who did not even support their own union.

The women never expressed any worries that the union leaders were doing anything other than carrying out their wishes, and there was a very strong sense of solidarity amongst all the strikers. Even among the women who never came down to the picket line and stayed at home, there were very few who had returned to work over the months of the strike. In any case these stories were a distraction; there were more urgent matters to attend to – such as winning equal pay!

SEXIST ATTITUDES

BOB MITCHELL

The blade assembly line had a lot of Asian women on it. But the area I was in was white, male dominated: 'Oh, what do you expect, they're just women'. But there was never those corny remarks made afterwards by certain people about getting back into the kitchen.

ANN FITZGERALD

Before the strike I found absolutely no problem with the men's attitudes. I didn't see any problem, you know, but maybe that was because I had just come over on the boat. Maybe I didn't take any notice. I'd never worked with men and women together, I'd always worked just with women … but I didn't find any problem.

But I did find it especially bad that some of our setters and charge-hands didn't support us. Before the strike we were getting out the work whenever they wanted it, and if they came and stopped the line and said 'oh I want this and this', we never refused, and we never said we couldn't do what they asked in that amount of time. We just did it.

So that part of it was bad, especially because they were friendly and we knew them, and it wasn't until this happened that it showed up their attitude. I really don't know whether they thought we weren't the equal to them. When you think of it, in some ways we were doing all the work – if they didn't have to come and set a machine or something like that they were just sitting at their desk and getting paid, and with higher money, and we were slogging.

It's very different now as you know. There's so many women top bosses the same as the men. But in those days the men were classed as superior and as the high earners, and we women were just … I don't know what word I'd use, but now it's very different as you know, since all this came along.

SEXIST ATTITUDES

PEGGY FARMER

You'd got managers, foremen, some a bit arrogant – you'd got your dictators. But generally the men were fine. I used to meet the men in the tool-room because I was a detail inspector. The boys in Development used to come down a lot to speak to me too, because of the job I was doing, and I found a couple of them very arrogant.

I remember there was a 'Miss Trico' competition. There was a picture of all these girls. One had very big boobs. She worked on the arm line. She was very pretty. Two of these guys were looking at these pictures. There was a crude remark passed between them. I knew this man had a daughter about the same age as this girl. I said 'Excuse me, if that was your daughter's photo up there and someone was talking about her boobs how would you feel?' He walked away and never spoke to me again. I disagreed with this 'Miss Trico', it was exploiting people. At the time of the strike a lot of the men were a bit contemptuous towards the women, arrogant, even though the women did all the work.

Men were nicer to women in other departments than their own. I think they were a bit frightened, afraid they were going to lose money, and they didn't want to lose the money. Maybe they were the sole breadwinners, maybe their wives didn't work. They couldn't see beyond that. They thought we were mucking around. They thought it funny at first – but they became unstuck.

'IF IT'S A WIPER – BLACK IT!'[2]

ONE OF THE MAIN obstacles to bringing full pressure to bear on the company to settle the dispute remained the patchy effects of calls for stopping Trico wipers from being delivered to car factories. Trico had given up running picket-busting convoys following the bad publicity from the 29 July events: they now resorted to smuggling parts out in the boots of employees' private cars. But within the wider trade union movement the boycott of Trico parts was not entirely effective, despite agreement by shop stewards to carry it out. For example, at Heathrow AUEW shop stewards constantly had to check freight shipments after it was found that Trico wipers and other products were still being sent out – in cases labelled 'computer parts'.

Despite the important decision of the British Leyland Combine Committee to boycott Trico products, effective action varied from plant to plant. In the absence of any official instruction from the AUEW National Executive Committee, the boycotting of Trico wipers was never robustly effective nationally, despite much local solidarity in many car plants, and the efforts that were made at some of the docks.

In any case, Leyland and Ford had neatly side-stepped the brunt of the Trico dispute by boosting their supplies of wipers from alternative sources, including Lucas Electric and AC Delco Division of General Motors, as well as West Germany's Bosch. As Mick Case, Deputy Convenor at Ford Langley, informed the strikers' mass meeting, although Langley had been boycotting Trico products for some time, production had not been affected because the company were importing Italian wipers. He therefore pledged to propose to the shop stewards at Fords to boycott all makes of wiper

[2] See Part Two, p90, note 7.

blades. Bill MacLaughlin for this very reason had called for a complete boycotting of all windscreen wipers whether or not made by Trico. So the slogan became 'If it's a wiper - BLACK IT!' Never before had windscreen wipers received such prominence in the public's conscience!

But there were some very positive developments coming from a number of other directions. The Greater London Association of Trades Councils had held their planned meeting to discuss practical ways to build further support for the strike, with nineteen Trades Councils in attendance. And they had pledged increased support for picketing, publicity, fundraising and boycotting Trico products. It was immensely cheering for all the strikers to hear about such efforts being made on their behalf.

STEPPING UP THE FIGHT

NICOLA TYRER, WRITING in the *Daily Mail*, had been correct to describe Trico as 'already well on the way to becoming the longest and most tenacious struggle by women in trade union history'. 'The Brentford Ladies' Excuse Me' – as she described it – 'showed no signs of petering out'. It was now early September and TUC Congress time, which could only mean one thing – the Trico women booking a coach and heading off for the Brighton Dome. They were not going to miss an opportunity to lobby delegates.

Betty Aiston told the strikers: 'We're going there to do a job of work – to get the TUC to take notice of us and look into the Equal Pay Act because it's a farce. We know that now ... We're carrying the rod for all women; let's see it through to the end.'

Trico strikers lobbying TUC Brighton

SOURCE UNKNOWN, IN S. GROVES'S PRIVATE COLLECTION

It was another lovely sunny day when the coach set off for Brighton with forty-five Trico strikers and supporters on board. Once there they made their presence felt outside the Dome. They set up the Southall AUEW District banner as well as their own home-made banners and placards, and handed out copies of the 'TUC special edition' of their Strike Bulletin to all the delegates filing in.

Judith Hunt, national women's organiser of TASS, the AUEW's white collar section, who was moving the composite equality motion, told Congress that the Equal Opportunities Commission should urgently review the workings of tribunals and the Equal Pay Act. 'Trade unionists like those at Trico fighting to extract equality from a reluctant American-owned multinational had their rights undermined by the one-sided deliberations of a tribunal.' Speaker after speaker supporting the motion cited Trico as an example of the Act's deficiencies and the need for it to be amended. The strike was becoming a household name. Pat Turner of the GMWU also held Trico up as an example, and pointed to the growing disquiet among many women over the use of tribunals to

STEPPING UP THE FIGHT | 135

LEADERSHIP

"

PHYLLIS GREEN

They were very strong working-class women. I knew Eileen best, and then Betty, too, would be there every morning when you went down. When they were going to meetings they wouldn't have gone by the time I got down there. They would always give you a report about what went on at the meetings, and they'd give you biscuits, and they'd always tell you if a convoy had gone in at night, and I remember them telling us about the boat coming up the canal one weekend and taking out wiper blades.

They were great organisers. They organised things fantastically. Without them people like me wouldn't have really known much, because I just went down there and picketed, but they were great. They'd keep you up to date with what was going on.

They were just ordinary working-class people. I wouldn't think they had had an awful lot of education, and for them to come out so strong ... and you know you wouldn't cross them either. I was afraid of them – well not afraid of them, but I thought 'I'm not getting my little Irish nose in here; these women know what they're talking about', you know.

And they'd have a little handbag with them, and a hat on sometimes – they looked like 1940s ladies – with the little skirts on, you know that kind of dress. I was there with my flares and my flowers in my hair and it was a completely different generation. But they were good. They were a lot better than my generation was, let's put it like that. They knew what they were out for, and they wouldn't be afraid to stand in front of lorries. I was kind of scared of that, when the lorries would come I would get in but I'd get behind somebody else. I was scared of those big lorries but they weren't. They'd stand in front of them and the lorries would nudge up and nudge up right up till they were where they were pushing them. I was well proud of those ladies of that age, of what they did. They were brilliant.

I was really surprised when we went down to that estate in Brentford. We were looking for Peggy Farmer's house, and every door we knocked on people knew Peggy, so I think she would have worked hard in the community as well.

Everyone in the community knew her. There was a lady whose daughter had died who was in a bad way, and Peggy went up to her house and got her back on her feet and brought her down to Trico's and got her a job. And the woman said she wouldn't have got over the shock, but Peggy got her out and got her back to work. I would say she was well respected.

There's a pub called the Nelson on the estate, and even now if I go down there they all know Peggy. Everyone knows her and she's still a strong character. She's an amazing woman and she still has got the fight in her as well. She hasn't lost that, not one bit.

She used to sit at the Trico back gate picket line. I used to see her when I was going past in the morning but I used to go round to the front gate. Well, I'd see more boys there, and I was more interested in the front gate! Peggy was great and she would never have missed a minute on that picket line, and she'd go in at weekends as well. She wasn't like me, a cowboy picketer only doing the five days a week!

It was a different generation to mine. They were really determined and there was nobody going to fob them off. They were very good – and Peggy still is.

I remember Roger well, too. He used to always come down. He came down nearly every day, or if he wasn't doing something he'd always pull up outside Trico's on the picket line and have a chat with us. I remember him speaking in one of the parks. He was very good. He supported it all the way. When you thought, 'Oh God, we're going to go nowhere', he'd come down and give you a lift, then you'd be alright, and you'd be fine until the next day.

BOB MITCHELL

I was quite impressed by Roger's involvement. I know he put a lot of his own personal time in rather than just time paid for because of being a full-time official, and I appreciated that at the time. It might not have been 24/7 but he was there round the clock sometimes, and when he wasn't actively on the picket line he was working in his office.

SANDRA (WARD) GRAY

My Mum [Eileen] was a Shop Steward and she really enjoyed it; it became a part of her life. John Inwood taught my Mum almost everything she knew, but she didn't always agree with everything he said. When the strike came along my Mum was really involved in it.

When the strike was called my Mum had quite a few restless nights. She was frightened that the girls would go back to work, especially as the strike went on so long. She really struggled to keep the girls out because nobody had realised it would go on the length that it did.

I think my Mum was the driving force behind all of us. She believed that what she was doing was right, and she was going to stick to it as long as she had the girls backing her up. And she would back the girls up. That's what kept her going, plus all the friends and the people that she got to know. They all helped as well.

The strike consumed everything at home, it consumed us all.

ERIC FUDGE

Roger was very good. He seemed to be able to explain things without getting too technical and baffling everybody with needless gobbledegook. The whole team did very well there in stating the facts without over-elaborating and confusing people. We were lucky in that respect – and they certainly stuck to their guns as well.

Eileen was very good; she did most of the speaking as I recollect. Again, she seemed to have the knack of getting some enthusiasm going when it was waning, and inspiring them to carry on. Betty Aiston, to a certain extent, and Betty Humphreys seemed much better at talking to people in small groups and getting them together – so you had all bases covered really with the three of them.

settle equal pay issues. She concluded with the comment: 'We haven't fought so long and so hard for equal rights only to be cheated at the end by unrepresentative bodies.' The Trico women couldn't have put it better themselves!

The strikers outside the conference hall were also pleased to learn that Billy Taylor, who was an active AUEW shop steward and Secretary of London Transport Acton Works' shop stewards committee, and a well-liked figure on their picket line, had fought for the right to speak on their behalf. Billy Taylor made an historic intervention at Congress when he became the first man of that week to speak on a specifically women's issue:

> In supporting this motion I welcome the opportunity to give an example of how the Act is not working. I refer to the case of Trico-Folberth. They make windscreen wipers, washers, etc. for the motor trade. The problem is that the women and the men at Trico's have been in dispute and out of work for sixteen weeks.
>
> The simple fact at Trico's is that the basic rates for piecework differ between men and women. A man producing 100 components finishes up with more money than a woman producing the same 100 components on the very same machine. The only equality I have seen there is in the treatment meted out to the pickets.
>
> People have come down from West London today; people of all races have come because we are all on the picket line. They are all out, to a woman, and some of the men. They have been outside the hall this morning handing out some of their literature. I ask you for support because in the words of William Butler Yeats, 'When you find that the women are equal a terrible beauty is born.'

He got loud cheers, including from a number of Trico women who had managed to get inside the conference. Many people were lobbied about the Trico women's cause that day, and £116 was raised outside the hall by the strikers, whilst inside there were repeated calls made to support the Trico workers in their historic struggle.

Their stand was fully vindicated by the open recognition that the Act was failing women and needed to be amended. The equality motion urged government to amend the Act in line with the International Labour Organisation's Convention 100, to provide for equal pay for work of equal value, instead

BRIGHTON

BILLY TAYLOR

In 1976 I was a delegate to the TUC Conference for the 25th Division, which covered the whole London area, and the night before the debate on equality I went to a social evening, a reception held by the AUEW for the officials and delegates to meet one another and mingle, and during that some of the TASS members, Judith Hunt in particular, came and talked to me, and I told them what I knew about the strike. They told me there was a debate on the next day regarding strikes and women's rights and women's wages, and they said you should get up and speak on the Trico strike. I was told you needed permission to speak but those who knew me said, 'Billy Taylor you never needed a way to find to speak, you'll manage!'

So the next day I had to go and see Reg Birch, our Executive Council member of the AUEW, to get permission to speak. It was my first time at the TUC, my second day on Congress. But I spoke to Reg Birch and asked permission. He said 'I can't give you permission but if you ask I'll have to refuse you permission'. So I just picked up my papers and left, and then, when they began to debate, during the speeches of many delegates, I got up and went to the platform and said I wanted to speak about Trico. We were discussing women's activities, and I wanted to speak on their strike. In the audience were Trico women who had come by coach, and they all cheered! Then I spoke for a few minutes and informed the TUC, and all the reporters there were made aware of the Trico strike.

That's how I got involved and after that I assisted in various things and all the rest of it. But the major thing after that was through my branch, through the SSC – Acton Works gave the strikers great support. Together we would take the banner regularly on the marches from Acton Works – we were well organised really. That was my major thing. As it happened, in 1979 I was elected as a full-time official and covered many factories, and I felt privileged to have been able to assist in the struggle of the Trico workers through my intervention at the TUC Conference of 1976, which in a way made more workers aware of that magnificent fight for equality.

MORE ON THE UNION

BELLA (DAVIS) YOUNG

The union was really good, it was lovely. It was a very strong union. Roger and Mac – they never let us down.

ROBERT (BOB) SINGH

I think the AUEW gave a significant amount of support but at the same time there was always this feeling that the strikers were pushing and pushing and pushing for what they wanted. Whilst the union locally gave fantastic support, nationally it looked like they wanted to resolve the dispute as soon as possible – as far as they were concerned strikes were not in their interests as bureaucrats. But the workers on the ground, and the local Southall AUEW, wanted us to get as much as we could.

It was a balancing act to make sure it remained official but at the same time not to allow the NEC of the union to get what they wanted.

BOB MITCHELL

The strike was being led by the strikers at the factory rather than the full-timers: the people taking the industrial action actually led the District Council and the full-timers. In retrospect I can see that's a very valid point. Also, the strike itself was obviously an embarrassment to the TUC.

PHYLLIS GREEN

The strike made me realise how good the trade union is. Before that I used to pay my trade union dues but I wouldn't bother with a meeting. I always belonged to a trade union but I wasn't really interested. It was only 45p a week or something like that. But when the strike was over, you realised how strong a trade union can be, and how you need it, and working people need a trade union. Then I started to get interested in politics. It would have been probably the Trico strike that got me involved in politics.

I mean, when the union calls a strike you go on strike, and that's it. There's no point moaning about it, and you know you're not going to go back in until you get what you get. Anyway not after sitting out there for four or five or six weeks – when it kept going on, you're thinking, well I might as well go up the road and get a job in some other factory – I'm not going back in there.

Maybe for some people it was more that the union called the strike, rather than the issue of equal rights. Once the union called the strike you went with it. We knew it was for equal rights though. No, they wouldn't have crossed the picket line. Once the union called out it was all out and they wouldn't have gone back whatever the husbands said.

of equal pay for work of the same or broadly similar nature. As it turned out, it was not until 1983 (after the European Commission had taken out infringement proceedings against the UK in the Court of Justice) that the Act was amended. But it was Trico that blazed the trail. As the women returned to Brentford that afternoon, singing on the coach, they were satisfied that they had done a good job of work that day.

Even the Equal Opportunities Commission were by now having to admit that the Act was proving 'a farce'. Many tribunal findings had been not only useless but also quite insulting to women. A short time before the TUC met, women quality controllers at the Kraft Cheese factory in Kirkby, Liverpool, had been refused equal pay because, according to management, they were unable to walk across a catwalk between departments in case men looked up their miniskirts. The women explained at the tribunal that they wore trousers to work, and that in any case miniskirts were five years out of date. But the tribunal accepted the management's argument, and as a result the women continued to get £12.45 a week less than the men!

Back at Brentford on the picket line everything was quiet after the layoffs, except for the war of words. The letters that had been set out before the layoffs threatening sackings or redundancies unless the strike was called off had been taken up with alacrity by the local papers, especially the *Middlesex Chronicle*, and this had prompted the Strike Committee to report the newspaper to the Press Council. Eileen Ward and Sally Groves wrote to the paper on the Committee's behalf, and it responded to this challenge to its partiality by hastily publishing the letter on their readers' letters page. The strikers' letter ended defiantly: 'Until the management come to their senses and talk with us, the strike goes on until justice is won.'

But few people knew how serious a threat there was to the very continuation of the strike at certain junctures. There were some critical points during the strike when official support was on a knife-edge. These did not result from any risk that a group of women would walk back in – this was always a fear rather than a reality – or from any lack of support from other trade unions and women's groups.

They were the result of the political complexion of the AUEW Executive Council, which at the time was almost entirely right-wing in complexion, apart from the lone figure of Reg Birch, the strikers' EC man. How important this was

Reg Birch talking to Betty Aiston, left, and Sally Groves.

for the women has only become publicly known recently.

The continuation of official support for the strike was crucial, but it was never a foregone conclusion. Without strike pay, which only came with continuing official endorsement of the strike, the women and their male supporters would not only have been demoralised and delegitimised in the eyes of the trade union movement: they would also have been starved back to work. The donations that were flooding in only provided funds for those who were suffering especial hardship. The rest of the strikers lived frugally off the strike pay that was provided by the national union.

The situation with the union's EC was nursed constantly by Roger Butler with Reg Birch. On at least one occasion they had to resort to a strategy of Roger Butler calling Reg Birch out of the EC meeting on pretext of urgent business. This was in order to avert official support for the Trico dispute being reviewed, on the grounds that Reg Birch would have been absent at the decisive moment when the item came up on the meeting's agenda.

But the Trico management were also facing difficulties. Even before the layoffs managers had been forced to close down the automatic power presses that produced parts still sent to Northampton for assembly, on health and safety grounds. Bill McLoughlin's comment was that people like Atkins and Slidders had a lot to answer for to the director:

> They have to answer for the enormous wage bill for no production. All they have produced is lies – public lies. If everything was so cosy and rosy why did they not carry on? As has been said all along, it is the Trico workers, the women, who produce the entire wealth of the company and they should be valued accordingly.

And, as Roger Butler stated:

> We have made our position clear from the word go. A return to work is easy but it requires negotiation. The company can't stand in the middle of the desert with their heads in the sand. This loyal employer, instead of kicking 522 workers out of the gate, should get around the negotiating table and talk with us about ending the dispute.

This was all reported in the Trico Strike Bulletins, which had begun to sport cartoons by the American cartoonist, Fred

"We're not seeing ourselves as the workers see us..."

Cartoon in Trico Strike Bulletin No 12, 10 September 1976

Wright. Fred, whose sharp humour took a swipe at the bosses, was one of only a very few cartoonists who have been able to capture the real flavour of the workers' everyday experience on the shop floor. It is said that his prolific pen played a major role in the survival of his union, the United Electrical, Radio and Machine Workers of America, in their struggle against the vicious political attacks of the McCarthyite period.

The production of these Strike Bulletins was the responsibility of Sally Groves, who was assisted hugely in this task by Jack Dromey at Brent Law Centre. Vernon Merritt, a local AUEW-TASS member, also gave enormous help. He was a delegate on Hounslow Trades Council, and at the time was unemployed, which gave him plenty of spare time!

By mid-September the Strike Committee had printed over 40,000 strike bulletins, and countless thousands of collection sheets. The strikers were surviving on their £9 per week official strike pay, plus £1.50 from the AUEW District levy. Hardship money over and above this amount could only be paid out according to the level of donations coming in; while the level of requests for help was increasing as women struggled to cope financially as the months

STRIKE BULLETINS

BOB BANISTER

The bulletins were very useful as a means of keeping all employees informed of developments from the point of view of those who were on strike. The regular bulletins forestalled any misinformation that the company put out. But the real value as far as I was concerned was circulating the bulletins among staff union members such as members of AUEW-TASS and ASTMS, to build sympathy and support by way of weekly collections for the strike fund for those in dispute, but also to use them as a basis for discussion and recruitment of non-union members.

Certainly, when the dispute was finally settled the trade unions were much better organised, with an established joint staff trade union committee that was connected through TASS to the shop floor union AUEW. Union membership amongst staff workers had also increased, with the result that one newly recruited woman even became a branch delegate to the TASS national conference within three years.

THANKS TO OUR FRIENDS

The following are just a few examples of what we have received in the past week; £50 from Eatons Basingstoke JSSC, £50 from Rolls Royce Harrow, £25 from the Merthyr District AUEW, £118 from a factory collection at Heniz in Brent organised by the TGWU, £22.50 from AEC Southall, £25 from FORD Langley JSSC, £50 from Leyland Lancs, £20 from the Morning Star, £20 from the TGWU Selly Oak Branch Birmingham, £20 from AUEW/TASS No 3 Divisional Council, £20 from the London North District of the AUEW, £77 from Earlsfield Womens Lib, £100 from Ambrose Shardlow JSSC Sheffield, £209.11 from the CAV Acton Dayshift and £56.10 from the CAV Nightshift.

A typical weekly report of donations, in Trico Strike Bulletin No 12, 10 September 1976

went by. To make ends meet, the Strike Committee needed at least £4000 in donations each week, especially given the numbers of single-parent families and single people amongst the strikers, who had no support from a partner, or those with unemployed or disabled partners. There were also the costs of running the strike itself: postage, telephone calls, delegations travelling around the whole of Britain, as well as the already mentioned publicity.

But despite the hardship faced by so many of those on strike, there was a great feeling of comradeship on the picket line and endless things to laugh about. Entertainment came not only from the varied groups that came along to support every day, but also from the fundraising socials and other events put on for the strikers. Then there were the theatre groups that seemed to come out of nowhere simply to entertain. At the beginning of the dispute folk singer Frankie Armstrong, working with the Broadside Mobile Workers Theatre, put on a show in Boston Manor Park. And Hammersmith Working Women's Charter organised a benefit at Greenford Hall in July that raised over £100, and featured the Broadside group again, along with folk singers Sandra Kerr, Bobby Campbell and others. Memorably, after the strike was over another group, the Women's Theatre Group, put on a play at the Bush Theatre in Shepherds Bush in honour of the Trico battle entitled *Out! On the Costa del Trico*.[3]

There was also a Disco-Benefit night in support of the Strike Fund at Ealing Technical College, sponsored by Hounslow and Ealing Trades Councils and Ealing Tech Students Union, which raised £46, and one at Brunel University that raised £52. And the Belt and Braces Roadshow put on a great show at the Park Hotel in Hanwell, packing in about 400 people, an event organised by the Socialist Workers Party locally.

On another occasion a bus company and the workers at Willesden bus garage got in touch to offer the strikers a trip to the seaside. Then Brighton Trades Council started to organise a holiday for some of the women with their kids with the idea that people would be put up in the Brighton trade unionists' homes. At the same time Crawley, Worthing, Eastbourne and Chichester Trades Councils began to take up the issue of support for Trico. And so the effort developed all around the country.

---

[3] During the 1970s and 1980s there was an explosion of radical fringe theatre groups – socialist and feminist – and they toured community venues throughout the country, including pubs, small theatres, shopping centres and picket lines, or anywhere that could offer a convenient space.

Broadside Theatre entertains Trico strikers in Boston Manor Park, 11 June 1976.

CHRIS DAVIES/REPORT ARCHIVE/ REPORTDIGITAL.CO.UK

'SARDINE SIDNEY'

TRICO MANAGEMENT NOW seemed to have run out of ideas on how to end the dispute, and the Engineering Employers Federation was, self-evidently, running out of patience with them. The Tribunal decision had failed to demoralise or divide the women, and the decision to lay off the rest of the shop floor was an admission by the company that they could not run the factory without them. They had won the Tribunal but not the campaign.

As Roger Butler told the mass meeting on 6 September: 'There's nowhere left to turn to apart from the union.'

Behind the scenes Trico approached ACAS, who arranged a fresh meeting for 13 September, when John Slidders and Sid Atkins met with Bill MacLaughlin and Roger Butler. The result was a further 50p (yes fifty pence!) offered in addition to the previous offers, making a total of £2.50, at a 120 performance measurement under Trico's labyrinthine payment by results system (see note 4, p15). This had nothing to do with equal pay, and, to add insult to injury, the proposed package included 'increased flexibility' and the ending of all shop agreements. The company letter sent out the following day, however, very misleadingly gave the impression that the offer was £5.50. They did this by including within the figure the 4½ per cent separate entitlement under the current round of the government's pay policy, which had nothing to do with the dispute. Readers have to bear in mind the very high inflation being experienced at this time, which made such increases essential.

Trico did not mention in this letter that they were not giving the 4½ per cent increase to the male operators – who would effectively get a wage cut. As spelt out once more in the Strike Committee Bulletin, the company needed to

Cartoon in Trico Strike Bulletin No 13, 16 September 1976

forget any ideas it had of avoiding equal pay by reducing the male rate to that of the women. Once again, equal pay in reverse!

The terrible twins Atkins and Slidders were told in no uncertain terms what to do with their extra 50p by a subsequent mass meeting of strikers. After discussion, all the hands went up, giving an enormous rebuff to this further insult. Mild-spoken John Inwood argued that acceptance would mean going back on even harsher terms than before: 'The management are not seeking a solution; their aim is to destroy the union. They want to break every shop agreement ever made in the payment by results areas, and you know what that will cost based on your own experience.'

Bill MacLaughlin spoke to the press after this meeting, and the gist of his statement was recorded in the Strike Bulletin of 23 September:

> There is no longer any point in the company threshing about trying to find ways to break the strike. They are

caught like rats in a trap – AND THE ONLY WAY OUT IS TO MEET THE UNION AND COME UP WITH A REALISTIC OFFER. We remain prepared at any time to meet the management to reach a solution to this dispute.

The rebuff was loud and clear.

Then, without any public announcement, a further meeting was arranged involving Atkins and Slidders with Reg Birch of the AUEW National Executive, Bill MacLaughlin and Roger Butler. Van Dyke, an American director of Trico, was also to be present. The meeting was to be held at ACAS under the chairmanship of Jim Mortimer, on 29 September.

Reg Birch informed the company side that no deal would be acceptable to the Executive Council that was not acceptable to Bill MacLaughlin and Roger Butler, who represented the strikers. This was a warning to the company that they should not try and make a deal with the AUEW National Executive behind the backs of the women and their local officials.

This really strengthened Bill MacLaughlin and Roger Butler's position. It seems that this meeting may have been set up by the then General Secretary of the AUEW, John Boyd, but Reg Birch had ensured that the company had no alternative but to deal with MacLaughlin and Butler from then on. The company could not go back to the NEC and come to a deal over their heads, if they wanted to settle the dispute.

The plight of some of the employees laid off by the company had around this time been taken up by the Brentford and Isleworth Conservative MP, Barney Hayhoe – along, of course, with 'the usual suspect' the *Brentford & Chiswick Times*. Hayhoe, who was Opposition spokesman for employment at the time, showed touching compassion for the scabs who had been laid off work three weeks previously – in sharp contrast to his lack of concern for the women's hardship over the previous three months and more.

He told the newspaper that he had already 'several times' approached Albert Booth, Secretary of State for employment, urging him to get talks going, and had requested his personal intervention. His hope was that Booth, as a former member of the AUEW, would 'respond and persuade his old union to get the dispute ended'. Is it possible that this pressure led to John Boyd taking the initiative to approach ACAS for a meeting?

Interestingly, it was Barney Hayhoe who was later to say – in 1978, as Jim Prior's deputy spokesman on employment – that collective bargaining was not necessarily synonymous with good industrial relations.

True to form, after the ACAS meeting the company sent out another letter in their 'correspondence course of con-tricks', to say that the £3 that had been offered was still conditional on increased flexibility and the scrapping of shop agreements. It wasn't in fact anything to do with equal pay at all.

As Eileen Ward said to cheers at the strikers' meeting on Friday 1 October, 'We're not in for a pay rise; we're in for bloody equal pay. Who the hell do they think they are?'

The strikers joked that the company must have 50p on the brain, which, they said, would hardly buy a tin of sardines. Hence when Sid Atkins arrived at the factory on Friday morning he found he had a new name, 'Sardine Sidney'!

Bill MacLaughlin told the company, 'We're always ready to sit down and have meetings any time, any place.' He continued: 'Just go on talking about money and we'll tell you when you've reached equal pay. We'll tell you when you are giving us too much.'

Meanwhile the campaign went on. Money was pouring into the hardship fund. At the following mass meeting, it was announced that, amongst other donations, £200 had been received from Middlesex Polytechnic and £100 from Heathrow airport workers. Roger Butler issued a statement on behalf of the AUEW Southall District Committee regarding the boycotting of alternative supplies of wipers:

> We appeal to the workers in the motor assembly industry, bus garages and transport depots to BLACK completely all alternative supplies or substitute wiper blades being brought into the country in an attempt to break our dispute and starve us back to work. Our members have shown by their magnificent unity, solidarity and determination that this will not happen. By this further BLACKING the motor industry could end this dispute tomorrow and bring a successful end to our fight for equal pay.

Just before this statement was issued a letter arrived from Switzerland from the International Metalworkers Federation asking for information about Trico and what they could do to assist the strike. The Federation said there was great interest on the continent in the women's struggle for equal pay.

A reply was sent by the AUEW officials listing the European firms that the British motor industry could use as alternative suppliers for windscreen wipers, and requesting that they take action during the dispute to ensure that no additional supplies came from these sources.

While this was happening Trico management were still attempting to smuggle out Trico goods in the boots of private cars. No wonder the strikers referred to them as 'bootleggers'! The materials were then being transferred to lorries hidden on a local housing estate.

Throughout this time many supporters came to the Trico picket lines, and some of them spoke at the regular mass meetings, not least Jo Richardson, MP for Barking, who addressed the strikers' meeting on 24 September. As Tam Dalyell wrote in his obituary for her in the *Independent* in February 1994, the prominence of women's issues in the affairs of the Labour Party at that time was 'due in no small measure to the day-in-day-out campaigning of Jo Richardson'. The Trico strikers were to find out, as Tam Dalyell said: 'Those who worked with her could be certain that if she promised to do something or see somebody she would do so.' It was Jo Richardson who raised the role of the police in the Trico strike in the House of Commons.

She told the strikers that the dispute had exposed crucial loopholes in the equal pay legislation, particularly in the operation of the industrial tribunals. She pledged that MPs would be mobilised to reorganise the legislation to block up the loopholes. She was a genuine supporter of the strikers' whole struggle for equal pay. After speaking at the mass meeting she also referred to the strike in an article she wrote for the *Morning Star* entitled 'Equal rights need laws – not lip service'. In that article she recounted the history of the new Equal Pay Act:

> We'd all been aware that in the years preceding the full implementation of the Act many employers had been busy finding ways round it, but even in our wildest nightmares we hadn't expected their continued resistance to be quite so blatant and quite so well backed-up by tribunals. The TRICO strike has in particular shown this up.

On 11 October the strike was discussed by the left-wing Tribune group of MPs at their meeting at the House of Commons. Syd Bidwell raised the issue along with Jo

Richardson, who, as secretary of the group, was requested to organise a deputation to see Albert Booth about the dispute and discuss how to bring it to a successful conclusion. They also pledged to call on the government to tighten up the Equal Pay Act.

These individual Labour MPs stand out for their support, in particular Jo Richardson. But some people have contended that the Labour Party in general gave the strike 'little to no formal recognition as being either politically or symbolically significant'.[4] It has also been suggested that Labour Party luminaries of that time such as Roy Hattersley, Jim Callaghan and even Tony Benn did not think 'the strike noteworthy enough to be considered in their accounts of the period' (ibid). In Callaghan's case this was despite commenting on the importance of women's equality in the foreword to Lucy Middleton's book *Women in the Labour Movement* in 1977.[5]

But whatever the case, none of this parliamentary activity meant that the need to raise money for hardship payments to strikers had diminished, in fact the reverse was true. Further delegations accordingly set off around the country. On 16 September, Sally Groves spoke at the AUEW shop stewards quarterly meeting in Oxford, while on the same day another delegation addressed the Birmingham East quarterly AUEW meeting. The Birmingham meeting of shop stewards and convenors raised £62 for the strike fund. The following day a delegation visited Birmingham factories and the British Leyland plant at Longbridge.

On 26 September Sally Groves set off with Bob Mitchell and Vernon Merritt for a two-day visit to lobby the Labour Party conference in Blackpool. Bob was amongst those who Sally Groves came to refer to as 'the diamonds' among the Trico men.

Further delegations travelled to Leeds, and the regular meetings with Trico workers at the Northampton plant continued; and donations of £200 each had been given by Nalgo and the CPSA. These donations were the life blood of the strike.

To lift the strikers' spirits, benefits and socials were still being organised. Southall District Committee held a dance for the strikers on 1 October. However, enjoyment of the event was marred by police harassment in the form of the attendance of half a dozen police squad cars. As Roger Butler commented at a later meeting, it was the first time they'd

[4] George Stevenson, 'The Forgotten Strike: Equality, Gender and Class in the Trico Equal Pay Strike', *Labour History Review*, Vol. 8, Issue 2, August 2016.
[5] Lucy Middleton, *Women in the Labour Movement*, Croom Helm 1977.

had the police turn up at one of their dances. He believed the police were just trying to provoke trouble, and asked the local Labour MP William Molloy to raise the matter with the Home Secretary, Merlyn Rees. At this same meeting Syd Bidwell described the strike as an enormous test of nerve and stamina and cheered the women on, urging the labour movement to strengthen its contribution to their struggle. On 5 October GLATC held a recall meeting in Hammersmith Town Hall to co-ordinate renewed calls for support for the strike amongst London Trades Councils. That same day a delegation left for a four-day visit to South Wales. And at the end of the week a social was held for the strikers at Chiswick Town Hall, organised by Hounslow Trades Council.

During the same week, at a mass meeting in the Methodist church hall, Eileen Ward responded to the company's latest 'final offer' with the contempt it deserved. 'We're out for equal pay, not half equal pay. When will Sardine Sid and the rest of Trico management get that into their heads?' Women got to their feet cheering. As reported by Mick Murray of *The Irish Times*, the company's offer was 'shredded into confetti by an enraged Eileen Ward', and 'tossed contemptuously into the air amidst wild applause'. Trico had had the women's answer to its 'final' offer.

After the meeting was over John O'Neill (Big John) told Mick Murray about his fund-raising trips to Scotland and Wales; and about the tremendous response there had been from the rank and file of the British labour movement. He added that he found it 'very difficult to understand the obduracy of Trico'. One of the two most plausible theories circulating at the time, he said, was that 'the company underestimated the feelings of the women, a very large number of whom were not even unionised prior to the dispute'. This is why they thought they could call the union's bluff, but now, five months and an industrial tribunal later, 'they are desperately threshing about for a face-saving solution'.

The second most likely theory put forward was that 'the Confederation of British Industry, mindful of the millions of women being paid well below the national average male rate, is secretly backing Trico and preventing a settlement being reached.'

As Mick Murray pointed out: 'One thing is certain though; the women have still a lot of fight left in them, and every day the support for their action is growing.'

VICTORY!

IT WAS ON THURSDAY 14 October that the final, crucial meeting took place – the meeting that the women and all their supporters had battled for over the past almost twenty-one weeks. From 11am onwards that day the AUEW officials met with Trico management at the Heathrow Hotel (now a Holiday Inn). It appears that this final meeting was arranged by Con Griffin from the London Association of the Engineering Employers Federation.

As Con Griffin conceded, the problem was that the company had won the Tribunal but that had not ended the strike as they had expected, and as a result they did not know how to end the dispute. Con Griffin met with Bill MacLaughlin and Roger Butler, and asked if they could think of a formula to give equal pay to end the dispute as they were totally exhausted. As the women's AUEW officials had said all along, they were happy to oblige! The final details of the settlement were thrashed out by Con Griffin and Roger Butler in the coffee shop of the hotel.

The company had caved in, fully conceding the women's demands. It was agreed that a common operational rate throughout the payment-by-results areas, regardless of sex, would be introduced – which was what the union had been demanding in negotiations for the twelve months prior to the dispute. The women would now get an average of £6.50 more a week.

At 7pm that evening an emergency meeting of the Strike Committee was called, attended by Bill MacLaughlin and Roger Butler. After hearing of the stunning breakthrough which gave them equal pay, the Committee unanimously agreed to recommend acceptance, as did the District Committee later that evening.

Eileen Ward addressing strikers at victory mass meeting, 15 October 1976.

ANDREW WIARD/
REPORTDIGITAL.CO.UK

The next day, the jubilant expression on the faces of the women who had packed themselves into St Faith's Church Hall in Brentford to hear the news said it all. Every hand was raised in acceptance of the settlement, the terms of which were read out to the crowded hall. It was agreed that there would be a victory march back into work on the Monday morning.

Roger Butler said:

> This is a lesson to the movement on how equal pay can be achieved. It won't be brought about by tribunals. It's only through trade union unity and working-class struggle that

Roger Butler addressing victory mass meeting (John Inwood on right), 15 October 1976.

CHRIS DAVIES/REPORT ARCHIVE/
REPORTDIGITAL.CO.UK

justice for women workers will be won. Our decision to boycott the industrial tribunal when the company took the case to it has been fully vindicated by this complete victory.

Celebrations went on that evening well into the night. It was like Christmas Eve in Brentford, and the bubbly was flowing!

The company and union issued a joint press statement intentionally ambiguously worded:

> As a result of exhaustive negotiations both parties agreed that the terms of the Equal Pay Act being satisfied ... a full

VICTORY! | 157

Jubilant Trico strikers voting for equal pay settlement at mass meeting, 15 October 1976.

Stella North in right foreground.

PETER ARKELL/REPORTDIGITAL.CO.UK

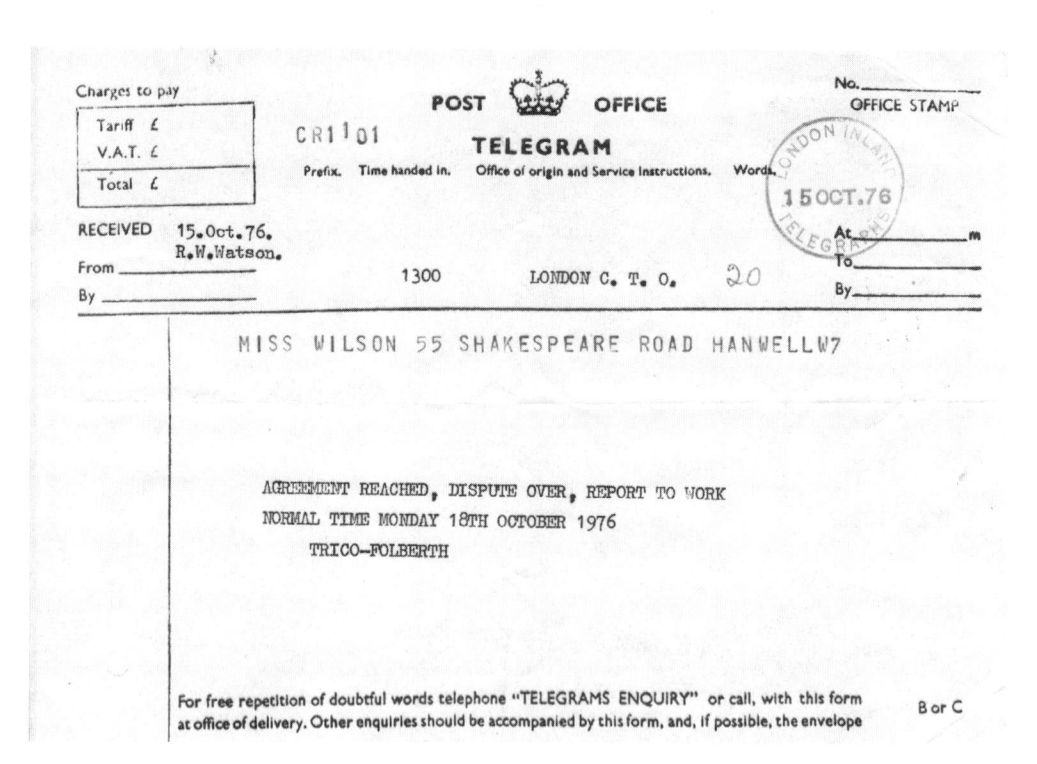

> Charges to pay
> Tariff £
> V.A.T. £
> Total £
>
> CR1¹01
> Prefix. Time handed in. Office of origin and Service Instructions. Words
>
> POST OFFICE
> TELEGRAM
>
> No.
> OFFICE STAMP
>
> 15 OCT 76
>
> RECEIVED 15.Oct.76.
> R.W.Watson.
> From _____
> By _____
>
> 1300   LONDON C. T. O.   20
>
> At _____ m
> To _____
> By _____
>
> MISS WILSON 55 SHAKESPEARE ROAD HANWELL W7
>
> AGREEMENT REACHED, DISPUTE OVER, REPORT TO WORK
> NORMAL TIME MONDAY 18TH OCTOBER 1976
>   TRICO-FOLBERTH
>
> For free repetition of doubtful words telephone "TELEGRAMS ENQUIRY" or call, with this form at office of delivery. Other enquiries should be accompanied by this form, and, if possible, the envelope
>
> B or C

Company telegram – welcoming us back!

return to normal working will take place on 18 October.

That agreement had been reached was kindly communicated to all Trico employees by telegram: 'AGREEMENT REACHED, DISPUTE OVER, REPORT TO WORK NORMAL TIME MONDAY 18 OCTOBER 1976. TRICO-FOLBERTH'.

The style of the return to work proved to be anything but normal, unless a cheering mass of women and men clocking into work with champagne, kisses and V-signs for victory is normal! And perhaps in honour of the women, the summer felt it could clock out with a downpour of rain, after months of blue skies and soaring temperatures that had turned the green grass of London's parks brown!

As the *Morning Star* described the scene that Monday:

> There was singing, chanting and hugging in the rain as the women and the men that had joined their marathon strike lined up outside … They returned to work in style after 21 weeks in which against them were stacked strike-breaking convoys aided by police, employers' threats of redundancy, and the court machinery of the Equal Pay Act.

Victory Strike Bulletin No 16, 18 October 1976

And with them went huge thanks to everyone, from building workers in N Wales to local factories, from trade union executives to women's groups who had helped them win through.

'I've learnt a lot in these twenty-one weeks', declared a happy Doll Wakefield. 'We want to thank everyone who gave us lots of encouragement and great support to our hardship fund. People brought food to us on the picket line, as well as money, and there were lots of people doing little things to help too.'

Roger Butler said, 'This is a lesson to the movement on how equal pay can be won.'

As it was reported at the time by *Spare Rib*:

We stood in the rain to cheer the strikers back to work – hundreds of women under umbrellas jostling on the pavement of the Great West Road at 7.30 am on Monday morning, 18 October.

'We are the champions', they sang. A pensioner (Bob Bunting) who had previously worked in Trico's tool room and picketed every day by the Great West Road started chanting:

Victory march, 18 October 1976. Front row, left to right, John Inwood, Roger Butler, Bill MacLaughlin, Betty Humphreys, Betty Aiston.

TRINITY MIRROR SOUTHERN (*EVENING MAIL*)

'What have we got?
Equal Pay
When have we got it?
NOW!'

Television cameras glared in the half-light, a young black woman hustled everyone to get into fours. Bill MacLaughlin, local AUEW official, asked people to fall in behind the Strike Committee – and then they marched through the gates, past the settee they'd sat on all summer, now soaking up the rain like a sponge.

The women laughed and waved to the crowd of supporters clustered round the gate – as we cheered and clapped I felt elated yet sad that victory had to mean return to the same old assembly lines.

Here Monica Harvey, one of the Trico strikers, describes what the victory meant to her:

Our equal pay strike is over. We went back to work on Monday having won a complete victory. What a bloody mockery this makes of the decision of the equal pay tribunal. They said we had no case but we've shown them

Roger Butler and Eileen Ward with bubbly outside Trico, 18 October 1976.

TRINITY MIRROR SOUTHERN
(EVENING MAIL)

otherwise. We refused to be pressurised by their decisions and our refusal to go back to work until we won showed that strength and spirit is what really matters. A strong shop-floor organisation is the way to win. It is worth a million Equal Pay Acts. We now have the same piece-work rate as the men. Together with a £2.30 wage increase, this gives us a total rise of £8.70. The financial support given to us by workers in factories and workplaces all over the country was a great help in keeping us going. This support amounted to hundreds of thousands of pounds, all given by brothers and sisters who committed themselves to our victory. Our full-time officials have also been great. Roger Butler, District Secretary, and Bill MacLaughlin, Divisional Organiser, refused to give even the time of day to the various pathetic offers made by management during the strike.

A massive celebration of the Trico victory had been organised for the following Friday by the GLATC. At least 600 people attended, and somewhere between £500 to £600 was raised. The event was held free of charge at Fulham Town Hall, courtesy of the Support Services Committee

VICTORY! | 163

LEGACY OF THE STRIKE AND PRIDE

"

BOB BANISTER
This dispute was the first in the fight for equal pay and deserves a place of honour in trade union history.

ERIC FUDGE
As far as the legacy is concerned, I think it's a lesson that you can achieve your aims if you are prepared to stick together and not be bullied, but you need to be strong-willed and prepared to put up with whatever hardship happens. No advances – in industrial relations at any rate, or a lot of other things for that matter – are achieved easily. It's far too easy to let a few control the many. They need to be reminded that everybody has a say, not just those at the top of the pile. These days, various governments, regardless of party, seem to think we are here to serve them instead of them being supposed to be serving us, the population. Until people get off their backsides and really get stuck into these people, that's what they are going to do. There are very few politicians of honest intentions these days.

Trouble is with things like this, it's the same with all of history, as time moves on it gets forgotten. New generations grow up and don't know, and half this stuff they don't teach now.

ANN FITZGERALD
Women saw that if we can do it, if they have a problem they can do it. And they think, 'why sit back, we'll voice our voice and go for it and stand up for ourselves'. And I think it did do good because of that. People thought, well if they can do it we won't sit back any more. And I think this is why today women are in so many positions. It's not the men any more, it's the women.

Well at least I can say that I never got up in the morning and said, 'oh blow I'm not going down there today'. I went down there with – in my head – a vengeance to fight and to be there. Maybe I would not be heard as much as I would be seen and, you know, go for it. We did our bit very well. I'm very proud of it, very proud to be part of it.

BOB MITCHELL
Trico got the ball rolling. You can always refer back to it. 'Well look at what happened at Trico in 1976. No one gave

LEGACY OF THE STRIKE AND PRIDE

them a hope in hell. Look at what they did because they all stood together.' And so it's good to have that hope.

Without a doubt on a personal level – and a national level – it was a matter of personal empowerment, having spoken to people who have known of the Trico strike, but didn't know the exact details, but actually got inspired by it.

I always knew – or I thought I knew – what was right and wrong because I grew up in the 1960s when there were things on the TV about civil rights in America and Martin Luther King and all that. I always thought I knew what was right and wrong but I could never do anything about it, and it wasn't until '76 that I even heard the term 'sexism'. I had never heard of it. I knew what racism was but not sexism.

Because I grew up in the 1960s and saw the civil rights movement in America, I knew about those ideas of this toilet is for blacks and this toilet is for whites, and the back of the bus is this way. And I knew in my own heart and brain that that was wrong. I can't say I was a socialist or something, or communist, but I just knew what was right and wrong. And when the Trico thing kicked in I thought, well, this is where I belong, and that is when I started meeting people, and, all of a sudden, I realised that I was a socialist ... the black and white thing seemed to translate into Brentford, not the black and white thing but the male-female thing ... It wasn't the fact that it was a male-female thing, it was just a human thing. I thought, it doesn't matter what sex you are, why should you earn less than me?

And since then it's educated me a hell of a lot because I met people who knew people, and then I did a little bit of research about the Suffragettes. And I thought, well, just because they're a different sex why can't they have the same vote as the guy that lives next door to them? And so it opened my mind ... and all of a sudden it came home to me, which made me feel pretty good, because I could get involved.

BELLA (DAVIS) YOUNG
People maybe think that they cannot do it, but if you want something you can do it. You could do anything if you are all together, and you know that what you're doing is right. If you come together you can do it. We did it and we were not rich!

It's like if you've got a girl and a boy, and you give more money for the boy,

LEGACY OF THE STRIKE AND PRIDE

"

and less money for the girl. Your girl, your daughter, will maybe say, 'Why you spend that money for him, and for me only this?' You know what I mean, it's the same. The men should get more than the girls. Why?

I have never been sorry I did it. I knew it was the right thing and I'm very proud of what I've done. I went on strike. I maybe have done things in my life I'm not so proud of. But I went on strike and I'm proud of what I did because I was in the right. The company was trying to use us as cheap labour, not as human beings. And the men just enjoyed it. The men always had it easier.

I knew I was in the right. No men could do the same job I do and get more money than me when I'm working hard. If I had to do it again I'd do it again.

ROBERT (BOB) SINGH

It was definitely an historical event. The Equal Pay Act had only just come into force and it hadn't really been implemented. There had been strikes for equal pay before that, and a major one at Ford's, but the Act itself had only just come into force, and it was important to have something that would crystallise people's view that actually equal pay was still an issue, that women were still not being paid the same. And the Trico strike did that. It said equal pay is still on the agenda and women were still not being paid the same despite the law. So that was the major legacy as far as I can see.

At a personal level, it made me appreciate the strength of people being together, working together. Even though you talked about it and had a theoretical understanding, to actually see it in practice was different. And you had a situation where women who were not political – were apolitical, quite frankly – were able to do something quite historic because they firmly believed in what they wanted, in what was right and what was wrong. That is definitely the legacy for me.

PHYLLIS GREEN

I was always taught that whatever men did, we could do as well as them and they could do as well as us – it was always equal with me. I never looked at men as being any stronger than us or doing anything better than us. It was a good time. I enjoyed the strike. I was glad I was there. I was glad I was part of women getting equal pay, well

LEGACY OF THE STRIKE AND PRIDE

equal pay as far as it went – there's still a way to go yet. I'm proud to have been in it. It was good fun. I got to know people I wouldn't have known otherwise – it was a great time!

RHODA (FRASER) WILLIAMS

I was glad I got the experience of what the strike was all about. I have no hard feelings towards that. I'm very proud of that, because nobody could have sent me back in there … I came out and I would go back when I want, when the strike is over. And I was very happy towards that. I did not have any pressure at all. I was proud of what I did. You never know, when people read the book, it might inspire them to do something if they are in trouble.

IZZY DAVIS

I remember my mum beaming and smiling with that triumphant look on her face when it ended, and coming home but still mentioning 'those flimmin' scabs'! It's funny you know, in the years that followed she never forgot about those people … from time to time she would mention them, and she'd say, I've not forgotten I suffered so much, 'those flimmin' scabs!' blah, blah'. She remembered. How could you forget that – by hook or crook, you have to stand up for what's right.

So there has been a feeling of being triumphant and that sense of pride till this day, but it was especially evident then – that pride that she got through and she survived and we kept our home and things returned to normal, and she could then give me pocket money – and I had my platform boots anyway!

I think the legacy is in the people, the experience – for myself and for anybody who witnessed what it was like to go on strike – not to forget how important it was to go through that and do that. And it probably helps you appreciate the working conditions now.

The party's over –
Trico picket line,
18 October 1976.

CHRIS DAVIES/REPORT ARCHIVE/
REPORTDIGITAL.CO.UK

Well done, Trico
strikers. Left to Right,
Peter Rowlands,
Roger Butler, Tom Durkin,
Jack Dromey outside
Trico gates,
18 October 1976.

CHRIS DAVIES/REPORT ARCHIVE/
REPORTDIGITAL.CO.UK

168 | THE RECKONING

> JOAN BAKEWELL
>
> Oct. 18. 76
>
> Dear Sally,
> Thanks for sending the good news! I was delighted for you all. Please offer my congratulations to all your colleagues. And my thanks to you for your assistance when I was writing the article.
> Sincerely
> Joan Bakewell.

of Hammersmith Council and Hammersmith Labour Party. Hammersmith Trades Council made all the arrangements. The actual organisation of the social was undertaken jointly by Brent and Hounslow Trades Councils.

A great many Trico strikers were present to enjoy the evening, along with thirty Grunwick strikers. It was agreed by the Trico shop stewards that half of the proceeds should go to the Grunwick Strike Committee. Following the Trico victory, it was announced that eighty new members had joined the AUEW in the factory, and Eileen Ward announced that after the elections there was now a total of fifteen women on the shop stewards committee. During the evening Tom Durkin, President of Brent Trades Council, read a poem that he had written in tribute to the Trico strikers, and the Trico song was sung by the strikers. Amongst the

from: Jo Richardson MP
House of Commons
London
SW1A 0AA
Telephone: 01-219 5028

Sally Groves
26 Ravensbourne Gardens
London
W 13

21
October
1976

Dear Sally: congratulations. I was really thrilled that the guts, persistence and solidarity of the TRICO workers won the day.

The Tribune Group, of which I'm secretary, had decided last week to send a deputation on your behalf to see Albert Booth, but of course in the event that was unnecessary. The Group has asked me to send all of you our good wishes.

Yours sincerely,

Jo Richardson

> **THE TRICO SONG**
> (to the tune of "THE RED FLAG")
>
> We print the song that has become part of the legend of our strike. The words are by Mary, one of the strikers, and her husband.
>
> The Trico Flag is stained with red
> With blood and tears our women shed
> We look towards the future day
> When Trico gives us Equal Pay
>
> Till then we'll keep our banners high
> We'll march along - we will not die
> Though poor we are and starve we may
> We'll see it through till Equal Pay
>
> Trico-Folberth's got no sense
> Keeps us all outside the fence
> For when it comes to Equal Pay
> Donkey-like they say nay! nay!
>
> Although the Pay Law gave us 'rights'
> Still through our action we must fight
> And never stop or hesitate
> To us the bosses can't dictate.

Trico song from Victory Strike Bulletin No 16, 18 October 1976, ending 'To us the bosses can't dictate!'

guests was Ken Gill, General Secretary of AUEW-TASS, the white-collar section of the engineering union.

After the social Frank Stiller, Secretary of GLATC, sent out a letter to all those that had been involved. It concluded:

> I would like to pay tribute once again to the magnificent men and women of TRICO. It has been a privilege for us to associate ourselves with them and their District Committee. They have set an example that will be hard to follow but one that has inspired and excited the whole trade union movement. We say 'Well done'!

**GREATER LONDON
ASSOCIATION OF TRADES COUNCILS**

TRICO BENEFIT

WITH A HOST OF MUSIC AND ENTERTAINMENT

on Friday 22nd October 1976

7.30 — 12 midnight

FULHAM TOWN HALL, FULHAM BROADWAY SW6

BAR AVAILABLE   £1.00 FOR A DOUBLE TICKET

VICTORY! | 171

LOOKING BACK

ERIC FUDGE

I don't think attitudes would be any different now. It would be just the bloody same, I think. There'd be a few of us who'd say, 'No, that's not right, we'll support you', and the majority would say 'Oh well it's nothing to do with me'. It's always someone else's problem, that's the attitude, and over the years that attitude has grown. Everybody's got their own self-interest at heart. They don't give a damn about anybody else, the rest of the population, how they have to live.

But you've got to stick together, you won't get anything if you just stand there saying, 'Can I have that please'. The answer will always be 'No'. And it's just as true today. I'm appalled by the attitude of people at the moment, actually, going on about the tube workers, bleating on about the money they earn. Well, as I point out, they earn that money because they stand and fight and they stick together. If you don't like it and you want more money, if you don't think you're paid enough for doing your job, do the same, otherwise shut up.

The tube workers have got strong leaders, a good union; they were prepared to put their heads on the block, so to speak, and take the bull by the horns. That's why they've got good pay and conditions, not because of the generosity of the employers.

At Trico everyone was very happy at the final mass meeting, and some were even elated. I think afterwards there was a great sense of relief really – hopefully things could go back to normal. However things can't go back to normal, and they never did. There's always that feeling about those that didn't go out on strike and yet were benefiting from the struggle of those that did and went through all that hardship. They didn't suffer anything, they didn't put any effort in to achieving the goal, yet they benefited from it.

BOB MITCHELL

Trico obviously got really good, positive publicity. And it evolved into Grunwick – looking back in 2016 and talking about the fortieth anniversary, it coincided with

172 | THE RECKONING

Grunwick, because one strike merged into another. It's great really. Both disputes couldn't have happened at a better time. And I know there were lots of people involved in our dispute that then joined the mass picket at Grunwick that the Yorkshire miners came down to, so that the whole of the TUC was more than aware. And now that I have been a trade union official for quite some time, I know there are lots of people that talk about Trico and Grunwick in the same breath.

ROBERT (BOB) SINGH

After the Trico strike started, the Grunwick strike started a few months later, and we went and supported them on their picket line. You had this strong bond between the different strikes, which spread to the wider trade union movement, and galvanised a lot of people's ideas about the rights of trade unionists and workers. But everything has its opposite, and the opposite to all that was the growth of Thatcherism. The ruling class – the upper classes and employers – realised that they needed something else to destroy the power of the trade unions, and Thatcher became that person, and that's why she became the leader of the Conservative Party. So those two strikes in a sense made the employers and the ruling classes aware that they needed something to destroy their movements. They wanted someone in power who was very determined and knew what she wanted. Don't forget there had already been talk about trade union legislation in the early 1970s, when they tried to bring in the legislation but didn't get away with it. I think that's why Thatcher became leader of the Conservatives because they wanted someone in power who was very determined and knew what she wanted to do.

Paul Sheldrick, arrested at Trico gates on 29 July, being congratulated by Roy Sheldrick and Trico workers after acquittal at Brentford Magistrates Court. Approx. November 1976.

TRINITY MIRROR SOUTHERN (*MIDDLESEX CHRONICLE*)

FORTY YEARS ON
– WHAT LESSONS FOR TODAY?

BOTH EQUAL PAY AND equal rights at work remain live issues for us today. Can something that occurred forty years ago tell us anything in the present situation? Perhaps the most significant lesson is that, when facing an intransigent employer, the right to withdraw labour as an ultimate weapon is important and has to be protected.

By any criteria, Trico was a stunning victory for women and equal pay and for the trade union and women's movements. It was a simple case of people taking a stand for their rights and then not letting themselves be ground down.

It was an example of the power of direct action when backed up by the organised muscle of a strong trade union. Without their union's support and assistance, it would have been difficult for the strikers to disregard the Tribunal and escape being drawn into the labyrinth of legal loopholes that was the Equal Pay Act at that time, sucked down a path that ultimately would lead nowhere.

It was also an example of a fight for equality with the backup of local AUEW officials who were left-wing in their politics, and threw themselves whole-heartedly into fighting the cause alongside the strikers.

John Slidders, the personnel executive at Trico, even admitted to a researcher after the strike that the union had played an enormous role, with the union officials doing what the workers asked them to do. His conclusion was that the union was 'too democratic'!

Interestingly, it was the first time that a strike by mainly female workers had been confronted by American-style picket-busting convoys of lorries and scab labour.

It turned out to be the longest successful strike for equal pay in British trade union history. (Needless to say, if all, or at least the majority, of the men on the shop floor had come out on strike in support of the women it would have forced the company to settle sooner.)

It was the first time that a trade union had boycotted a Tribunal and refused to attend; and it was also the first time that an employer had presented the trade union case to a Tribunal. In addition to this, the negotiated settlement was in the end larger than the original claim. This was illegal, as a Tribunal had previously decided that the women were already in receipt of equal pay!

Significantly, it was the first time a trade union had negotiated a settlement despite a Tribunal decision against it.

It needs to be pointed out here that going to a Tribunal is only an option, not a requirement – although without a strong trade union it may be the only channel available for workers seeking redress. Judging by the sanctimonious attitude of much of the press in 1976, however, you would have thought it was a moral obligation!

In some ways our case was unusual, and in many other situations going to a Tribunal with your grievance may be the best – if not the only – route to take; and this is something that is considered a democratic right in a modern society. Yet, in a move with the clear intention of reducing workers' access to this right, the Conservative government has imposed prohibitive charges for anyone seeking adjudication through this route.

The women at Trico astonished the company managers when they walked out; and they dumbfounded them when they stayed out, shattering all the stereotypes of 'girls' not having the staying power or guts of 'the men' – and, of course, refuting the jibe that women only worked for 'pin money'.

One important factor in the staying power of the Trico women was the close bonds of friendship, family and community that existed in the factory prior to the strike. As Louise Raw has highlighted through her research: 'close bonds between women have been extremely beneficial in providing a ready-made basis for collective action, helping to maintain solidarity during strikes and ultimately promoting class consciousness'.[1] This kind of collective consciousness has been insufficiently studied in labour movement history, and was certainly a crucial factor at Trico.

---

[1] Ardis Cameron, in S. Moore (1986), *Women, Industrialisation and Protest in Bradford, 1780-1845*, PhD thesis for University of Essex 1986, p14, cited in L. Raw, *Striking a Light*, Continuum International Publishing Group, 2011, p88.

TRICO AND GRUNWICK

THE WORKERS AT the Grunwick film processing factory in Willesden, Brent, only eight miles from Trico, who were more than 60 per cent female, also astounded people when they came out on strike in August 1976, only a few months after the Trico strike had begun.

It was thought that immigrants were even less likely to go on strike than women: they would accept low pay and bad conditions and would never go on strike.

Women workers were supposed to be so tame and obliging that Grunwick took on women at low pay even before they tried their hand at immigrants. But the women at Grunwick proved to be at least as militant, if not more militant, than the men.[2]

Likewise, at Trico the women proved to be the most militant, once the spark had been ignited! And the Trico women, too, although they were not aware of it at the time, had for years been used as cheap labour on the production lines, with their skills and co-operation taken for granted.

From August until October 1976 the strikes at Trico and Grunwick were running simultaneously, and affection, respect and admiration for one another's cause was felt on both sides; this was underlined when the Grunwick Strike Committee members expressed a wish to give some money to their sisters at Trico, who had by then been out for about four months – until it was pointed out that they really were not in a position to do so as they themselves were on strike!

The workers at Grunwick had been paid considerably less than the Trico women, and had been blatantly exploited by their managers. A key difference here was that they had had no union to represent or protect them.

[2] J. Dromey and G. Taylor, *Grunwick: The Workers' Story*, Lawrence & Wishart, 1978, p49.

Laurie Pavitt, Labour MP for Brent South at the time, told Parliament that 'Grunwick was a sweat shop lifted straight out of the Dickens era'. Yet Grunwick was little different from thousands of small- to medium-sized firms around Britain at the time. Over time, types of employment have changed considerably from those days, but no-one can say that exploitation has disappeared: the scandal now is the huge numbers of working people on zero hours and short-term contracts, or enforced self-employment. Today we have an increasingly casualised workforce – yet another way of employers seeking to undermine organisation in the workplace.

Both strikes were confronted with a big, co-ordinated police operation. At Trico it was launched in conjunction with the company, to help ensure that the scab lorries got materials and goods in and out the factory. (The huge sums of money spent on these operations by the company could have been better spent on giving us equal pay in the first place.) Given that the picketing was mainly being done by women, we would have been unable to challenge these convoys without other trade unionists coming to our assistance. And this solidarity was also repeated at Grunwick.

Perhaps the police tactics on 29 July at Trico can be seen as a small dress rehearsal for what was to take place at Grunwick, where there were huge numbers of trade unionists and supporters lined up every morning (including sometimes, spectacularly, coachloads of miners) to show solidarity and try to stop the daily bus from going into the factory with its scab workforce on board. Each day the police also lined up to force a way through the picket lines for the bus. The notorious Special Patrol Group was deployed alongside the police, and their violence resulted in many injuries to pickets.

The diminutive figure of strike leader Jayaban Desai became the face of Grunwick, and she became an inspiration for other immigrant workers taking a stand against a bad employer, and for the right to organise in a trade union. As has been said before (most recently by Jeremy Corbyn): 'ordinary people do extraordinary things'.[3] This was true at Grunwick and at Trico, and is true of all the many other struggles and campaigns for rights and justice over the years.

As we have seen, one means of bringing pressure to bear on a perverse employer is through other workers organising to boycott their goods or services. At Trico, however, stopping the supply of Trico windscreen wipers and other products in this way was never more than partially successful:

[3] Jeremy Corbyn, speaking on You Tube Jayaben Desai documentary.

the car industry had become adept at swapping to alternative suppliers, and the company resorted to every trick they knew to smuggle parts in and out the factory. These difficulties helped prolong the strike.

In contrast to this, at Grunwick the local postal workers at Cricklewood made a spontaneous decision to boycott the Grunwick post, so cutting off the company's lifeblood, given that the films it processed were distributed through mail order. This confronted the Managing Director, George Ward, with the shocking realisation that he might be forced to negotiate with his workforce, or even to recognise the trade union! At this point, however, he was 'saved' by the ultra-right-wing National Association for Freedom (now called The Freedom Association): one of its members, Conservative MP for Hendon John Gorst, organised over 100 Conservative MPs (with support from Maggie Thatcher, already by then leader of the Tory Party) to demand a debate in the House of Commons about what they saw as a gross infringement of the rights of employers. It was this that catapulted Grunwick into the national headlines, and the strike became one of the key 1970s battles over the role of unions in society. The idea that trade unions had too much power was a theme that was constantly repeated by the new right during the 1970s, and one of Margaret Thatcher's main aims as Tory leader was to destroy them.

As the right-wing media made a cult victim figure out of George Ward, and collaborated with the Tories in their denouncement of the trade union movement, the right wing of the TUC and the Callaghan government capitulated to the pressure. The resulting lack of support from the mainstream Labour establishment meant that the strikers were forced into compromises that allowed George Ward to play the Conciliation Service (ACAS) along for months on end. This policy of delaying tactics then continued with the setting up of the Scarman Court of Inquiry, which, although it eventually found in the strikers' favour, was totally ignored by George Ward. In the end the brave and intrepid strikers finally had to call off the dispute after more than eighteen months.

As Tom Durkin commented, the key lessons from the Grunwick dispute were, 'first, the difference between left and right within our movement, second, the dangers of over-reliance upon procedures laid down by law, and, third, the lessons for the movement on the relationship of the immigrant community to the Trade Union movement'.[4]

At Trico it was certainly crucial to victory that the local officials were from the left, and gave unwavering support to the women; and it was also important that they were able to keep all the negotiations in their own hands. What's more, the Strike Committee and their officials understood the dangers inherent in relying on a law rigged in favour of the employers (in our case the Equal Pay Act), and they knew the power of working-class collective action for the securing of a just result.

It was lucky, too, for the Trico women that no opportunity presented itself for an organisation such as the National Association for Freedom to get involved in the dispute. Trico did have the powerful Engineering Employers Federation to represent and advise them, and to bail them out financially, but the EEF was an employers' association, in contrast to the NAFF, which was a crusading ultra-right political pressure group.

But, as the strike progressed, there was often a wish expressed on the picket line that the TUC and the Labour government would speak out on behalf of the women, or, at least, that Betty Lockwood from the Equal Opportunities Commission would show some disquiet at the failure of the Tribunal system to find in favour of the women. It is an indictment of the Labour establishment that the only MPs to lobby on behalf of the strikers were members of the left Tribune group and the local Ealing Southall MP Syd Bidwell.

On the other hand, this lack of support from the Labour and TUC leadership meant that all the negotiations with the company were kept firmly under the control of the local AUEW officials, as well as the region's AUEW Executive Committee member Reg Birch. It was Reg Birch who ensured that the EEF did not ultimately take over and negotiate directly with the AUEW Executive Council, which would have taken the final settlement out of the hands of the strikers' representatives.

---

[4] Tom Durkin, *Bravery and Betrayal, an assessment of the Grunwick dispute*, Brent Trades Council, May 1978.

LESSONS FOR TRADE UNIONISTS

THE REASON IT IS important to remember a strike for equal pay that took place forty years ago is that it is impossible to understand the significance of what is happening to ordinary people in the present day without a knowledge of what happened to them in the past. The British media is owned, with a few exceptions, by multi-millionaires, which makes it unsurprising that the press gives a distorted view of ordinary working people's lives – especially when it comes to organisations, such as trade unions, that have the ability to represent us, challenge employers and protect and improve pay and conditions at work. As an ex-editor of the *Sun* once said, the news that is deliberately ignored by the papers is often of equal – if not greater – significance than what is included!

So the fact that the media has generally chosen to forget the importance and current relevance of the women's victory at Trico in 1976, along with so much of our working-class and trade union history, is hardly a great surprise.

But the equal pay victory of the women at Trico remains relevant today – and not only because women still earn 9 per cent less than their male counterparts in full-time employment, and, even more shockingly, 19 per cent less if working part-time. It is also relevant because it shows the importance of unions: without their union the Trico women could not have won. Yet successive pieces of anti-trade union legislation, starting with those of the Thatcher government, have made it increasingly difficult to win legitimate battles against bad employers, as employment rights have been whittled away – and as the right wing and their press allies continue to batter away at the theme of overbearing unions.

We seem to be sleepwalking towards a more authoritarian society, with laws increasingly aimed at attacking ordinary working people, not to mention migrants and refugees escaping war and persecution.

The Trade Union Act 2016 is a further sinister assault on our democratic rights as citizens. It is easy to think that such new laws 'won't affect me'. We were in that position before the strike: we never dreamt we would have to be out on a picket line for months on end, fighting for our basic rights. Basic rights at work are a necessity for all workers: without them it is very difficult to stand up to an abusive employer.

The 2016 report of the United Nations Joint Committee on Human Rights concluded that the Trade Union Bill raised a number of human rights concerns, and the International Labour Organisation Committee of Experts came to a similar verdict.[5] These bodies have the authority to comment on British law because the right to strike is a fundamental right embodied in the UN International Covenant on Economic, Social and Cultural Rights, 1966; and this right has been protected by the ILO supervisory bodies for over sixty years. A body of principles on the right to strike is broadly shared by the international community, and is based on the general principles of freedom of association.[6]

Under the terms of the 2016 Act, in order to make any industrial action legal, unions will have to achieve a 50 per cent turnout in any industrial ballot – a requirement that would make elections in many other organisations in the UK invalid, including a substantial proportion of local councils. And as if this wasn't discriminatory enough, what have been newly defined as 'important public services' (health, education, transport and border security) will have to meet a threshold of support from at least 40 per cent of all those entitled to vote in the ballot for any proposed strike to be legal. By including in these provisions huge swathes of workers in the transport and education sectors the government has ignored the international standard of 'essential public service' in its own much broader definition. The ILO Committee of Experts has stated that this threshold would have the effect of constituting 'an obstacle to the right of workers' organisations to carry out their activities without interference'.[7] It will mean that workers at the sharp end of resistance to privatisation and cuts will find it virtually impossible to take strike action.

At Trico the women voted by a show of hands at the

---

[5] TUC Trade Union Bill, JCHR Report and ILO opinion briefing report, 2016.
[6] Carolyn Jones, 'The Tory Trade Union Bill breaches international law', *Morning Star*, 22.2.16.
[7] Carolyn Jones, 'Unjust New Law Spells Trouble', *Morning Star*, 12.5.16.

mass meeting in the park. They reconfirmed their support for the strike almost weekly at further mass meetings. This would now be illegal. Employment law has enforced secret ballots of the entire workforce since at least 1984. A ballot of the whole workforce at Trico, as now required, would have led to the strike action being defeated, as the great majority of the men were apathetic about, if not openly hostile to, the women's equal pay cause.

Would men's attitudes be so different now? We think it is fair to say that some attitudes have changed today: nowadays not many men would say that women work for 'pin money'! And there is less fear today than there was at Trico in 1976 that any increase in pay for women would undermine men's own pay or 'craft' status. As with many such fears, the opposite proved true at Trico: while the women were being used as cheap labour, all the factory wages were being held down. This was shown to be the case following the strike, when the outcome led to significant wage increases throughout the factory, to maintain the differentials.

As Carolyn Jones of the Institute of Employment Rights comments, in the new Act we face 'a government determined to silence political opposition, cull collective action, criminalise solidarity on the picket line and strangle unions with bureaucratic red tape …'[8]

Ironically it was David Davis speaking in a House of Commons debate in 2015, who described the new picketing provisions in the Trade Union Bill as something out of 'Franco's Spain'. The Act requires trade unions to appoint a picket supervisor for all picket lines, and to supply that person with a letter of authorisation; furthermore, the union or supervisor will be required to supply the police with the supervisor's name and contact details. Failure to comply with any of these obligations would mean the union loses legal protection and could result in an injunction, the picketing being stopped, and damages being claimed against the union.

This means that in a dispute with a company with many workplace sites – for example, the London Underground, where there are hundreds of stations – supplying a picket supervisor for each workplace would require the appointment of hundreds of picket supervisors and the delivery of hundreds of letters of authorisation. This would also apply to organisations with shift systems: when the shift changes another picket supervisor would have to get a letter of authority. Clearly the whole aim is to present the unions

[8] Ibid.

with demands that are impossible to meet.

It is very likely that information on picket supervisors will be collated and stored by law and order agencies (though this is likely to be denied). There is also a risk that a disgruntled member of the public could demand to see the details of any picket supervisor – and perhaps post it on social media. A manager could also demand the information, and it remains to be seen whether in practice this information will be shared between employers, or between employers and the police. The police did indeed work very closely with managers at Trico.

This almost certainly will lead to further blacklisting of shop stewards and activists, and is not compatible with the blacklists regulations 2010, which are designed to stop the compiling of lists of trade union activists. As Ellie Mae O'Hagan has pointed out, the construction industry in particular has a 'murky history of monitoring trade unionists ... thousands of ordinary workers were blacklisted and left unemployed for decades after committing such appalling crimes as informing their employer of health and safety risks'.[9]

Few people today know about the construction industry's persecution of trade unionists in the 1970s, or the imprisonment of building workers Des Warren, Ricky Tomlinson and John McKinsie Jones – 'the Shrewsbury Three' – in 1973-74, on antiquated charges of conspiracy. Yet they became, in effect, 'political prisoners' of the British state, as a result of a legal system loaded in favour of employers and against trade unionists.

The 2016 Act also assigned new powers to the Certification Officer (CO), the government regulator for trade unions and employers' associations, giving it the ability to fine trade unions as much as £20,000 for breaches of reporting rules, and to require an annual audit of a union's protests and pickets. Furthermore, the CO's investigations are to be paid for by the unions. The CO now has unprecedented powers to access and remove union records. The only conclusion to draw is that the government intends to cripple the unions with bureaucracy.

In addition, although a proposal to allow bussing in agency workers to replace strikers was not included in the Act, this omission was a concession made only to make sure it was passed. And, as Liberty, the civil liberties and human rights organisation, has pointed out, the government has left itself space for secondary legislation to be introduced at a

[9] Ellie Mae O'Hagan, 'This sinister trade union bill is an assault on the rights of working people', *Guardian*, 16.9.15.

later stage. If such a proposal were introduced in the future it would have the same effect as an outright strike ban. Faced with agency workers taking over their production jobs the Trico women would never have achieved equal pay.

As with earlier attempts to use the law to prevent trade unions organising, the Trade Union Act 2016 was drawn up because of a fear of trade unions' ability to represent, protect and improve their members' wages and conditions. Trade unions are seen as a threat to all who are determined to maximise profits by maintaining a workforce on low wages and insecure contracts with scant employment rights.

As Ellie Mae O'Hagan states: 'None of the better employers in the UK have called for this clampdown on trade union activity, because frequent strikes and poor relations with unions are something you find only in the worst workplaces.'[10] As an example of poor management O'Hagan cites British Airways, where in 2010 Chief Executive Willie Walsh was accused of trying to break the union in order to impose wage cuts that left some cabin crew relying on working tax credits on salaries as low as £12,000 a year (in 2013 Walsh was paid £5 million). Another example is Sports Direct, whose billionaire owner Mike Ashley is so hostile to trade unions that all organising work was driven underground, and the union was made to feel it was organising the 'French Resistance'.[11] In companies such as these, destroying trade union organisation is seen as an integral part of the drive to keep wages and conditions as poor as possible.

Measures put in place by successive Tory governments (and left largely unrepealed by Labour when in office) have drastically curbed legitimate trade union activity and put civil liberties and industrial relations at risk. Taken together, they would have made our legitimate right to fight for equal pay at Trico unlawful. Is that compatible with a modern, democratic state?

We would never have been able to achieve equal pay at Trico under the draconian new Act. Almost certainly our union would have been unable to meet all the incessant daily requirements: our picketing would have been stopped and injunctions served on the union.

---

[10] Ellie Mae O'Hagan, 'If you curb the power of trade unions, you reduce the rights of working people', *Independent*, 15.7.15.
[11] Ibid.

LESSONS FOR FEMINISM

IT WAS NOT IDEAS ABOUT feminism as such that compelled the Trico women to take up the fight for equal pay. It was the stark injustice of getting less pay than the male operators doing identical work. From the experience of being out on strike for five months they then became aware of being part of a much wider trade union and working-class movement that had come to their aid with overwhelming practical and financial support. If we allow the organisations that can provide that kind of support to workers to be strangled by bureaucracy and criminalised, we will have forfeited some of our most fundamental civil liberties, including our right to strike.

We will never forget the Women's Liberation groups who put on socials and outings and raised impressive amounts of money for our hardship fund, or the Working Women's Charter, which, embedded as it was in the Trades Council structure, had closer links with the trade union movement and played a major role in supporting us. But, ultimately, it was the trade unions that were our life-force.

Fast forward to the feminist debates of today, and the media focus on women reaching the top, and the differences are clear to see.

Yasmin Alibhai-Brown comments that:

> High profile, middle-class activists are extraordinarily concerned about boardrooms and Parliament, pay and bonuses, hardly ever about lone mothers too poor to feed their children, discrimination faced by black and Asian women or exploited workers. It is necessary to criticise and sometimes damn women who do not care about other women, about men, children, a decent society.[12]

[12] Yasmin Alibhai-Brown, 'Suffragette shows feminism's success – and its flaws', Independent, 12 October 2015.

Alibhai-Brown also notes that: 'Some feminists believe a woman who has broken through glass ceilings must always be supported.' And women on the Trico picket line would have been among the first to cheer women for beating competition and winning jobs previously the preserve of males, usually white males.

But generally their experience would make them deplore a Conservative prime minister like Thatcher, with her calculated defeat of the miners and destruction of their entire communities, especially given that it was just such people – the miners, steelworkers, car-workers, print-workers and dockers – who helped us win at Trico.

What we learnt was that you have to take collective action, and show determination and guts in face of all the brickbats and abuse hurled at you, as well as the more sophisticated lies peddled about your cause in certain sections of the media. As time goes on, it becomes all about holding your nerve and standing your ground.

The only way to do this is to meet and listen to your own people – your supporters in the trade unions, in the Labour Party, in our case in the women's organisations, people who understood our situation and actually wanted us to win! We found that it was working-class people, ordinary folk, even down to pensioners who could only afford to send a few stamps to help – it was these people that were our backbone.

REMEMBERING OUR HISTORY

IT'S AN INDICTMENT of our society that we still need to fight for equality. Over the years since Thatcher's time in power there has been a redistribution of wealth in favour of the very rich, and this has accelerated since 2010 with the piece-by-piece dismantling of the welfare state and public services. But far fewer people would accept this state of affairs if it were not for the right-wing media in Britain, mostly owned by a few ultra-rich and powerful individuals in alliance with big business, who have government ministers in their pocket. It is this media that tells the official story, or distorts and distracts us from the real story.

The 1970s was in many ways a turning point. It was the decade during which the welfare state started to come under attack, and nationalised industries started to be seen as a drag on the economy. In fact they were subsidising underperforming private industry, which was suffering from underinvestment: Britain was investing less in its industries at that time than a number of other European countries, including France, Germany and Italy.

But in the 1970s the myth was peddled that Britain was a failing economy, and this was caused by 'greedy unions' making too many demands. In reality, it was the economic policy of Heath's Tory government that had led to rampant inflation at the beginning of the 1970s. And after Harold Wilson was elected as prime minister in 1974, the unions showed a lot of restraint under the social contract pay policy, and worked with the government to try to help stabilise the economy. But then in 1978 the Labour government (by then led by James Callaghan), taking union support for granted, demanded too great a sacrifice from low-paid workers. The fourth phase of incomes policy restricted pay increases for workers in the public sector to under 5 per cent (effectively a pay cut given that the government had not succeeded in controlling inflation), and it was this which triggered the so-called 'winter of discontent'.

As John Medhurst and many others have noted, the media significantly exaggerated the impact of the strikes of winter 1979-80, in order to discredit Labour and assist Thatcher.[13] In contrast to genuine catastrophes such as the collapse of UK manufacturing in the 1980s under Thatcher, or the banking crisis of 2008, it had very little economic impact. Despite this, the legend of the 'winter of discontent' is now set in stone, impervious even to the admission of Derek Jameson, editor of the *Daily Express* in 1979, who said, 'We pulled every dirty trick in the book. We made it look like it was general, universal and eternal, whereas it was in reality scattered, here and there, and no great problem.'[14]

The Trico equal pay settlement was portrayed as being exempt from government pay policy – hence the careful wording of the negotiated final settlement. But in fact it went against it, for two reasons. First, the Tribunal had ruled that the women were not eligible for equal pay, and, second, the AUEW had negotiated a settlement that was a little bit in excess of equal pay!

Trico was one of the most outstanding examples of a strike for women's rights arising from the expectations created by the new Equal Pay Act. At the time, as George Stevenson's research shows, the Trico strike was seen as a symbol of women's fight for equality, and it was perceived as being highly significant to the trade union movement, the women's liberation movement and the left.[15]

It was hard for establishment commentators to demonise the Trico women, as they didn't fit the stereotype of 'greedy' trade unionists so beloved of the media. Yet any tribute to the achievement of the Trico women is also a tribute to their AUEW union officials and the strength of the trade union movement – which is anathema for the right-wing media and the establishment.

Yet, as Stevenson points out, 'even the national press saw it as "the first great battle in the equal pay campaign" and as a "trial of strength" between employers and unions with "far wider significance" for the entire industry.'[16]

Since that time, however, the importance of the 1976 Trico strike has been neglected, especially in comparison with

[13] J. Medhurst, 'The Myth of the 1970s', *Red Pepper*, October 2014.
[14] Ibid.
[15] George Stevenson, 'The Forgotten Strike: Equality, Gender and Class in the Trico Equal Pay Strike', *Labour History Review*, Vol. 81, Issue 2, August 2016.
[16] Ibid.

the Ford women's dispute eight years earlier or Grunwick, which began a few months later. Stevenson argues that this neglect 'undoubtedly owes much to the dispute's successful resolution for the strikers and the discordant note this strikes with the dominant historiographical trend which understands the late 1970s as a period of progressive retreat and symbolic defeats'.[17]

It is also true that, as Stevenson points out, despite outstanding support from a handful of Labour MPs and tireless assistance from hundreds of trade unionists, the 'two most symbolically important institutions of the labour movement, the Labour Party and the TUC, failed to explicitly recognise the significance of the dispute for trade unionism, the women's movement and class politics'.

As a result, most people, especially the younger generation, are unaware of the events in Brentford during that long hot summer.

Many people today work in a place where there is no trade union to represent them. Trade union membership is much reduced since the 1980s, even though the current Tory government's neoliberal austerity programme is, if anything, even more devastating than the Thatcher regime, making trade union organisation more important than ever.

There are numerous groups across Britain taking action against cuts and privatisation, the sanctioning of benefit claimants, and the wholesale attack on working-class communities and council housing in the Housing Act 2016. And where there are campaigns, women – who are among those most affected by the loss of public services – are often at the forefront. As at Trico, once women take up a cause they run with it. The challenge appears to be to find ways to build alliances between these groups. Within the trade union movement Unite Community's network of branches open to diverse membership has given a lead. And the People's Assembly movement reaches out to be inclusive. The rise of left-wing activism in the Labour Party is also a welcome new development, despite the British establishment, mainstream media and right-wing elements within the Labour Party who sought to undermine the leadership of Jeremy Corbyn following his election as party leader in September 2014.

The Trico women's strike has an important place in history: the strikers were remarkable role models in the struggle for equality, and understood the importance of building alliances of solidarity and inclusiveness. The story of

[17] Ibid.

their victory on equal pay offers an opportunity for younger people to get a better understanding of the importance of collective rather than individualised action in pursuit of equal rights and a more just society.

Trico is the story of ordinary women, and the men that stood by them, who came out on strike for the principle of equal pay. It was their collective action and unity that finally brought about victory.

As Bob Crow, the late RMT General Secretary, commented:

> If you fight you won't always win!
> But if you don't fight you will always lose!

The women at Trico put up a fight and won. Let that be the inspiration for future generations of young people to follow.

Celebration outside Trico gates, 1st anniversary of strike, 24 May 1977.
Left to Right, Betty Humphreys, Bella (Davis) Young, May Dawes, Sally Groves,
Sandra (Ward) Gray, Monica Harvey.

TRINITY MIRROR SOUTHERN (EVENING MAIL)

FIGHTING FOR OUR RIGHTS

WOMEN WORKERS AND EQUAL PAY BEFORE THE 1960S

WOMEN'S STRUGGLE FOR equal pay has a long history, often ignored by the British press and establishment, if not trivialised and occasionally demonised. In contrast, the trade union movement has taken some pride in these achievements.

The exclusion of women from history is also an intrinsic part of our education system, and, as Dale Spender comments, this 'has directly affected the way generations of women feel about themselves and their abilities, and the value society places on them'.[1]

The Matchwomen's strike of 1888 is often seen as the first time that women organised themselves effectively, but women had been involved in workplace battles for many years before that – putting up a fight against being used as cheap labour, as well as for the right to unionise. Those early pioneers were either very brave or desperate, probably both: they had to confront an employer without any union organisation or strike funds to support and assist them.[2] A brief sketch of some of that history is given below, as a background to the equal pay struggles that began in the 1960s.

In the first half of the nineteenth century there were many examples of women taking action, especially in the textile industry. The formation of the Grand National Consolidated Trade Union (GNCTU) in 1834, which led to an explosion of union membership in Britain, was important for women – the new union allowed women to be members of its Lodges of Industrious Females. As Sarah Boston points out, the

---

[1] D. Spender, *Women of Ideas and What Men Have Done to Them*, cited by L. Raw, *Striking a Light*, Continuum, revised edition 2011, p230, herself citing E.J. Yeo (ed), *Radical Femininity: Women's Self-Representation in the Public Sphere*, Manchester University Press 1998, p178.
[2] S. Boston, *Women Workers and the Trade Unions*, Lawrence & Wishart, third edition, 2015, p19.

textile unions were the first to negotiate rates based on 'the rate for the job' and not the rate for 'the sex of the worker doing the job' – which effectively was equal pay.

The GNCTU soon counted membership of half a million. Strikes and lockouts around the country occurred, on issues of wages, hours of work and union membership, and women played a not inconsiderable part in these battles.[3]

The establishment responded by going on to the attack, and sought out for this purpose what they saw as the weakest link in this new Big Union: the agricultural labourers. The persecution of trade union organisation in this sphere culminated in the trial and deportation of the six agricultural workers who became known as the Tolpuddle Martyrs. Although women's involvement is largely hidden from this history, there is little doubt that women played a significant role in the successful nationwide protest campaign that supported the Martyrs and their families and eventually secured their freedom.

But this earlier model of general industrial unionism was eclipsed in the mid-nineteenth century by a newly emerging model of craft trade unions, usually organised around single industries or groups of workers, and these tended to be focused on defending the vested sectional interests of their members rather than challenging the employing class as a whole. This was at a time that Victorian Britain was claiming its position of industrial monopoly of the world.

A number of concessions were won for the two main groups that benefited from Britain's new prosperity: the textile workers, who gained greatly from the Ten Hour Act of 1847, and the skilled artisans in the metalworking and building trades. It was at this time that the Amalgamated Society of Engineers (ASE), forerunner of the AEU/AUEW, was established, in 1851. But this new 'aristocracy of labour' was in the main removed from the main mass of the working class, and women were largely excluded from these unions, which were organised around a narrow and elitist craft outlook. Despite this, positive gains in laws on employment were made by these trade unionists, such as the shorter working week and the nine-hour day, whose effect was to improve the conditions of all workers.

Then in the late 1880s, with the active assistance of socialists such as Eleanor Marx, a new more radical general unionism emerged, which sought to once more organise unskilled workers into general unions. One of the first harbingers of

[3] Ibid, p23.

this New Unionism was the Bryant & May strike of 1888.

When about 1400 young women, many of Irish descent, walked out of the Bryant & May factory in the East End of London in the summer of 1888 little did they know that they were about to make history – and nor were they in a position to foresee the distortions and myths that would later be spun around them.

Annie Besant, at that time a socialist journalist and campaigner, had written a sensational exposé of the appalling conditions in the factory, and in response the company asked the young women to sign a statement that the article was untrue, which they refused. This was a contributory factor to the dispute, but the strike itself arose from incidents inside the factory, rather than originating with Besant, as the company claimed.

It has taken 120 years and historian Louise Raw's meticulous and fascinating research to demonstrate that these women were neither helpless 'little match girls' nor slatternly 'factory girls'. They were factory workers, working-class women, many of them colourful characters, who took 'deliberate, independent action' against a powerful employer that was a pillar of the British establishment.[4] They were also very much part of their own community in the East End, which was at that time a hub of socialist and Irish causes.

Historians have tended to focus on the well-known personalities involved in the strike, particularly Annie Besant, to the exclusion of the workers themselves. In addition, they have often overlooked the importance of the strike as the first in the strike wave of New Unionism, which is usually seen as starting with the Great Dock Strike of 1889. As Louise Raw argues, although the strike was short-lived, it 'ultimately transformed the image of poor unskilled workers, and their view of themselves'.[5]

The Women's Protective and Provident League, the first women's trade union, was set up in 1874, and had given a big boost to women's organisation at work. In 1903 it changed its name to the Women's Trade Union League, and after it was restructured the number of women affiliated to it increased from 2000 to more than 70,000. By this point many of the women in its leadership could be described as middle-class reformers.

In 1888, Clementina Black, Secretary of the League, moved the first equal pay motion to be adopted by the TUC Congress: it stated that 'it is desirable, in the interests of both

[4] L. Raw, op cit, p229.
[5] Ibid, p231.

men and women, they shall receive equal payment'. It was an historic moment. But it did little to change women's abysmally low pay. The real struggle was to change the attitude that a woman's wage was the 'secondary wage', despite the fact that in a large number of households it was the primary wage, and often the sole wage.

In 1906, Mary Macarthur founded the National Federation of Women Workers (which was closely linked to the Women's Trade Union League), with the intention of increasing unionism amongst women. In 1907 the organisation founded a monthly newspaper for women trade unionists, *The Woman Worker*. One battle to which Macarthur and NFWW gave invaluable assistance was that of the women chain-makers of Cradley Heath in the Midlands, in 1910. After a ten-week strike, the women won a crucial battle that established, for the first time, the right to a legal minimum wage.[6] This victory changed the lives of thousands of workers who were earning little more than starvation wages. It was Macarthur who commented that 'women are unorganised because they are badly paid, and poorly paid because they are unorganised'.[7]

During the First World War large numbers of women took over men's jobs while the men were at the front. Regrettably, however, women remained excluded from membership of the ASE, the union that represented male workers in the munitions industry. Most women were paid less than the male rate, but the government started to pay the same rate as for men when there was talk in the press of government-induced 'sweated conditions' for women in the factories.

Apart from in munitions work, however, the government refused to pay equal pay for the same work as men had done. The best equal rates of pay for women during the war were those that were won on the Clyde, as a result of the strength of the newly formed shop stewards movement, and in transport, where the NUR negotiated equal basic rates for women employed in jobs formerly undertaken by men. There was also a successful strike for equal pay in 1918, when the women tramway workers took action against an unequal war bonus, a dispute which spread to towns in the south east and London Underground.

Women had high hopes for the post-war years, and expected some recognition of their rights as citizens and workers, but within five months of the end of the war more than 600,000 women had become unemployed. Although

[6] Boston, op cit, pp65-8.
[7] Ibid, p62.

the Sex Disqualification (Removal) Act of 1919 opened up higher education and most of the professions to women, women could still be barred from work if they were married. Thousands of married women lost their jobs after the war, or were prevented from working, because of the 'marriage bar'. The Act was not applied to trade union agreements that barred women from a variety of jobs, which were widespread in almost every industry.[8] All these exceptions to the Act were made because of a fear that women would undercut men's wages, and men's belief that they were the breadwinners and had the first right to any job.[9]

The fight for equal pay for equal work in the years after 1918 was almost entirely confined to the National Union of Women Teachers and the National Federation of Women Civil Servants, as well as some workers in local government.

During the Second World War women took on, and proved themselves capable in, every conceivable job – surprising everyone, including sometimes themselves. This dispelled the myth that women working alongside men would make it impossible for either sex to concentrate and would be morally dangerous! Women joined trade unions in their droves during the war, and equal pay remained a burning issue. An Equal Pay Campaign Committee and a Royal Commission on Equal Pay were set up, but the wheels turned slowly.

The ASE's successor union, the AEU, adopted a different position from that taken in the First World War. Despite continuing fears that the war-time employment of women could be used to erode the status and wages of skilled men, the union opened membership to women in 1943, and Jack Tanner, then President of the union, spoke against the economic discrimination faced by women.

But, needless to say, at the end of the war the same prejudiced views about women in society prevailed: that society was based around family units with a male breadwinner, while the role of married women in the workforce was secondary to their home responsibilities.

The Royal Commission on Equal Pay eventually recommended equal pay for teachers and civil servants, but it took strenuous campaigns before equal pay was introduced for (non-industrial) civil servants in 1955. And even here there was a catch: it was to be phased in over seven years! Teachers had to wait until 1961 before they achieved equal pay. Let's not forget, however, that even in white-collar public sector jobs, half of the women were employed in women-only jobs

[8] Ibid, p134.
[9] Ibid, p145.

or grades and fell outside the criteria for equal pay, which relied on comparison with a male doing the same work.

The 1950s was an especially bleak time for women in private industry, given that the government and most trade unions accepted the dubious argument that the British economy would collapse if women obtained pay parity with men.[10]

THE CAMPAIGN FOR EQUAL PAY

THE LABOUR PARTY'S 1964 election manifesto included as part of its Charter of Rights for all employees 'the right to equal pay for equal work'. But this was not acted upon until 1970, the year in which the Labour government also ratified the International Labour Organisation's Convention 100 of 1951, on equal remuneration.

Harold Wilson's Labour government was elected in 1964 and again in 1966, but the issue of equal pay was shelved until almost the end of Labour's period of office. It was the high-profile strike action of the women sewing machinists at Fords, Dagenham, in pursuit of a re-grading demand, that eventually galvanised the movement to campaign vigorously against government and trade union inaction on the whole question of equal pay. This 1968 dispute has recently become better known to a new generation because of the film *Made in Dagenham*.

The dispute was important because it was about the way in which women's work was graded. This has been a consistent feature of equal pay battles: women's work is frequently classified as less skilled than men's, allowing employers to pay them less while avoiding the accusation of unequal pay.

In 1985 Bernie Passingham, the real-life Convenor of Ford River Plant (portrayed by Bob Hoskins in the film), described the conflict and bitterness that surrounded the job

[10] M. Davis, *An Historical Introduction to the Campaign for Equal Pay*, TUC Libraries Collection.

grading and job profile of the Ford women sewing machinists, disputes over which had by then continued for seventeen years.[11] He saw this as part of 'the practice of occupational sex discrimination prevalent throughout British industry since the industrial revolution'.[12]

In 1967 a joint management/trade union divisional review committee at the plant found that the intermediate sewing machinists' job profile had been significantly under-assessed, and recommended uprating, but the company's consultants disregarded their report. It was this arbitrary action by the company that led to the historic strike, which became one of the catalysts for the eventual introduction of the Equal Pay Act 1970.

More immediately, a government Court of Inquiry was set up, but this failed to find in the women's favour. Although they did receive a wage rise and returned to work, the women had not achieved the skills recognition that had been their goal in going on strike – it was only in 1984, after a further strike and many more battles (see below), that they achieved this long-fought-for aim.

Although the Dagenham strike did not achieve all its goals, it helped to inspire a renewed campaign for equal pay in the UK, spearheaded by a new organisation called the National Joint Action Campaign Committee for Women's Equal Rights. The Action Committee organised a huge equal pay demonstration on 18 May 1969, while in September an amendment to a TUC motion on equal pay was passed that called for TUC-affiliated unions to support any strike action for equal pay. This was followed by a TUC one-day conference on equal pay in November. It was at this point that Barbara Castle, the employment secretary, decided to introduce the Equal Pay Act 1970, perhaps to forestall any further unrest. It appears that the Act was also passed in anticipation of Britain's entry into the EEC, which would mean that Article 119 of the Treaty of Rome, on equal pay, would need to be transposed into law.

The EPA was duly passed in 1970, but was not to come into force until 29 December 1975, giving employers over five years to make 'adjustments'. As Mary Davis aptly sums up, the Equal Pay Act 1970 highlighted what had been apparent throughout the history of women's paid employment in the nineteenth and twentieth centuries (and is still the case in the twenty-first): 'the real cause of women's low and unequal pay is the issue of job segregation and the consequential

[11] B. Passingham, Convenor, Ford River Plant, *The Trade Union Case for Upgrading the Ford Sewing Machinists*, March 1985.
[12] Ibid.

undervaluing of women's skills'.[13]

During those five generous years of delay between 1970 and the end of 1975, employers were kept busy planning how to avoid equal pay, advised and assisted in this by their employers' associations. Some companies worked towards implementing equal pay, but others simply took no action to rectify their discriminatory pay structures.

The dawn of the equal pay era duly occurred at the end of 1975, but women soon found that the Industrial Tribunals entrusted with the task of interpreting the new legislation were more than happy to go along with the attempts of employers to turn the Equal Pay Act into a levelling down rather than a levelling up exercise.

Of the legion of loopholes in the Act, one in particular became a favourite – the claim that a group of higher paid men were an anomaly, and that once these men were no longer employed in this role, through natural wastage, the lower women's rate would prevail for both men and women. This ruse, known as 'red circling', was used at Trico in regard to the former night shift men who had come onto day work.

This ploy was spelled out in a case that came before a Tribunal early in 1976, Bedwell v Hellerman Deutsch. The proceedings were described in one of the Trico Strike Bulletins:

> The employer brought in a new grading scheme before the Equal Pay Act came into force. Before the new grading scheme, there were, among others, three job types – 1. Inspector (men), 2. Senior Viewer (women) and 3. Viewer (women). A job evaluation scheme showed that these jobs were broadly the same. But the women were paid on the lower hourly rate, while the greater bargaining strength of the men had got them 'staff status' and higher pay.
>
> One job was now created – that of 'Inspector' and that was to include the women as well. But, instead of paying the higher men's rate, the employer decided to try and avoid the Equal Pay Act by downgrading the new job to the lower women's rate.
>
> They realised that to reduce the men's actual wages would provoke an industrial dispute and so they treated the existing male staff as an 'anomaly'. They continued to pay them the higher rate until such time as this 'anomaly' disappeared by natural wastage. In this way, the employer

[13] M. Davis, op cit.

hoped to avoid both the Equal Pay Act and an industrial dispute. The Tribunal agreed to this. So the result of this case was:

The women that claimed equal pay didn't get it.
All new applicants for that job would get the lower rate.[14]

In the Tribunal ruling in the Trico case, they quite blatantly accepted that there was no difference at all between the work the men were doing and that which the women were doing. With a certain lack of subtlety, they went on to say that the company must therefore rely upon the 'escape provision' contained in sub-section (3) of Section 1 of the Act i.e. the material difference clause.[15] The Tribunal helpfully referred the company to a recent case of a Mrs Elizabeth Harrower and others v Glen Alva Ltd, where a Scottish Tribunal had held that the fact of working permanently at night amounted per se to a material difference as compared with work carried out permanently by day.

Clearly, even if the Trico women had attended the Tribunal and disputed the claim that the men had been more 'flexible', they would never have overcome the legal hurdles stacked against them. Their success is historic because not only did they defy the biased legal route, but they also won despite a Tribunal decision against them.

By the time of the Trico strike it was already clear that Tribunal decisions on the EPA were not only 'a bit odd' – as described by the Institute of Personnel Management – but, as Judith Hunt, AUEW-TASS women's organiser, pointed out, were also quite often simply 'insane'.

In the first six months of the Act, to June 1976, Tribunals had upheld thirty-one equal pay claims and rejected seventy-nine.

Cases at the time were sometimes reported seriously in the media, but often with mirth and hilarity:

Ms Hobson worked a machine which put wrappers on boxes of Black Magic chocolates. She wanted equal pay with the men who wrapped Kit Kats. But the Tribunal accepted Rowntree-Mackintosh's explanation that the men were 'concerned with the product which is to be consumed by the customer whereas the applicant is concerned only with the outer wrapping'.[16]

Then there was the case of the community worker, Sue Waddington, who worked for Leicester Council for Voluntary

[14] Trico Strike Committee Bulletin, No 4, Thursday 22 July 1976.
[15] The Tribunal decision goes on to say: 'It must be noted that here it is not the work which must differ but "the case".' It concludes: 'The sole purpose in the variation between the remuneration of the five men and that of the female operatives, and indeed the other male operatives recruited to the day shift, is in order to compensate those five men for the loss of the pecuniary benefits of the night shift. The variation is a transitional provision only and is in the process of being phased out over a comparatively short period. The case of the five men therefore is genuinely due to a material difference, other than the difference of sex, between the two cases.'
[16] Patricia Ashdown-Sharp, 'Women's Rights: The Missed Opportunity', *Sunday Times*, 20.2.77.

Service, and was told by the Tribunal that she didn't qualify for equal pay with the play leader she supervised, who was paid £500 more than her, because she was *more* experienced, *more* highly qualified and her job *more* responsible!

In another case, Reyrolle Parsons Ltd tried to explain why they paid one group of women workers £10 a week less than the men. 'A male toilet attendant has to approach his job from the labouring point of view and a female toilet attendant approaches it from a housekeeping point of view.'[17]

In this case, however, the Tribunal actually found in the women's favour.

Patricia Ashdown-Sharp also reported the case of Yvonne Wilson, a rifle packer, who was doing heavier work than men in the same department and therefore claimed equal pay. But the men also did clerical tasks, and for that reason their higher pay was upheld by the Tribunal. Mrs Wilson commented bitterly: 'if it had been the women who were doing the clerical work they'd say the men should have more money because they were doing heavier work'.[18]

The case of the women working at Electrolux in Luton is a significant one, partly because they belonged to the AUEW, the same union as the Trico strikers.

The women were doing virtually the same job as the men on the assembly line – assembling the thermostats for fridges. So they thought they should get the same rate of pay as the men but Electrolux disagreed!

After the Equal Pay Act was passed in 1970, the company put the men onto a different contract from the women, under which they *might* be required to work at night, although many were never required to do so.

In June 1975 the company made a small pay offer to the women, still short of equal pay, so in July they decided to go on strike, supported by the men. The strike ended when the company agreed to more negotiations with the AUEW, during which it made further small offers, though still short of equal pay, which the women again refused. The following day their AUEW district official called a meeting of all the women, where he called for 'Hands up those who want £50 a week?'[19] Before the women shop stewards could point out that this still wouldn't amount to equal pay, nearly everyone present had accepted. But subsequently the official did say he'd support anyone who went to the Tribunal once the Act came into force.

[17] Ibid.
[18] Ibid.
[19] G. Search, 'Equal Pay: The Fight We Haven't Won Yet', *Woman*, 1977.

Ann Hutchinson, the leading shop steward, and six of her workmates did then apply to the Tribunal, and duly approached their official for support, only to get the response, 'If you think you're entitled to equal pay, see it through on your own. We're not supporting you.'[20]

In this instance, the women won at the Tribunal, but their joy was short-lived when they heard that the company was going to appeal. The Employment Appeal Tribunal also then upheld their case, but experience had taught the women caution. Sure enough, the following Monday morning the company told them, as Ann Hutchinson recounts: 'we, personally, had won equal pay, not our jobs, so they were moving us on to what had always been men's jobs and moving women into our old jobs at our old, lower rate of pay!'[21] – i.e. the ruling applied to the individual not the job. The women who had gone to the Tribunal were moved to jobs that paid the men's rate, and all the other women in the factory remained in the same position as before.

This was in line with the intention Electrolux had made clear all along – that even if the six women won, every other woman would have to prove her case individually at Tribunal. As a result, 227 further women employees at Electrolux then submitted claims to the Tribunal! This was the case that finally forced Betty Lockwood and the Equal Opportunities Commission, on the prompting of Merlyn Rees, to take up a formal investigation – nearly a year after Ann Hutchinson and her colleagues had, individually, been awarded equal pay.

According to Ashdown-Sharp, it was 'paradoxical' that the union that gave full backing to the Trico women had failed to support the women at Electrolux.[22] But it would seem that the difference was not so much paradoxical as political. The Trico women were fortunate to have politically progressive officials representing them, who gave them unswerving support, whilst the Electrolux AUEW official and majority of the shop stewards committee at the factory clearly had not stood by them. Needless to say, if it had been up to the majority of men working at Trico, the women there would also not have received any support.

The outcry against the blatant pro-employer bias of the new Equal Pay Act gradually gained momentum. Voices were raised throughout the British trade union and women's movement. The European Commission was prompted

[20] Ibid.
[21] Ibid.
[22] Ashdown-Sharp, op cit.

to carry out infringement proceedings after the Equal Opportunities Commission raised the fact that the Act was defining equal work more narrowly than it was defined in European law.

Women within the trade unions called for a widespread campaign to fight for higher wages for women and for the wording of the Act to be broadened to provide for equal remuneration for women and men for work of equal value. This would bring the law in line with the provisions of the ILO Convention 100.

WORK OF EQUAL VALUE

FINALLY, IN 1983 the Equal Pay Act 1970 was amended to include 'work of equal value', in terms of demands made under such headings as effort, skill and decision-making. Claims were now pursued through the Employment Tribunal system.

By now Ford had been denying the women sewing machinists their legitimate entitlement to upgrading, and real recognition of their skills, for seventeen years.[23] The Ford trade unions' case had been rejected by the company in 1970, 1974, 1981, 1982 and 1983!

After the EPA had been amended to include work of equal value, the women walked out on strike again, in November 1984. The dispute lasted six weeks and cost the company £239 million in lost car production. The women and the trade unions prepared an independent job evaluation which the company rejected for six weeks, but finally agreed to in January 1985, in order to secure a resumption of work. The women's skill grade was finally raised to C grade later in 1985 – although, arguably, this still fell short of full recognition of the women's skills.

In 1985 women fish packers in Hull won the first case

[23] Passingham, op cit.

brought to a tribunal under the new equal value amendment of the Equal Pay Act, claiming their work was of equal value to that of a male labourer engaged on general duties. Pete Allen, their TGWU official, emboldened by their success, went on to win seventeen out of eighteen further cases taken to tribunal! As a result, the women's skill status and wages in the Hull fish-processing industry was significantly improved.

A new feature of these battles over equal value claims was the increasing reliance by companies and even tribunals on management consultants with proprietary job evaluation schemes. Given the cost of hiring consultants, this expertise was available almost exclusively to employers. Among the dubious practices adopted by some consultants was the inflation of differences between jobs.[24]

The biggest cause of any narrowing in the gender pay gap remained employee complaints, equal pay cases and legislation requirements – and most frequently some form of direct action by women. The law itself was 'remedial': it only provided backdated pay or damages to a woman who had managed to argue she should be paid more. There was no duty on employers to secure equality of pay.[25]

A major problem in securing equal value claims was the battle over how to evaluate skills that were generally regarded as being either 'male' or 'female', especially in a context of continuing job separation. In the absence of a proper evaluation study, the question of equal value was often decided by finding a male comparator employed in the same employment against whose pay the woman's pay could be measured. Where there was no such comparator, the different value placed on 'male' and 'female' skills operated to overvalue men's traditional skills and undervalue those of women.

Indeed, the new concept of equal pay for work of equal value was much more challenging than the idea of equal pay for equal or broadly similar work. As Sarah Boston points out, it directly challenges male prejudice and the often underlying sexism of many wage structures, most of which had been negotiated by trade unions.[26]

Louise Raw makes a related point about dominant attitudes to women being reflected in trade union leaderships when she argues that under-representation of women in the decision-making processes and structures of unions became a matter of widespread concern only in the 1980s, when political and economic changes began to undermine traditional male membership.[27] It was only after these changes, in 1994,

[24] Passingham, op cit.
[25] Incomes Data Services Report 461, November 1985.
[26] Boston, op cit, pp371-2.
[27] Raw, op cit, p231.

that the TUC launched a New Unionism campaign to tackle the issue.

As Raw argues, if the movement had learned the lesson from the matchwomen's strike about the capability and solidarity of women workers, it is possible that these belated changes would never have become necessary. Similarly, had the labour and trade union movement recognised the capability and solidarity of the Trico women and the importance of their strike in 1976, it would today be given its rightful place in our working-class history.

In the second half of the 1990s the issue of equal pay was given some recognition in two major agreements in public sector pay structures – the 1997 Single Status Agreement in local government and 1999's Agenda for Change in the NHS.

The Single Status Agreement was ground-breaking in that it put equal pay at the centre of a new grading structure, through a job evaluation scheme that was equal-pay-based and jointly agreed. Local authorities were committed to implement the agreement by 2007. In that same year a new Gender Equality Duty also came into effect. This imposed a general duty on all public authorities to eliminate unlawful discrimination and harassment and to promote equality of opportunity for men and women.[28]

However, by 2010 only 65 per cent of local authorities had implemented the Single Status Agreement, while a further 15 per cent were progressing towards it. Unsurprisingly, some councils viewed single status as a useful strategy for levelling down wages to the women's lower rates of pay.

In some authorities trade unions had failed to pursue equal pay claims on behalf of their women members. This was highlighted by the success of one solicitor, Stefan Cross, who set up his own law firm simply to pursue equal pay claims, and went on to take up 3000 claims against Unison, Unite, TGWU, GMB and the Royal College of Nursing. Many of the difficulties faced by women had arisen from the legacy of the systemic sex bias of many trade union agreements over a long period of time.

The 1999 government paper *Agenda for Change; Modernising the NHS pay system* inaugurated a similar major restructuring of pay scales involving a single job-evaluation process in the NHS. One of the catalysts for this was the substantial number of equal value claims that were being brought to employment tribunals, a notable example of which was the

[28] Boston, op cit, p405.

case of the speech and language therapists, who argued that their work should be compared to that of clinical psychologists and clinical pharmacists. It was to take fifteen years, but the speech therapists finally won their fight at the European Court of Justice.

Unison also won a major victory in 2002, after a four-year battle in Carlisle for nurses, cooks, domestics, porters and administrative and clerical staff. This was after the tribunal found in each case that the women should be on a par with the top-rated comparator.[29]

Many women did benefit as a result of Agenda for Change. But the biggest threat today to those gains is the current gradual undermining of the national NHS pay system through escalating privatisation and the fragmentation of the service.

For decades the Equal Pay Act had struggled to have any lasting impact on women's pay, and then, ironically, many landmark victories were won just as Conservative austerity measures were beginning to severely affect women and low-paid workers after 2010. These victories happened as a result of a series of long-running campaigns by poorly paid local authority women workers, who pursued their cases through the courts and opened up major new ground.

About 170 former Birmingham City Council employees, including women who had worked as cooks, cleaners and care assistants but who had left their employment several years earlier, argued that the equal pay compensation paid to their colleagues who had remained in employment should also be paid to them. The claim concerned compensation for the bonuses and other benefits that had been paid to men in traditionally male-dominated jobs such as refuse collecting and street cleaning. The women were represented by solicitors Leigh Day & Co rather than their trade unions, and they took the women's fight all the way to the Supreme Court, which ruled three to two in the claimants' favour.

This had huge implications, mainly because it extended the time limit for equal pay claims from six months to six years. This was 'the biggest change to equal pay legislation since it was introduced in 1970'.[30] The lawyers claimed that it was their bold approach to litigation that had made such a result possible, pointing out that since the EPA 1970 no one had previously thought to bring their claims in the High Court.[31]

In a further landmark case, in October 2012 Unison

[29] Ibid, p409.
[30] Patrick Butler and agencies, *Guardian*, 24.10.12.
[31] Malcolm Burns, *Morning Star*, 27.10.12.

WORK OF EQUAL VALUE | 207

reached a settlement with Edinburgh Council on long-standing equal pay claims, mainly affecting women based in schools. Edinburgh Council had maintained that women who worked in schools in roles such as classroom assistants, librarians or nursery nurses should not be paid equally with male refuse collectors, road workers or gardeners – because they had different workplaces. The union finally won the case in a judgment in November 2011 at the Court of Session in Edinburgh. The council at first decided to appeal to the UK Supreme Court, but then withdrew the appeal as part of the 2012 settlement.

At the time of writing, the long-running battle for equal pay by thousands of low-paid council employees of North Lanarkshire Council, which had resulted from its original Single Status Agreement, had still not been completely settled. This was partly due to problems with the GMB, which had agreed a settlement with the council that was backdated only for three years – well short of settlements reached by other unions and private legal firms who had represented the vast majority of workers in the authority.

EQUAL PAY AFTER 2010

AS WELL AS THIS BACKLOG of equal value claims, the Conservative-led Coalition government of 2010 also inherited the Equality Act 2010, a ground-breaking piece of legislation that was the result of fourteen years of campaigning by equality specialists and human rights organisations. But, as Catherine Barnard noted, it was unfortunate that such a radical agenda was to be implemented in 'a hostile economic and political climate'. There was a severe risk that much of its radicalism would be neutered by a government with a determined deregulatory agenda: 'The British beacon may be reduced to more of a flicker.'[32]

The Act incorporated nine pieces of legislation, including the Equal Pay Act 1970. Among other measures, it gave government the power to impose pay auditing – though it did not require employers to take any action to address any inequalities highlighted by such auditing.

True to form, the Coalition government shelved the audit provision. It was not until 2015 that the new Conservative government agreed to implement the audit – in companies employing over 250 employees.

A further major problem for women's pay equality has been the economic changes brought about by neoliberalism, beginning in the 1980s and carrying on under all subsequent governments, whether New Labour, Coalition or Tory. The pattern of employment has changed, with a big shift in employment from full to part-time; and the internal market that has been introduced into public services and the NHS has seen incremental increases in the outsourcing of services to private providers, as well as the introduction of competitive tendering. All this has had a detrimental effect on women's pay levels. Zero-hour contracts, a feature of cost-cutting and the general casualisation of large swathes of the workforce, have also had serious effects on women's pay equality.

Women have also been disproportionately affected by austerity and the shrinkage of public service. Women account for about 65 per cent of public sector jobs and have therefore borne the brunt of the disappearance of so many jobs in this sector.

An analysis by the House of Commons Library showed that in 1997 the pay gap between men and women was 27.5 per cent. Over the intervening years it narrowed, but in 2013 it rose for the first time, from 19.6 per cent to 19.7 per cent. In 2016, the Institute for Fiscal Studies found the hourly wage gap to be down to 18 per cent. The gap is smallest for 20- to 30-year-olds, but for the mid-level and highly educated the gender wage gap is the same as it was twenty years ago. Women also lose out because so many more of them work in part-time jobs to balance family and domestic responsibilities, and these jobs are subject to lower pay and poorer career and promotion prospects.

There remains a continuing strong link between the gender pay gap and women's poverty in Britain. This gap is still largely caused by occupational job segregation, as well as by women's continuing greater family and childcare

[32] Catherine Barnard, 'The Equality Act 2010', *European Gender Equality Law Review*, No. 1/2011, The European Network of Legal Experts in the Field of Gender Equality.

responsibilities, the consequence of which is fewer opportunities for promotion, discrimination in pay structures, and more widespread part-time working by women.

In the Equalities Act 2010, Harriet Harman initiated the idea of a legal requirement for companies to publish information about the gender pay gap among their employees. However, Cameron's coalition government declined to enact these provisions, instead favouring a voluntary approach. Its paper on closing the gender pay gap, *Trailblazing Transparency*, written in partnership with Deloitte, was little more than a glossy document focusing almost entirely on inequality amongst top earners.[33] Companies employing over 250 staff are now, finally, required to publish information about their gender pay gap by April 2018, with the first collection of data starting in April 2017. But there are currently no penalties for non-compliance.

The Cameron government's Ministry for Women and Equalities also announced in February 2016 that Sir Philip Hampton of GlaxoSmithKline was to lead their effort to increase the number of female executives at Britain's 350 biggest companies. As one observer on social media commented: 'So government has appointed a man to the top job of a new campaign to appoint more women to top jobs!'[34]

It is also ironic that it is the chairman of GlaxoSmithKline that was appointed, given that it is GSK that now occupies the site that, over forty years ago, witnessed one of the most intrepid battles for equal pay in British trade union history.

One thing is certain: it will not be the chairman of a transnational company that secures equality for women. It will be brought about by the determination, solidarity and, ultimately, direct action of ordinary women themselves, and their trade unions, as it has been throughout history.

---

[33] Government Equalities Office in partnership with Deloitte, *Trailblazing Transparency: Mending the Gap*, 9.2.16.
[34] Tom Pride, on Twitter, February 2016.

Eileen Ward- equal pay pioneer

It is with great sadness that we report the death of Sis. Eileen Ward, who had been a Shop Steward and convener for nearly two decades at Trico Folberth at Brentford, Middlesex (West London District). Thousands will remember her from the historic 23 week Equal Pay Strike in 1976, which achieved total victory with full Equal Pay. Eileen was a pillar of strength and an example to all, both during and since the dispute. She organised a team of mainly women who built up Union to 100% membership. No mean achievement in a multi-racial factory of over a 1000 workers. In addition to all this, she still found time to sit on the West London District Committee for a number of years and in the last couple of years she became Branch Secretary of the Brentford Branch. At all time she was given 100% support from her husband, George, and her children. Eileen always led from the front and was a credit to our Union and on behalf of our Union and we wish to express our appreciation for all the help and support that Eileen gave to all in need of assistance. She will be greatly missed, not only in the factory but throughout the West London District. Our deepest condolences to her family. She will not be forgotten!

Eileen Ward obituary in AEU journal, October 1990

ABBREVIATIONS

ACAS Arbitration, Conciliation and Advisory Service. In 1896 the government launched a voluntary conciliation and arbitration service which also gave free advice to employers and unions on industrial relations and personnel problems. It was separated from government control in 1975 and then in 1976 made a statutory body by the Employment Protection Act 1975.

Following the Grunwick dispute for trade union recognition ACAS ceased to have a statutory role in recognition cases and in 1993 its statutory duty to promote collective bargaining was removed.

Its role has reduced with the decline in trade union membership and the contraction of industries and services covered by collective bargaining agreements.

APEX Association of Professional, Executive and Clerical Staff. APEX originated from the National Union of Clerks or Clerks' Union formed in 1890 and the Association of Shorthand Writers and Typists which started in 1903. After various name changes and an amalgamation, the Clerical and Administrative Workers' Union was formed in 1941 which changed its name to APEX in 1972.

Perhaps it is most remembered for its association with the Grunwick strike after the strikers made it their union of choice and Roy Grantham, as General Secretary, became embroiled in endless legal processes with Grunwick's George Ward.

In 1989 APEX merged with the GMB.

ASTMS Association of Scientific, Technical and Managerial Staffs. This was created in 1969 when ASSET merged with AScW. By the end of 1970 Clive Jenkins had become sole

General Secretary.

In 1988 ASTMS merged with TASS to form MSF and then amalgamated with the AEEU in 2002 to form AMICUS. It is now part of Unite.

AUEW Amalgamated Union of Engineering Workers. There are records of engineering societies going back to the early nineteenth century but they were banned by law until 1824.

The ASE, Amalgamated Society of Engineers, was formed in 1851. It expanded into the AEU, Amalgamated Engineering Union, in 1920 after absorbing nine craft unions in the industry.

The AEU did not admit women to membership until 1943 during the Second World War when the pressure to do so became overwhelming. 100,000 women joined almost immediately.

A further merger with the foundry workers led to the union becoming the AUEFW in 1967 and then the AUEW in 1971 when it merged with DATA, the Draughtsmen and Allied Technicians' Association. DATA then became AUEW-TASS and, from 1974, was led by Ken Gill. In 1988 TASS left the AUEW to merge with white-collar union ASTMS led by Clive Jenkins to form MSF.

At this time the AUEW returned to the AEU name. In 1992 the AEU merged with the electricians and plumbing union EEPTU to form the AEEU.

AMICUS was formed in 2001 as a result of a merger between the AEEU and MSF and later with the TGWU to form Unite in 2007. Unite is currently the largest trade union in Britain.

CPSA Civil and Public Services Association. The union was originally called the Civil Service Clerical Association (CSCA) and formed in 1921 after an amalgamation.

In 1969 the union renamed itself the CPSA. In 1998 the CPSA merged with the Public Services, Tax and Commercial Services Union to form the Public and Commercial Services Union (PCS). Since 2000 Mark Serwotka has been the elected General Secretary.

CSEU Confederation of Shipbuilding and Engineering Unions. The CSEU was founded in 1890 by small craft unions such as the Federation of Engineering and Shipbuilding Trades, primarily in response to the employers forming their own federation. It began to concentrate on making national agreements for the engineering and shipbuilding industries. It adopted its current name in 1936. With the decline in trade union membership and loss of our industrial and manufacturing base in Britain the organisation is now less prominent. It currently has six trade unions affiliated.

EOC Equal Opportunities Commission. The EOC was set up under the Sex Discrimination Act 1975 and had statutory powers to help enforce this Act, the Equal Pay Act 1970 and other gender equality legislation. In 2007 it became part of a new single equality body, the Equality and Human Rights Commission, arising from the Equality Act 2006.

EPA Equal Pay Act 1970. See Appendix for more details about the history of the struggle for equal pay in Britain.

GLATC Greater London Association of Trades Councils. GLATC was the successor body to the London Trades Council which was founded in 1860.

It is now called GLATUC and is the largest County Association of Trades Union Councils in the UK and covers the Greater London area. It is part of the TUC.

GLATUC is the trade union body for London. It is made up of delegates from the trade union councils covering the thirty-one London boroughs. It fits into the TUC national structure through the Southern and Eastern Region of the TUC (SERTUC).

It aims to be the co-ordinating body for rank and file trade union action across London and its trades councils.

GMWU General and Municipal Workers Union. Will Thorne, the outstanding trade unionist and Labour movement leader, helped found a national gasworkers' union in 1889 and led the fight for the eight-hour day won that year. The GMWU was formed in 1924 as a result of a series of mergers. Following further mergers, the union officially adopted its current name GMB in 1987 although it has used the abbreviation GMB since 1982. Its full name is General, Municipal, Boilermakers and Allied Trade Union.

ILO International Labour Organisation. The ILO was founded in 1919 in the wake of the destruction of the First World War as an agency of the League of Nations to pursue a vision based on the premise that universal lasting peace can be established only if it is based on social justice. The ILO became the first specialised agency of the UN in 1946.

NALGO National and Local Government Officers Association. The union mostly represented local government white-collar workers. It was formed in 1905 as the National Association of Local Government Officers but changed its full name in 1952 while retaining its acronym NALGO. By 1977 it was the largest UK public sector trade union with over 700,000 members. NALGO merged with NUPE (National Union of Public Employees) and COHSE (Confederation of Health Service Employees) in 1993 to form UNISON.

NUJ The NUJ is the largest trade union of journalists in the UK representing about 38,000 members. It was formed in 1907. It is mainly concerned with members' pay and conditions of work but this includes professional ethics and a substantial part of the NUJ's work concerns professional practice and ethics.

Its current General Secretary is Michelle Stanistreet, the first woman to hold this post in the NUJ's history.

RMT National Union of Rail, Maritime and Transport Workers was formed in 1990 as a result of a merger of the NUR and NUS. The RMT places emphasis on being a specialist Transport Union.

Under the charismatic leadership of Bob Crow, its membership rose from 57,000 in 2002 to over 80,000 in 2015.

Unite the Union See under AUEW for details of its formation. Unite is Britain's biggest union with approximately 1.42 million members.

WWC Working Women's Charter. The WWC was launched by the London Trades Council in 1974 but was given force by local charter campaign groups around the country. It tried to link trade unionism to feminism and pledged to agitate and organise to achieve its 10-point charter for women. This included the rate for the job, equal opportunities, equal education and training, removal of legal impediments to equality, improved provision of local authority day nurseries, and 18-week maternity leave with full pay. The campaign was active during the 1970s and 1980s.

APPENDIX
OF DOCUMENTS NOT INCLUDED IN THE TEXT

The Trico strike donation book was lost when the Trico factory in Brentford was demolished. On the following pages are the only remaining records of the magnificent support the strikers received.

BALANCE SHEET

Income	£	Expenditure	£
Receipts (donations, etc.)	27,000.15	Payments (hardship, etc.)	29,051.23
District Levy	6,822.45	Bad cheques	29.50
Transfer from Branch	600.00	Transfer to Strike fund	1,840.00
Trico AUEW Levy	222.00	Repaid to Branch	600.00
		Transfer to levy	300.00
		Transfer to D.C. fund	600.00
		Balance in Hand	2,223.87
	34,644.60		34,644.60
Cumulative surplus (Misc. collections)	965.31		
Balance Cash Book	1,258.56	Total Balance in Hand	2,223.87
	2,223.87		2,223.87

Trico Strike Fund Balance Sheet, November 1976

SOLIDARITY

Our delegation to the Kent Miners last Friday returned with a cheque for £200. The miners have also agreed to a levy on every member to guarentee weekly funds. We salute their unselfish support. It will not be forgotten!

Further examples of recent large donations are as follows; £200 from the King Street (Birmingham) Shop Stewards, £125 from the Magnatex Joint Shop Stewards, £58 from Park Royal Vehicles, £35 from the APEX Great West Road Branch, £30 from the BSC Davy Ashmore, £43.20 from the AUEW Yeading Lane Branch, £34.70 from Hoovers, £50.00 from the Rolls Royce/ Mulliner Park Wards Joint Shop Stewards Committee, £33.00 from the Hammersmith Working Womens Charter Campaign and £50.00 from the Hammersmith Branch of NALGO.

Strike Bulletin 15 July

WITH A LITTLE HELP FROM OUR FRIENDS

The Trade Union movement throughout the country is responding to our cause. We especially thank all those loyal Trade Unionists who rush to our aid at any time of the day or night on the picket line. Again, we list a few examples in the past week of donations to the strike fund; £50.00 from ASTMS West London Branch, £35.00 from ASTMS TRICO-Folberth, £214.00 from AUEW/TASS Designs Leighrell Ltd., £50.00 from Vehicle Builders, Longbourne, Chertsey, £20.00 from AUEW Fleet Street Branch, £80.00 from Magnatex, £10.00 from Harrow Trades Council, £45.00 from NATSOPA Press Association Clerical Chapel, £72.75 from Park Royal Vehicles, £50.00 from Eaton Ltd., Basingstoke, £30.00 from NUJ St. James Press Chapel, £34.50 from BCC Ltd., £12.73 from COHSE St. Bernards Hospital and £35.60 from Crossfield Electronics.

Strike Bulletin 29 July

THE TRADE UNION MOVEMENT STANDS WITH US

Many thanks once again to all those who have donated to the Strike Appeal so magnificently. Some examples from those received last week are as follows; £50.00 from the AUEW Southall District Committee, £50.00 from the Ealing and Southall Labour Party, £50.00 from Mrs. Z. Nittim, a patient in University College Hospital, £25.00 from Everett Medical Products, £53.00 from AEC in Southall, £7.75 from the TASS members in TRICO, £54.00 from the Time Out Strike Fund, £16.50 from Heinz in Harlesden, £70.00 from NATTKE Thames TV at Teddington, £30.00 from the Central London Branch of the Musicians Union, £20.00 from the UCATT Chiswick Branch, £15.80 from the teachers and pupils of the Faraday High School, £100.00 from OI/524 TGWU/ACTS, £30.31 from EMI Hayes, £24.00 from the TUC Office Staff, £5.00 from Sid Bidwell, MP, £40.75 from SULZER Bros. of Leeds, £20.00 from Wolf Electric AUEW, £50.00 from Davy United of Sheffield, £20.00 from the National Assembly of Women and £20.00 from British Steel of Rotheram. WE CANNOT THANK YOU ENOUGH FOR YOUR HELP!

Strike Bulletin 6 August

APPENDIX | 219

The day previous, Tuesday, 10th. August, a delegation visited South Wales and, in the evening, spoke to and gained the support of the local District Committee of the AUEW. We thank them and all those who have continued to donate so generously. The past week's post has included, amongst many others, the following donations: £100 from the British Leylands Convenors' meeting, £50 from the London Co-Operative Society Political Committee, £50 from the TGWU at EMI in Hayes, £30 from the ASTMS at Dominion House, EC1, £26.50 from New World Gas Spares Joint Shop Stewards, £25 each from the Hackney and Lewisham Branches of NALGO, £20 from the British Airways Overseas Division, £15.75 from Lyons Maid, Greenford, £15.25 from HM Customs and Excise CPSA, £15.15 from Walls Meat Co., Southall, £25 from an ex-TRICO worker now living abroad, £100 from a couple living in Holland Road, W14, and £20 from TGWU Express Dairies Cricklewood Branch.

Strike Bulletin 12 August

FINANCIAL SUPPORT

We have continued to receive magnificent support from all over the country. The following are just a few of the donations that we have been sent in the past week; £150 from BOAC Heathrow AUEW, £100 from Parsons Newcastle TASS, £70 from NALGO Hamilton Training Course, £50 from Leyland Shop Stewards Committee, Birmingham, £50 from Bathgate Shop Stewards Committee, West Lothian, £50 from Reyrolle Shop Stewards Committee, Tyne and Weir, £30 from Frigidaire Shop Stewards Committee, £25 from British Leylands Coventry Engines, £15 from Associated Automation Joint Shop Stewards Committee and £32 from the ASTMS members in TRICO.

Strike Bulletin 20 August

Money continues to flow in. The following are just a few examples of what we have received in the past week; £464 from Martin Bakers in Denham, £66.50 from AEC Joint Shop Stewards Committee (they have now donated a total of £616), £34.55 from UCATT Battersea, £20.40 from Walls Meat TGWU, £25.00 from the Sheffield District Committee of the AUEW, £40 from the Doncaster Sheffield Joint Shop Stewards Committee, Labour Party Transport House members donated £15, £56.91 from a collection taken by the Shop Stewards Committee at McVities and Price, Harlesden, £32.50 from the GMWU Wandsworth and District Branch, £50 from NATSOPA Joint Branches, London, £63.66 from the Union of Post Office Workers London Overseas Telephone Branch, £25 from the British Leyland Joint Shop Stewards Committee, Wellingborough, £44 from Park Royal Vehicles, £30 from Firth Brown, £50 from Stuart Plastics Croydon Joint Shop Stewards Committee and £50 from Shardlows, Sheffield.

Strike Bulletin 25 August

We continue to receive magnificent financial support but, in the fourth month of our strike, we need even more. Some examples of donations in the past week are as follows; £50 from the British Leyland Preston Joint Works Committee, £25 from a pensioner, Miss Harris, £20 from Harrow Trades Council, £24 from Glacier Metals Works Committee, £25 from NALGO Hammersmith Hospital, £100 from Davy United JSSC Sheffield, £50 from Yarrow JSSC Glasgow, £25 from Albion Motors JSSC Glasgow, £25 Kilmarnock Trades Council, £100 from Watneys Isleworth, £25 each from the Magazine and Books Branches of the NUJ, £60 from the Stratford Depot collections, including from the ASLEF Branch, £40 from Magnatex JSSC and £50 from Cannon JSSC Wolverhampton. OUR THANKS TO THEM ALL!

Strike Bulletin 3 September

THANKS TO OUR FRIENDS

The following are just a few examples of what we have received in the past week; £50 from Eatons Basingstoke JSSC, £50 from Rolls Royce Harrow, £25 from the Merthyr District AUEW, £118 from a factory collection at Heniz in Brent organised by the TGWU, £22.50 from AEC Southall, £25 from FORD Langley JSSC, £50 from Leyland Lancs, £20 from the Morning Star, £20 from the TGWU Selly Oak Branch Birmingham, £20 from AUEW/TASS No 3 Divisional Council, £20 from the London North District of the AUEW, £77 from Earlsfield Womens Lib, £100 from Ambrose Shardlow JSSC Sheffield, £209.11 from the CAV Acton Dayshift and £56.10 from the CAV Nightshift.

Strike Bulletin 10 September

IN THE LAST WEEK...

we have received the following magnificent donations, amongst many others, although we must stress the urgent and continuing need for the Trade Union movement to redouble its efforts in our support; £39.79 from a collection taken at the Shop Stewards Quarterly meeting of the Southall District Committee of the AUEW, £22.50 from Mercury Display Ltd Wandsworth, £100.00 from LUCAS Great King Street Shop Stewards Committee Birmingham, £44.00 from Park Royal Vehicles JSSC, £58.69 from Transport House TGWU Branch, £25.00 from British Leyland UK Morris Engineers Coventry, £25 from Mollins AUEW Shop Stewards Committee, £25 from Goodyear Maintenance Fund Wolverhampton, £50 from Davy United JSSC Sheffield, £25 from British Airways Laundry Section and £37 from the Pathway Further Education Centre in Southall. Finally, at a social organised in our benefit by 01/724 TGWU (Kilburn), £63 was raised. As we have said so many times, there are not words to thank you all enough.

Strike Bulletin 16 September

IN THE PAST WEEK...

we have received so many donations that we can only record a few of them at this stage. However, we wish to make it clear that, after 18 weeks, we are paying out a great deal of money in hardship payments and we need every penny that we can get. Thanks to the following:

£81.30 from Acton Works AUEW
£37.00 from Fidelity Radio, NW10
£50.00 from Magnatex JSSC
£50.00 from British Leyland Cowley
£29.40 from collection at Fords Langley
£60.00 from the Sheet Metal Workers at London Airport
£20.00 from NUPE South West Middx Group Hospital Branch
£43.40 from the AUEW Oxford District Shop Stewards Quarterly
£100.0 from TGWU 01/1530-05
£50.00 from ASTMS Paddington Branch
£46.50 from British Leyland Body Plant AUEW
£50.00 from ASTMS West End Branch
£24.39 from Peckham Labour Party
£31.00 from Rotaprint
£21.00 collection from the September meeting of the GLATC
£20.00 from the POEU NW London Branch
£30.00 from the Glacier Metals JSSC
£23.80 from the NUT Wandsworth
£120.70 from a collection taken by the Young Liberals at the Liberal Party Annual Conference
£35.00 from the Dockers in the Royal Group
£71.00 from the Pontins Site Fund Levy
£17.50 from the NUJ Chapel at the Evening Mail

Two things - first, please redouble your efforts and, second, when we have won, we will produce a full list of all those who have donated so generously. THANKS ONCE AGAIN!

Strike Bulletin 23 September

UNITY IS STRENGTH

Once again, there are'nt words to thank you enough for your continuing magnificent financial support. As the weeks go by, we need your help more than ever. WE NEED TO RAISE £4,000 PER WEEK - PLEASE KEEP YOUR EFFORTS UP. The following are some of the contributions that we have received in the past two weeks:

£200 from NALGO Hammersmith Branch
£200 from CPSA National Executive Committee
£76.30 from Hawker Siddeley JSSC
£50.00 from Camden Trades Council
£57.00 from Southwark Trades Council
£367.50 from levy at Lyons Greenford
£69.00 and £63.00 from Pontins Site levy
£92.15 from Scotsoun Marine JSSC
£30.00 from AUEW Lansing Bagnall
£30.00 from Witney and District Trades Council
£50.00 from Davy United JSSC
£25.00 from Glacier Metals JSSC
£30.00 from NATKE ATV Studio Borehamwood
£50.00 from Burroughs JSSC Scotland
£50.00 from Massey Ferguson JSSC
£35.00 from Feltham and Heston Labour Party
£20.00 from Rolls Royce JSSC Hillington
£100.00 from British Airways European Division
£25.00 from GEC Sheffield JSSC
£50.00 from Magnatex JSSC
£20.00 from COHSE St Thomas Hospital
£30.00 from NUJ St James Press
£32.72 from Gestetner SSC
£50.00 from Western International Market Southall
£20.18 from Sikh Temple Southall
£69.30 from LPYS meeting at Blackpool Conference

plus from socials:

£45.00 from "Jam Today" and £75.00 from the Camden Cuts Campaign (EGA Benefit)

Strike Bulletin 8 October

INDEX

Abbreviations, 213-16
Acton Works, London Underground, 26-7, 51, 73, 118, 138, 139
airport workers, 48, 133
Aiston, Betty (leading shop steward), 25, 31, 37*i*, 48, 52*i*, 53, 78, 88, 113, 142*i*, 162*i*
   delegations, 99, 101, 115-16
   AUEW meeting 27 May, 39
   on financial hardship and inequality, 114-15
   on TUC lobby, 134
   Trico names as co respondent, 71
Alibhai Brown, Yasmin, 186-7
Allen, Pete (TGWU), and Hull women fish packers, 204-5
Amalgamated Society of Engineers (ASE), 194, 196
Amalgamated Union of Engineering Workers (AUEW/AEU), xii-xiii, 26-7, 197, 202, 214
   ACAS meetings on Trico offers, 33-4, 39-40, 67-71, 148-51
      Trico accepts AUEW/EEF equal pay formula, 155, 157, 160, 189
   and Industrial Tribunal
      first ever TU boycott, 50, 104-8, 175, 176
   AUEW-TASS, 10, 51, 73
   Hunt, Judith, national women's organiser, 135, 139, 201

   National Executive, 48-9, 118, 133, 141, 143
   Southall District Committee, 39, 51, 61*i*, 68*i*, 95-8, 135*i*, 153, 169, 175
      'flying pickets', 61
      on wipers boycott, 151
      votes in strike pay levy, 99
   Trico factory AUEW, 10, 22-3, 28-9, 140, 153, 189
      and pay rates, 14-15
      apologies from scab hauliers, 90
American style industrial practices, 10, 60, 135
   picket busting, 95, 104, 175
   and UK industrial unrest, 7, 10
Anders, Andy, Strike Committee, 53
Angela (striker), xvii, 111*i*
APEX, 10, 213
Arab, Rosy, 70*i*
Arab, Susy, 69*i*, 70*i*
Arbitration Conciliation and Advisory Services (ACAS), 213
   Grunwick and, 179
   Trico and, 33-4, 39-40, 67-71, 150
      meetings, 39-40, 67-71, 148, 150-1
      Trico accepts AUEW/EEF equal pay formula, 155
Ashdown Sharp, Patricia, on EPA decision, 202
Ashley, Mike, (Sports Direct), 185
ASTMS, 10, 89, 102-3, 110, 213-14

Atkins, Sidney (Trico works manager), 7, 15, 34, 50, 51, 79, 82, 105, 143, 148-51

Bakewell, Joan, 43, 169*i*
Banister, Bob, anecdotes, 5, 12, 24, 77-8, 102-3, 145, 164
Barnard, Catherine, on Equality Act 2010, 208-9
BBC news, 84, 97
Bedwell v Hellerman Deutsch, 200-1
Belt and Braces Roadshow, 146
Benn, Tony, 153
Besant, Annie, 195
Bidwell, Sydney MP, 95, 153, 180
Big Flame, 43
Birch, Reg, 48, 142*i*, 143, 150
Birmingham City Council employees, 207-8
Birmingham delegation, 99, 153
Black, Clementina, TUC equal pay motion 1888, 195-6
blacklists regulations 2010, 184
Bodilly, Sir Jocelyn, 105-6
Booth, Albert MP, 95, 150, 153
Boston, Sarah, 193-4, 205
Boyd, John, 150, 151
Bracher, John, support, 65*i*, 98, 118
Braithwaite, Loretta, 9, 12, 47*i*, 75-6, 120
Braithwaite, Reggie, 12
Brent Law Centre, 98, 144
Brent Trades Council, 51, 73, 76, 98
Brent Working Women's Charter, 73, 110, 116*i*, 186
Brentford, Police Station, protest delegation to, 66, 66*i*
Brentford & Chiswick Times, hostility, 41, 42, 104, 127, 130, 150, 189
Brighton Trades Council, 146
Brighton, TUC lobby, 48, 134-5, 135*i*, 138-41
British Airways, 51, 73, 185

British European Airways shop stewards, 110
British Leyland, 99, 133, 153
Broadside Mobile Workers Theatre, 146, 147*i*
Brooks, George, 113
Brunel University, 146
Bryant & May strike 1888, 193, 195, 206
building workers, imprisoned, 184
Bunting, Bob, 74*i*, 161-2
Butler, Roger, xiii, 22-3, 26, 35, 59, 98, 137, 148, 150, 168*i*
 and strikers, 35, 39-41, 89, 106, 110-11, 143, 153-5
 and scab lorries, 90, 92
 at victory, 156-7, 157*i*, 161, 162*i*, 163, 163*i*

Callaghan, James, government, 18*n*, 103, 153, 179, 189
Cameron, David, government, Ministry for Women and Equalities, 210
Campbell, Bobby, 146
Carlisle NHS equal pay, Unison success, 207
Carty, John, 100, 118
Case, Mick, 113, 133-4
Castle, Barbara MP, Equal Pay Act 1970, 199
Certification Officer (CO), 2016 Act powers, 184
'Champion', 36*i*
Chandler, Ivy, 66*i*, 90, 91*i*, 109*i*
Chichester Trades Council, 146
Choulerton, Len, 52*i*
Chrysler Linwood, 100, 118
Claimants' Union, Handbook for Strikers, 62, 64*i*
Clark, Win, 58*i*, 66*i*
Clyde women, First World War equal pay, 196

228 | INDEX

Confederation of British Industry (CBI) and Trico, 154
Confederation of Shipbuilding and Engineering Unions (CSEU), 22, 214-15
Connors, John, 47*i*
Cook, Don, 26
Cook, Rosie, 74*i*
Cooke, G.B. (Trico director), 7, 10
Coomber, Derek, exposes scab hauliers, 92
Corbyn, Jeremy, 178, 190
Coventry delegation, 101
CPSA, 153, 214
Craven, Peter, 66*i*, 100, 117
Crawley Trades Council, 146
Cross, Stefan (solicitor) equal pay claims, 206
Crow, Bob (RMT), 191

Dagenham women sewing machinists (1968 & 1984), 14, 190, 198-9, 204-5
Daily Express 'winter of discontent', 189
Daily Mail, 134
Daily Mirror, 43, 113
Davis, David MP, 183
Davis, Izzy, anecdotes, 123-4, 167
Davis, Mary, on EPA 1970, 199-200
Dawes, May, 192*i*
Deloitte, 210
Dempsey, Mary, 58*i*, 88, 90, 91*i*
Desai, Jayaban, 178
DHSS
  and gender inequality, 114-15
  and strikers' financial hardship, 62-3
Dimbleby, David, 41*n*
dockers and Trico boycott, 48, 118
donations, 42, 119, 145*i*, 153, 217-23
Dromey, Jack, later MP, 88, 98, 144, 168*i*
Durkin, Tom, 98, 168*i*, 169, 179-80

Bravery and Betrayal, 83*n*
Duvalls, 102

Ealing DHSS, 62
Ealing Gazette, 112
Ealing North Constituency Labour Party, picketing, 73
Ealing Technical College, 146
Ealing Trades Council, 51
Eastbourne Trades Council, 146
Edinburgh Council equal pay claims, Unison win, 208
Electrolux women (1975-6), 108, 202-3
Emmy (striker), 58*i*
Employment Acts, 1980s, 90*n*
Employment Appeal Tribunal, and Electrolux, 203
employment rights, 175, 181-5, 193-201, 209-10
Engineering Employers Federation, 11, 50, 111, 148, 155, 180
Engineering Voice (Broad Left), meeting, 100, 117, 118
Equal Opportunities Commission (EOC), 141, 203, 215
Equal Pay Act 1970 (EPA), 11, 14-15, 152-3, 199-200, 215
  1983 amendment, 198-209
  European Commission and, 141, 203-4
  implementation/avoidance, 33-4, 50, 175, 198-205, 207-8
  Industrial Tribunal and, 105-8
equal pay campaign, 196-210
equal pay issues, 16-17, 175, 181, 209-11
Equality Act 2010, 209-11
Evening Mail, 41, 43*i*, 106
Evening Standard, 103

Farmer, Peggy, 38*i*, 108*i*, 117-18, 136-7

anecdotes, 5, 8, 17, 25, 31, 77, 100-1, 108, 132
financial hardship, 61, 62-3, 64, 114-15, 120-4
Financial Times, 43, 127
Firestones, 101, 102, 115
First World War, equal pay successes, 196
Fitzgerald, Ann, 47*i*, 52*i*, 102, 110*i*, 115
 anecdotes, 5-6, 19-20, 77, 96, 120, 129, 131, 164
'flexibility', male, and pay rates, 15, 106, 148-9, 151, 201
flying pickets, 61-2, 73
Ford, 110, 133
 Dagenham women sewing machinists (1968 & 1984), 14, 190, 198-9, 204-5
Fowler, Eileen, 58*i*
Freedom Association (NAFF), supports Grunwick, 179-80
Freighting World, exposes scab hauliers, 92
Fryer, John, 43
Fudge, Eric, 65*i*
 anecdotes, 6, 16-17, 19, 25, 30, 34, 85, 97, 102, 107, 121, 126, 129, 137, 164, 172

Gay Socialists, picketing, 73
gender inequality and financial hardship, 114-15, 210
 see also equal pay headings
Gender Equality Duty 2007, 206
General and Municipal Workers' Union (GMWU), Trico membership, 10, 215
General Express Services, apologises to AUEW, 90-1, 92
General Motors, and UK industrial unrest, 7
Gibbard, Arthur (AUEW), 40, 49, 52*i*, 95-6
Gill, Ken (AUEW TASS), 171

Glacier Metals, 51, 73, 118
Glasgow, 100, 117
GMB, and equal pay claims, 206, 208
Golden Mile, 3, 76
Gorst, John MP, supports Grunwick, 179
Grand National Consolidated Trade Union (GNCTU) 1834, 193-4
Gray, Sandra (Ward), 13, 121, 137, 192*i*
Great Dock Strike 1889, 195
Greater London Association of Trades Councils (GLATC/GLATUC), 98, 134, 154, 215
 victory celebration, 163, 169, 171, 171*i*
Green, Phyllis, 72, 115
 anecdotes, 9, 17, 19, 24, 31, 34, 44, 49, 78, 80, 97, 101, 121-3, 129, 136-7, 140, 166-7
Greenwich Trades Council, 101
Griffin, Con (EEF), asks for formula, 155
Griffin pub (strike HQ), 43*i*, 44, 49, 53, 121
Groves, Sally, 6, 31, 43*i*, 44, 53, 65, 66*i*, 142*i*, 153, 192*i*
 and Sheffield AUEW, 116
 and Strike Bulletins, 144
 Labour Party Conference, 103
 letter in *Middlesex Chronicle*, 141
 on claiming DHSS benefits, 62-3
 on Industrial Tribunal, 106, 50
 pursuing convoy, 86-7
 Trico names as co-respondent, 71
 tries to stop convoy lorry, 84, 84*i*
Grunwick strike, 76, 169, 177, 179
 and ACAS, 179
 contrast with Trico, 177-80
 police and, 83*n*
 postal workers boycott, 179
Guardian, The 43

230 | INDEX

Halpin, Kelvin, and Wales delegation, 99
Hammersmith Council, 169
Hammersmith Trades Council, 169
Hammersmith Labour Party, 169
Hammersmith Working Women's Charter, 119, 146
Hampton, Sir Philip (GlaxoSmithKline), 210
Harman, Harriet, later MP, 98, 210
Harroway, Sid, 113
Harvey, Monica, 36*i*, 100-1, 162-3, 117, 192*i*
Hattersley, Roy MP, 153
haulage firms
  regular, respect picket line, 29
  strike breaking, midnight convoys, 59-61, 64-6, 71-3, 79-93
    convoy turned away 27 July, 79-81, 81*i*
  deny involvement, 90-2
Hayhoe, Barney MP, on plight of scabs, 150-1
Healey, Denis MP, 18*n*
Heath government, and rampant inflation, 188
Hewland, Helen, 106
Hoover, 102
Hounslow DHSS, calls police, 62-3
Hounslow Evening Mail, 127
Hounslow Trades Council, 48, 51, 98, 144, 154
Housing Act 2016, 190
Hull women fish packers, EPA success, 204-5
Humphreys, Betty, 38*i*, 58*i*, 66*i*, 109*i*, 113, 162*i*, 192*i*
Humphries, Jean, picketing, 73
Hunt, Judith, TASS, 135, 139, 201
Hutchinson, Ann, Electrolux, 203

Industrial Tribunal, 104-9, 152, 201
  and Equal Pay Act, 105-8

'flexibility', male, and pay rates, 15, 106, 148-9, 151, 201
and Trico
  14 July, 50, 67-71, 148, 201
  first ever TU boycott, 175, 176
Conservatives prohibitive charges for, 176
Institute for Fiscal Studies, on gender pay gap, 210
Institute of Employment Rights, 183
International Labour Organisation (ILO), 215
  Committee of Experts, on TU Act 2016, 182
  Convention 100, 88, 138, 141, 198, 204
International Metalworkers Federation, and wipers boycott, 151-2
Inwood, John, 22-3, 25, 29, 39, 53, 77, 88, 157*i*, 162*i*
  on Tribunal, 108
  on Trico offer, 149
  on Trico women workers, achievement, xi-xiii
Irish Times, 154

Jameson, Derek, on 'winter of discontent', 189
Jenkins, Roy, Home Secretary, 95
Jinks, George, 53, 99, 100-1, 117
Jones, Carolyn, on TU Act 2016, 183
Jones, John McKinsie, 184

Kemp, Trico lawyer, 105
Kent miners, 118
Kerr, Russell MP, 63
Kerr, Sandra, 146
King, Lou, 70*i*, 95
Kraft Cheese factory, women lose case, 141

Labour governments, 180, 185
    capitulate over Grunwick, 179
    election programme, and EPA, 108
    manifesto 1964, 198
Labour Party, 18, 190
    and Trico, 153, 190
Labour Weekly, 88
Le Monde, 44
Leeds delegation, 153
Leicester Council for Voluntary
    Service, EPA decision, 202
Leigh Day & Co (solicitor), and
    Birmingham claim, 207-8
Lesbians and Gays Support the Miners,
    73n
Lewis, Marie, on police, 95
Liberty, on 2016 TU Act secondary
    legislation, 184-5
Lockwood, Betty, and Electrolux
    investigation, 203
Lodges of Industrious Females, 193
London Transport Acton Works, 26-7,
    51, 73, 118, 138, 139
London Underground, First World
    War equal pay, 196
Long, Peggy, anecdote, 115

Macarthur, Mary, National Federation
    of Women Workers, 196
MacLaughlin, Bill (Mac), xiii, 25, 52,
    52*i*, 69*i*, 98, 113, 148, 150, 162,
    162*i*
    all wipers boycott, 134
    and ACAS, 67, 69
    equal pay formula, 155
    on layoffs, 125, 127
    on strikers' holiday pay, 111
    on Trico management, 143
    on Trico offers, 149-50, 151
    on Trico and picket, 88
Made in Dagenham (film), 198
Magnatex, 51, 73, 118
Manchester, fundraising, 102

Marx, Eleanor, 194
Matchwomen's strike 1888, 193, 195,
    206
McCarthyite period, 144
Medhurst, John, on 'winter of discontent', 189
media, right wing, 181, 188, 189
    and Grunwick, 179
    Trico and, 59, 60
    see also press
men
    'flexibility', and pay rates, 15, 106,
    148-9, 151, 201
    Trico
        in support, 28-9, 31, 49
        transferred from night shift, pay,
        14-15, 16-17, 18, 22
        wage reductions, 200-1
Merritt, Vernon, 86-7, 88, 103, 144,
    153
Middlesex Chronicle, 108, 141
Middleton, Lucy, Women in the
    Labour Movement, 153
migrant community, 177, 180, 182
Militant, 43
Millican, Arthur, 100, 117
miners, 118, 187
Ministry for Women and Equalities,
    210
Mitchell, Bob, 81*i*, 110*i*, 153
    anecdotes, 6, 13, 17, 20, 27, 31, 76,
    80, 85, 96, 103, 107, 116, 126, 128-9,
    131, 137, 140, 164-5, 172-3
Molloy, William MP, 154
Moorehead, Caroline, 43-4
Morning Star, 43, 95, 106, 152, 160-1
Murdoch, Rupert, 43
Murray, Mick, 154

NALGO, donations, 110, 153, 216
Nation Union of Railwaymen, 196
National Association for Freedom
    (NAFF), supports Grunwick, 179-80

232 | INDEX

National Day of Action on Unemployment, 22
National Federation of Women Civil Servants, 197
National Federation of Women Workers, 196
National Front, 40, 127
National Health Service (NHS), 206-7
National Joint Action Campaign for Women's Equal Rights, 14, 199
National Union of Journalists (NUJ), 42, 41n, 216
National Union of Women Teachers, 197
New Unionism campaign (TUC), 195, 206
Newcastle AUEW, 115-16
Newsline, 43, 108
North Lanarkshire Council settlements, 208
North, Stella, 47i, 110i, 159i
Northampton, pursuing convoy to, 86-7, 88
Northampton Post, 87
Northfield Women's Liberation, 119
NUPE member arrested 29 July, 84, 88

O'Hagan, Ellie Mae, 184, 185
O'Neill, John (Big John), 53, 79, 101, 154
Orme, Stan MP, 63
Oshei, John R. (Trico founder), 10n
Oshei, R.J., (Trico Corp president), 10
Oxford delegation, 153

Pamela (striker), 45i
Parrish, Lisa, 119
Passingham, Bernie, on Dagenham grading, 198-9
Pavitt, Laurie MP, on Grunwick, 178
People's Assembly movement, 190

Phoenix Transport visit, 91i
picket lines
  supervision provisions, TU Act 2016, 183-4
  Trico *see* Trico women's strike
Pike, Alan, 43
Pinner, Frances, 38i, 108i
Pirate Jenny Theatre Company, 57n, 116
police
  and Grunwick dispute, 83n, 178
  and picket supervisor information, 184
  and Trico strike breaking, 59-60, 65-6, 95, 113, 152
    and benefits claimants, 63
    break up picket, 29 July, 82-4, 88-9, 95-7
    harass Southall AEUW dance, 153-4
    surveillance suspected, 71, 72
  Special Patrol Group, violence, 178
police station, protest delegation to, 66, 66i
Pontypool, Trico relocation, 3
Porter, Olga, 108-9
postal workers, boycott Grunwick post, 179
Pound, Steve, later MP, picketing, 73
press, 44
  and scab lorries, 90, 92
  attitudes to strike, 40-1, 42-4, 181
  photographers attend 26 May meeting, 35
  see also media
Prestatyn building workers, 118
Prior, Jim MP, 150
public services, 188, 209-10
  civil servants (non industrial), equal pay 1955, 197-8
  cuts, campaigns against, 190
  Gender Equality Duty 2007, 206
  'important', TU Act 2016 and, 182

INDEX | 233

Rabstein, Martin, on police and strikers, 95
Racal AUEW stewards, 110
Rainer, Peter, Phoenix Transport, 91*i*
Ranton Plastics, 51
Raw, Louise, 176
    on Bryant & May strike 1888, 195-6
    on TU leaderships and women, 205-6
Rees, Merlyn MP, 154, 203
Reid, Jimmy, 100-1, 117, 118
Reidford, John, 100, 117
Reyrolle Parsons Ltd, EPA decision, 202
Richardson, Jo MP, 152-3, 170*i*
Right to Work marchers, 103
Ritchie, Jamie, support, 98
RMT, 191, 216
Roberts, ACAS Conciliation Officer, 67
Robinson, Derek, 103
Robinson, Monica, Strike Committee, 53
Rose (striker), 45*i*
Rowlands, Peter, 18 October, 168*i*
Rowntree Mackintosh, EPA decision, 202
Royal College of Nursing, and equal pay claims, 206
Royal Commission on Equal Pay, Second World War, 197
Royal Group dockers, 118

Scanlon, Hugh, 103, 127, 130
Scarman Court of Inquiry, Grunwick, 179
Scotland delegation, 100-1
Scotstoun Marine, 117
Seath, Joyce, 38*i*, 91*i*
Second World War, women join TUs, 197
Sex Disqualification (Removal) Act 1919, 197

Sheffield, 118
    AUEW, 116
    Trades Council, 101, 116
Sheldrick, Paul (arrested picket), 84, 174*i*
Sheldrick, Roy, 8, 174*i*
Sheridan, Geoffrey, 43
Shrew magazine, 114
Shrewsbury Three, 184
Sikh temples, fundraising, 115
Singh, Robert (Bob), 27, 81*i*, 110*i*, 116
    anecdotes, 6, 9, 17, 20-1, 25, 30, 44, 85, 96, 101-2, 126, 128, 140, 166, 173
Single Status Agreement 206
Slidders, John Millner (Trico personnel executive), 15, 7, 32, 50, 82, 105-6, 112-13, 143, 148, 149, 150, 175
Social Contract (Labour Party TUC), 18
social security (DHSS), 62-3, 114-15
Social Security Act 1971, 62
Socialist Worker, 43
Socialist Workers Party, 146
SOGAT print chapel, 110
South Wales delegation, 154
Spare Rib, 43, 50, 161-3
Special Patrol Group, violence, 178
Spender, Dale, on women exclusion from history, 193
Sports Direct, and TUs, 185
Stevenson, George, 'Forgotten Strike...', 153, 189-90
Stiller, Frank (GLATC), 171
strike *see* Trico women's strike
Strike Bulletin, 69, 79-81, 81*i*, 98, 105-6, 135, 144-5, 146, 148, 149-50, 149*i*, 161*i*, 170*i*, 200-1
    donations weekly reports, 145*i*, 217-23
Sun, 42, 113, 181
Sunday Times, The, 43

Supreme Court, equal pay claims time limit extension, 207-8
Syed, Begonia, 'Flower', xvii

Tanner, Jack (AEU), 197
Taylor, Billy, 26-7, 138, 139
teachers, equal pay 1961, 198
Ten Hour Act 1847, 194
Thatcher, Margaret MP, Government, 90*n*, 179, 187
theatre groups, radical, 57n, 116, 146, 147*i*
Times, The, 43
Tolpuddle Martyrs, 194
Tomlinson, Ricky, 184
Trade Union Act 2016, 181-5
Trade Union and Labour Relations Act 1974, 61, 83
Trade Union Congress (TUC), 179, 190, 206
  Brighton lobby, 48, 134-5, 135*i*, 138-41
  equal pay policy, 14, 196, 199
Trade Union Industrial Relations Act 1990/1992, 90*n*
trade unions, 181-5, 190
  Trico workers and, 10-13, 46-9, 61, 64, 115-18, 175
  see also specific unions; Trico women's strike
Trades Councils, 73, 98, 110, 118, 186
  see also specific Trades Councils
Transport and General Workers' Union (TGWU), 10, 118, 206
Treaty of Rome, Article 107, 199
Treesbank TU recreational centre, 117, 100
Tribunal see Industrial Tribunal
Tribune Group, 152-3, 180
Trico Brentford
  workforce, 8-9
    pay & conditions, 4, 5-6, 19-21
    men's wage 'anomaly', 200-1
    night shift, phased out, 11, 16-17
    piecework rates, male & female, 11, 14-15, 16-17
    'twilight' shift, 16
    womens' reaction to men's higher pay, 14-15, 16-17, 18
  strike, non striker attitudes, 39-41, 89-90, 178
Trico Folberth Limited
  and Equal Pay Act 1970, 11, 14-15, 18, 22
  'equal pay' to be women's rate, 33
  'flexibility', male, and pay rates, 15, 106, 148-9, 151, 201
  ACAS, 33-4, 39-40, 67-71, 148-51
    accepts AUEW/EEF equal pay formula, 155, 157, 160, 189
  Industrial Tribunal, 33-4, 50, 67-71, 104-13
  industrial relations, xii-xiii, 7, 10, 7, 10-13, 40, 125, 127, 143
  delays strikers' holiday pay, 111-12
  freezes male day shift pay, 18
  layoffs, 125, 126-7, 127-30
  letters to workforce, 33-5, 41, 141, 148, 151, 160*i*
  owner: Trico Products Corporation of Buffalo NY, 2i, 3-6, 7
  trading during strike, 57-66, 57*n*, 71-89, 136
    American style industrial practices, 7, 10, 60, 135
    picket busting, 95, 104, 175
    midnight convoys, 59-61, 64-6, 71-3, 79-81, 81*i*, 82-9
  paying non strikers to do nothing, 32, 40
  wipers boycott, and smuggling, 48, 133-4, 151, 152, 178-3
  see also haulage firms

INDEX | 235

Trico Northampton, 10-11, 57, 143
  convoys to, 71-3, 86-7, 88, 143
  workforce, 39, 11, 99, 125, 153
    delegation to, 99
Trico women's strike
  begins
    24 May, 22-3, 24-7, 28-9, 30-1, 32-7
    26 May meeting, 35, 36, 37*i*
    27 May official, 35-7, 39
    29 June march, 37*i*, 38*i*, 51*i*, 51-3, 52*i*
  continuing
    delegations, 98-103, 115-18
    mass meeting & picket 23 August, 109-11*i*, 110-11
    meeting, Boston Manor Park, 65*i*
    TUC Brighton lobby, 134-5, 135*i*, 138-41
  fundraising, 100-3, 115-19, 145-7, 151, 153-4, 98-103
    donations weekly reports, 145*i*, 217-23
    general public, donations, 119
  picket line, 46-9, 58*i*, 74*i*, 75-8, 146, 168*i*
    midnight convoys, 59-61, 64-6, 71-3, 79-81, 81*i*, 82-9, 109-13
    duties, 29, 32-4, 46-9, 59-66, 70*i*, 71-89
    'flying pickets', 61-2, 73
    police break up 29 July, 82-4, 88-9, 95-7
    pressure/support, 61, 62-3, 64-6
    visitors, 73, 75, 77, 78
  police and *see* police
  strike breakers, 57-66, 128-9
    see also Trico management, trading during strike
  strike bulletin *see Strike Bulletin*
  strike committee, 53, 61-2, 76
    ACAS meeting on Trico offers, 67-71
    accepts AUEW/EEF equal pay formula, 155
    boycotts Industrial Tribunal, 104-8
  strikers, 46-9, 147*i*, 176
    and Paul Sheldrick, 174*i*
    benefits/entertainments, 146
    financial hardship, 61, 62-3, 64, 74-5
      strike fund, 42, 48, 144, 146
      see also donations
    Trico song, 169, 171*i*
  victory
    Trico accepts AUEW/EEF equal pay formula, 155
    see also Arbitration Conciliation and Advisory Services (ACAS)
    mass meeting 15 October, 156-7*i*, 158-9*i*
    celebration, 163, 169-71
    victory march, 18 October, 162, 162*i*
    victory Strike Bulletin, 161*i*, 170*i*
  aftermath, xi-xiii, 164, 175, 176, 185, 206
    achievement/firsts
    first anniversary celebration, 192*i*
    Grunwick contrast, 177-80
    political perceptions, 188-91
    women, post-29 July fame, 96-7
Trott, Fred, 101
Tumulty, Peter, 66*i*
Turner, Pat (GMWU), on EPA, 135, 138
Tyrer, Nicola, 'The Brentford Ladies' Excuse Me', 134

Unison, 206, 207, 208
Unite The Union, 190, 206, 216
United Electrical, Radio and Machine Workers of America, 144
United Nations
  International Covenant on … Rights 1966, 182
  on UK TU Act 2016, 182
Upper Clyde Shipbuilders, 117

Van Dyck, Rene (Trico MD), 7, 10, 150
24 Heures, 44

Waddington, Sue, EPA decision, 201-18
Wakefield, Dora (Doll), 109, 161
Wales delegation, 99
Walsh, Willie (BA Chief Executive), 185
Ward, Betty, 8
Ward, Eileen, leading shop steward, xv, 8, 25, 31, 37*i*, 52*i*, 53, 78, 136, 137
   addresses strikers, 29, 35, 35*i*
   and women on shop stewards committee, 169
   at victory, 156*i*, 163*i*
   AUEW meeting 27 May, 39
   Coventry, 101
   letter in *Middlesex Chronicle*, 141
   on Trico 29 September offer, 151, 154
   on Trico intimidation, 113, 125
   tries to stop convoy lorry, 83*i*, 84
   obituary, 211
Ward, George (Grunwick MD), 179
Warren, Des, 184
Whyman, Bill, AUEW Northampton, 39
Wilcox, Sally, thesis on Trico equal pay strike, 105
Willesden bus garage workers, 146
Williams, Rhoda (Fraser), 5, 9, 13, 21, 51*i*, 75, 120-1, 167
Wilson, Harold, government, 18*n*, 188
Wilson, Maria (May), on EPA, 108
Wilson, Yvonne, EPA tribunal decision, 202
'Winning Equal Pay' TUC history website, 193
'winter of discontent', media and, 189
Woman Worker, The (1907), 196

women workers
   as cheap labour, held down wages, 183
   chain makers strike, Cradley Heath, 196
   Dagenham sewing machinists (1968 & 1984), 14, 190, 198-9, 204-5
   fish packers, EPA success, 205
   GNCTU Lodges of Industrious Females, 193
   Grunwick, 177
   Matchwomen's strike 1888, 193, 195, 206
   trade unionists and equal pay pre-1960s, 193-8
   unemployment post First World War, 197
women's groups, and Trico strikers, 116, 119, 186
Women's Charter, 43
Women's Protective and Provident League, 195-6
Women's Theatre Group, *Out! On the Costa del Trico*, 146
Women's Trade Union League, 195-6
Women's Voice, 43, 115
workers' anecdotes
   AUEW, 140
   convoys, 85-7
   determination, 96-7
   early days, 30-1
   equal pay issue awareness, 16-17
   financial hardship, 62-3, 120-4
   fundraising/delegations, 100-3
   jobs, 19-21
   layoffs, 126
   leadership, 136-7
   looking back, 172-3
   men in support, 49
   picketing and solidarity, 75-8
   political awareness, 80
   press, 44
   sexist attitudes, 131-2
   strike breakers, 128-9

strike legacy, 164
strike meeting 24 May, 24-7
surveillance, 72
Trico letters, 34
TUC Brighton lobby, 139-40
union membership, 12-13
workforce and community, 8-9
working at Trico, 5-6
working people, 181, 182, 187-8
Working Women's Charter (WWC), 73, 110, 116*i*, 119, 146, 186, 216
workplace picket supervisors, TU Act 2016, 183-4
World War I, *see* First World War

World War II, *see* Second World War
Worth, Kathy, 109*i*
Worthing Trades Council, 146
Wright, Fred, cartoons, 112, 144, 144*i*, 149*i*

Young, Bella (Davis), 26, 63, 75, 120, 128, 140, 165-6, 192*i*
Young Liberals, 119

zero hours contracts, 178, 210